Baedeker

# Cologne

www.baedeker.com
Verlag Karl Baedeker

# SIGHTSEEING HIGHLIGHTS ★★

**Cologne has much more to offer than its wonderful cathedral, Rhine panorama and Kölsch beer: the charming and fascinating Old Town, outstanding museums and no less than a dozen Romanesque churches make it one of Germany's most attractive historic cities and provide a packed programme of sightseeing. We have selected the highlights for you.**

**★★ Altstadt · Old Town**
A quarter of narrow cobbled lanes, charming courtyards and historic pubs full of atmosphere ► **page 150**

**★★ Dom · Cathedral**
The emblem and focal point of the city, visited by millions each year
► **page 166**

**Cologne Cathedral**
*Figures on the south entrance*

**Gross St Martin**
*The church tower rises majestically above the Old Town.*

**★★ Gross St Martin**
This 12th-century church with its massive tower rises above the maze of alleys in the Old Town. ► **page 178**

**★★ Museum Ludwig**
The world's third-largest collection of Picassos and a high-quality exhibition of works by famous modern and contemporary international artists. ► **page 193**

**✶✶ Rathaus · City Hall**
The oldest city hall in Germany has a beautiful Renaissance loggia and a 15th-century tower adorned with over 100 statues. ▸ **page 205**

**✶✶ Römisch-Germanisches Museum**
The Roman and Frankish history of the city is presented right next to the cathedral.
▸ **page 218**

**✶✶ Schloss Augustusburg**
This Rococo palace in the nearby town of Brühl set new standards for princely living in the 18th century. Artists such as Balthasar Neumann and Carlo Carlone carried out the sumptuous interior decoration. ▸ **page 220**

**✶✶ St Aposteln**
The east end of this Romanesque church with its »trefoil« choir is a remarkable architectural ensemble. ▸ **page 232**

**✶✶ St Gereon**
According to legend early Christians were martyred on the site of this church. Its core is a late Roman building, over which a magnificent dome was built in the early 13th century. ▸ **page 237**

**✶✶ St Maria im Kapitol**
The Church of the Nativity in Bethlehem was the model for this church, which stands on the foundations of a Roman temple. ▸ **page 241**

**✶✶ St Pantaleon**
This church, which was dedicated in 980, is one of the oldest in the city and a fine example of early Romanesque architecture, built for a member of the imperial family.
▸ **page 246**

**✶✶ Wallraf-Richartz-Museum · Fondation Courboud**
An extensive art collection covering the period from the Middle Ages to the 19th century ▸ **page 254**

**Römisch-Germanisches Museum**
*Time for a rest on Roncalliplatz before learning about Roman history*

# BAEDEKER'S BEST TIPS

**Of all the Baedeker tips in this book, we've collected the most interesting ones for you here. Experience and enjoy the cathedral city of Cologne from its best side!**

### Models of the city

The history museum in the Zeughaus has a beautiful model of Cologne in 1571, the inner courtyard of the Spanischer Bau next to the city hall a model of modern Cologne. ► page 47

### Get really wet

On the Mediapark lake children can let off steam in the pedaloes, which are equipped with water pistols. ► page 76

### Authentic Christmas taste

Home-made Stollen cake and genuine Lebkuchen from Nuremberg make excellent Christmas gifts. ► page 78

### A popular beer garden

On the lake named Aachener Weiher there is a large beer garden with a view of the swans. ► page 79

### Old Love

Could there be a better name for this houseboat café on the Rhine in Rodenkirchen, upstream from the city centre? ► page 81

### Asparagus time

In May white asparagus features heavily on the menus of German restaurants. The local produce tastes best! ► page 89

### Museum Mondays

Not every museum closes on Monday: see innovative architecture and thought-provoking art in Kolumba, the work of goldsmiths in the cathedral treasury, or a photo exhibition in the Mediapark. ► page 112

**With a head for heights ...**
*... passengers in the cable car can enjoy this view of the city while crossing the Rhine.*

**Romanesque night**
*Once a year performances of church music go on into the small hours in St Maria im Kapitol.*

**Eau de Cologne**
A museum of perfume in the shop owned by the Farina family, where the inventor of eau de Cologne worked 300 years ago
► **page 118**

**Tours by rickshaw**
Hire a bike in the Old Town – or if that is too strenuous, see the sights from a rickshaw and let the guide do the pedalling. ► **page 126**

**The Cologne Riviera**
The Rhine bank at Rodenkirchen is a popular place for walking and cycling.
► **page 144**

**High above the river**
A cable car across the Rhine provides a wonderful view of the city.
► **page 162**

**Superb panorama**
The skyscraper called KölnTriangle, across the river from the cathedral, has a viewing deck on the 29th floor – and, unlike the cathedral, a lift. ► **page 164**

**Church café**
Café Stanton is a stylish place to stop in the middle of the shopping zone. Drink coffee, have an excellent meal, and support the church at the same time.
► **page 182**

**For children**
The animal enclosure in the extensive, wooded Stadtwald park provides entertainment for young visitors. ► **page 184**

**Flickering candlelight**
A visit to the old Melaten cemetery at dusk on 1 November, the day when the dead are remembered, is an unforgettable experience. ► **page 185**

**Museum café**
The café of the Museum of Applied Art is a tranquil place to take refreshments, near the cathedral and the shops.
► **page 192**

**Flowers and confetti**
Come to the city hall to see how the people of Cologne greet the bride and groom as they emerge from the registry office. ► **page 210**

**A day at the zoo ...**
*... is a popular family attraction.*

**A new landmark ...**

*... of steel and glass makes a trip across the Rhine worthwhile. The LanxessArena with its arched roof seats 18,000 spectators for concerts and sporting events.*

► page 165

## BACKGROUND



**Julia Agrippina**

*The city owes its name to the wife of Emperor Claudius.*

## PRACTICALITIES

## TOURS



## SIGHTS FROM A to Z

**Kölsch …**
*… is the local beer, which may only be brewed in and around Cologne.*

**Price categories**

***Hotels***
Luxury (cat. I): over 150 €
Mid-range (cat. II): 100 – 150 €
Budget: (cat. III): under 100 €
Two persons in a double room

***Restaurants***
Expensive (cat. I). over 25 €
Moderate (cat. II): 15 – 25 €
Inexpensive (cat. III). under 15 €
For a main course

**Cologne Cathedral**
*The best views of the city's landmark are from the right bank of the Rhine.*
▸ **page 166**

# Background

COLOGNE IS ONE OF GERMANY'S LIVELIEST CITIES. IN ADDITION TO THE FAMOUS CATHEDRAL, IT HAS MANY FINE MEDIEVAL AND MODERN BUILDINGS, HIGH-CLASS MUSEUMS, AN INNOVATIVE CULTURAL SCENE, EXCELLENT PUBS AND A VARIED NIGHT-LIFE.

# VIBRANT CITY ON THE RHINE

**Cologne – Köln in German – is one of the liveliest cities in Germany. Each year millions of visitors come to the Rhine to see one of the world's great cathedrals, impressive museums, a range of shops, cultural attractions, sports and leisure facilities to suit all tastes, and all-year-round events from carnival to the Christmas markets.**

2000 years of history have visibly made their mark on Germany's fourth-largest and oldest city. Visitors arriving in Cologne from the east and crossing the Rhine on the railway bridge or the Deutzer Brücke are treated to a memorable view. The twin spires of the majestic cathedral, the landmark of the city, dominate the skyline, and further south the panorama continues with the massive tower of St Martin, one of twelve fine Romanesque churches, and the 600-year-old tower of the city hall, which is adorned with over 100 statues of people who have shaped the destiny of this historic city since Roman times. Down by the Rhine the colourful little houses of the Old Town cluster around these great monuments, and at a discreet distance some recent high-rise buildings add a modern touch.

**Street life**
*Skateboarders show off their tricks on the square by the cathedral.*

## Strong Traditions

A walk along the banks of the river and through the narrow cobbled streets of the charming Old Town are an essential part of a visit to the city. One of the most popular attractions here is an evening in a traditional *Brauhaus*, a brewery pub. There are about 20 different kinds of local beer, which is known as *Kölsch*, and the people of Cologne are strongly attached to their customs – in terms of what they drink, their pride in the life and history of the city, the dialect they speak and above all in their carnival celebrations, when costumed revellers throng the streets, hundreds of thousands watch or take part in processions, and every pub is packed to the doors. Rhinelanders have a justified reputation for being friendly and easy-going, and give the lie to outdated preconceptions that Germany is a joyless and over-disciplined place.

The city has a great deal to offer both to serious sightseers and to those looking for more relaxed amusement. There are first-class art

**Carnival**
*A true-born Cologner never misses the parade on carnival Monday.*

**Old Town**
*Coffee and Kölsch beer on Fischmarkt, with picturesque old houses as a backdrop.*

**Schildergasse**
*In the pedestrianized streets of the shopping district, many stores stay open in the evening.*

**Trip on the Rhine**
*Boats run from the centre to Rodenkirchen in the south of the city.*

**Roman remains**
*The funeral monument of Poblicius in the Römisch-Germanisches Museum is one of the most impressive survivals from ancient times.*

**Nightlife**
*Bars, clubs and pubs for every taste give Cologne a real buzz at night.*

galleries – the Museum Ludwig for modern art, the Wallraf-Richartz Museum for the medieval period through to the Impressionists, and Kolumba, an inspiring new building housing religious art – as well as Roman remains, historical museums and many interesting churches. The shopping scene encompasses boutiques run by creative designers, excellent galleries for art and antiques, good specialist stores and all manner of markets. In the evening the activities on offer range from opera and classical concerts to fringe theatre and dance clubs large and small. The restaurants, bars and pubs cater for all tastes and budgets.

## A Major City

Cologne is not just a varied and interesting destination for leisure and tourism, but also one of the outstanding central European cities for business and science.

As a venue for trade fairs and congresses, Cologne is internationally important. It is also a centre for media, especially broadcasting, as the site of TV production studios and headquarters both of the leading European private broadcaster, RTL, and of the largest German public broadcasting corporation, WDR. Cologne University is the biggest and second-oldest in Germany. The presence of a number of other schools of higher education, especially the schools of music and media art and the German Sport University, and of such institutions as the German Aerospace Centre (DLR), reinforce the reputation of Cologne for learning and science, and the large population of students and people from creative professions is noticeable in the lively, creative atmosphere of the city.

**Holiday atmosphere** *in the Beach Club by the Rhine*

The Rhine is a major traffic artery, both for tourist ships and freight transport: Cologne's five harbours make it the second-largest inland port in Germany. The autobahn connections in all directions are excellent, and the 1300 trains that stop each day at the main station mean it is a leading European rail hub, now with high-speed links to Paris and Brussels, where connections to Eurostar have brought Cologne within five hours of London by rail. For those who prefer to fly, the city has one of the fastest-growing German airports with good international connections.

# Facts

**In ancient times, and even more in the Middle Ages, Cologne was the most important trading centre on the Rhine. Today the city has one of the world's largest congress and exhibition centres and has become a leading European media metropolis.**

# Population · Government · Economy

## Population

Changes in population

In Roman times, when Cologne was already an important settlement, the number of residents within the city walls was probably over 20,000 and possibly as high as 40,000. In the post-Roman period the population fell, but rose again at the end of the first millennium as the economy grew and the city became seat of an archbishop. By the 13th or 14th century the city had 40,000 inhabitants. In 1794, at the start of the period of French rule, the number was 44,500. Industrialization led to a rapid increase: between 1820 and 1910 the population trebled to reach over half a million. At the outbreak of the Second World War 768,352 residents were recorded – and at the end of the war fewer than 40,000. Over 80% of the houses had been more or less severely damaged, and over 90% of the buildings in the inner city completely destroyed. However, by 1946 the population had already risen to almost 500,000, and has grown fairly steadily since then to reach 1,020,000 today. 330,000 are from immigrant families, of whom 178,000 do not have German citizenship and 57,000 are immigrants of German descent, e.g. ethnic Germans from Russia. Against the national trend, slight population growth is predicted in Cologne for the coming decades.

**? DID YOU KNOW ...?**

- ... that in Cologne, traditionally a bastion of the Roman Catholic church, only 41.4 % of the population are Catholic? About 12% are Muslim.

## Government

Government

As early as the 12th century the citizens of Cologne gained political influence through the so-called college of jurors. By the constitution of 1396 the craft guilds, each of which was represented in a political organization known as a »Gaffel«, elected the city council. This is unremarkable by modern standards, but was a sensational development at the time: Cologne had the **first city constitution with a strong democratic element** outside Italy. About 10% of the citizens were enfranchised through their membership of a guild. This constitution remained in force for four centuries. The form of government was changed under French rule in 1794, then again in 1856 when the city was governed by Prussia, and once more in 1933 by the National Socialists.

← *During Carnival in Cologne everyone is a »lord of misrule«.*

## *Facts and Figures* Cologne

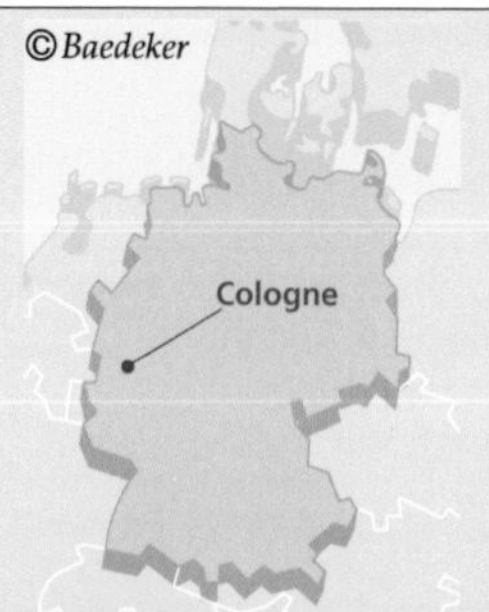


**Location**

- basin on lower Rhine
- latitude 50° 56' north
  longitude 6° 57' east
- altitude 56m/184ft above sea level

**Area**

- area of city: 405 sq km/156 sq mi
- city perimeter: 130km/81mi
- east-west extent: 27.6km/17.1mi
  north-south extent: 28.1km/17.5mi
- tallest buildings:
  - Colonius TV tower 249m/817ft
  - cathedral 157m/515ft
  - KölnTurm in MediaPark 148m/486ft

**Population**

- total population 1.02 million
- population density 2380 persons per sq km/6170 per sq mi
- residents without German nationality 178,000 (17.3%)

**Government**

- state in Federal Republic: North Rhine-Westphalia
- head of city government (Oberbürgermeister): since 2000 Fritz Schramma, Christian Democratic Union
- 9 city districts (Chorweiler, Ehrenfeld, Innenstadt, Kalk, Lindenthal, Mülheim, Nippes, Porz, Rodenkirchen)
- 85 city quarters
- coat of arms: three crowns for the Three Magi (Three Kings), whose relics were brought to Cologne in 1164, and eleven flames or drops of blood in memory of the legend of St Ursula and the 11,000 virgins, whose martyrdom is said to have saved Cologne from the Huns.

**Economy**

- GDP: approx. 42 million euros
- employment
  - 81.7% service sector
  - 18.1% manufacturing, construction
  - 0.02% agriculture
- rate of unemployment (2006): 14.6%

**Tourism**

- visitors staying overnight: 2.5 million (2007)

Today's city government was constituted in 1946, originally based on the British model with a council (Stadtrat, the decision-making body chaired by a lord mayor) and the administration (the executive arm headed by the Oberstadtdirektor). Since 1999 the lord mayor (Oberbürgermeister) has also been the head of the city administration and is now directly elected every 9 years. The council consists of 90 elected representatives. Three further mayors (Bürgermeister) act as deputies for the Oberbürgermeister.

## Economy

**History**

The geographical position of Cologne at the crossing of major trade routes gave the city international importance for commerce and manufacturing at an early date. Goods being transported along the Rhine were transferred here from the flat-bottomed boats that used the middle and upper reaches of the river to vessels with a deeper draught that could sail down the lower Rhine and across the sea. This made the city a great market place that attracted many merchants. The **right of staple of 1259** specified that all Rhine ships had to stop in Cologne and offer their cargo for sale on the markets there for three days. No other German city had such far-reaching or varied commercial contacts in the Middle Ages as Cologne. This was an important reason for the early political independence of the city. The next period of economic growth, in the 19th century, revolved particularly around agriculture, mining and engineering.

**Industry**

Cologne is still a major centre for manufacturing and commerce. The city's largest employer is the Ford automobile factory, and other car companies such as Toyota have their German headquarters here. Other significant industries are engineering – Klöckner-Humboldt-Deutz AG, a manufacturer of diesel engines, originated when Nikolaus Otto built the first-ever four-stroke engine in Cologne in 1876 – the chemical and pharmaceutical industries, electronics and oil refining.

The world-famous perfume eau de Cologne is no longer made in the city, but many companies in the building, steel, textile and food industries remain. Cologne is also the main retail centre for a large surrounding region.

**Banking and insurance**

Since the Middle Ages Cologne has been one of Germany's main banking centres: the first joint-stock bank in the Prussian state was established in Cologne in 1848. Sal. Oppenheim, Germany's largest private bank, was founded in the city 200 years ago. Since the 19th century Cologne has also had a leading role in the insurance business. National and international takeovers have reduced the importance of this sector for the local economy in recent years, but the insurance business is still a major employer. The offices of banks and insurance companies are prominent on the Ring (inner ring road) and the streets Unter Sachsenhausen and Gereonstrasse.

**Trade fairs**

The tradition of trade fairs in Cologne goes back to the granting of the right of staple in 1259 and beyond. Today around 70 international trade fairs and exhibitions (►p.162), including Anuga, an important show for the food & beverage industry; the **Art Cologne** art fair; Orgatec, the world's largest office fair: and photokina, the world's leading exhibition for the imaging business. 44,000 exhibitors from about 120 countries attract 2.5 million visitors annually to the trade

CINEDOM

fair complex. The organizer, KölnMesse, also hosts about 2000 congresses and events each year as well as numerous special exhibitions.

**Media city**

Cologne rightfully claims the title of media city and **TV capital of Germany**. Producers from all media sectors, from TV studios and publishers of newspapers and magazines to book publishers, e-commerce companies and multi-media agencies, are based in the city. No other German city has as many TV and radio broadcasters as Cologne; about 60 book publishers, over 200 printers and almost 70 newspaper and magazine publishers produce their print media here. This has encouraged the establishment of many smaller businesses related to the media industry. Cologne is also the seat of Germany's only institute of higher education for audio-visual media. Hundreds of journalists, film producers, TV studios, press and PR agencies and other suppliers, freelancers and management companies associated with the media business swell the employment figures to the point where one in ten jobs is connected to media and communications, a higher figure than in any other German city. The **MediaPark**, which occupies an area of 200,000 square metres (over 2 million square feet) in an excellent inner-city location, is a prominent forum for the information and communications sector.

◄ TV

Radio and TV stations are the leading players on the Cologne media scene. **Westdeutsche Rundfunk (WDR)** is the largest German public broadcaster of radio and television. It has been in operation since 1952, and produces long-running soap operas that are nationally popular in studios in the suburb of Bocklemünd.

**RTL**, which has a higher turnover than any other European private TV company, is Cologne's second broadcasting giant. RTL has been based in the city since 1984 and in 2008 moved from the outskirts to renovated premises in the Rheinhallen, a heritage-protected building complex with a central location on the right bank of the Rhine. This move has secured the future of Cologne as a media city.

Several other broadcasters, including **Super RTL**, in which the Walt Disney Company has a major stake, also operate from Cologne.

← *The Cinedom is a modern multiplex cinema in the Media Park.*

# History

**Beneath the present city hall the remains of the palace of the Roman governors is a reminder of the status of ancient Colonia as a provincial capital; magnificent Romanesque churches and the famous cathedral testify to the status of Cologne as a holy city in the Middle Ages. And high-quality recent architecture shows that Cologne is today still a vibrant place.**

# Prehistory · Roman and Frankish Rule

| | |
|---|---|
| **100,000 BC** | First human settlement |
| **AD 50** | The town gains Roman municipal rights and the name Colonia Claudia Ara Agrippinensium. |
| **5th century** | Frankish rule begins. |

**First settlement**

In prehistoric times humans occupied the territory that is now the city of Cologne and the surrounding area, between a line of hills to the west (Vorgebirge) and the hilly country to the east of the Rhine (Bergisches Land). The first traces of settlement date back to the **Palaeolithic period** about 100,000 years ago. However, the history of the city begins just over 2000 years ago, a few years before the birth of Christ, with the arrival of the Romans.

**Romans found Ubii settlement**

Around 50 BC Roman forces led by **Gaius Julius Caesar** conquered Gaul. Caesar exterminated the Eburoni tribe, who occupied areas between the rivers Rhine and Maas. Some years later the Roman general Agrippa settled the Ubii, a tribe who originally lived to the east of the Rhine, in the depopulated area. The main urban settlement of the Ubii, from which Cologne developed, is likely to have been founded around 5 BC.

In AD 50 **Agrippina**, the wife of Emperor Claudius and mother of Emperor Nero, who was born in Cologne, gained municipal rights for the town of her birth. The city was now named **Colonia Claudia Ara Agrippinensium** (meaning »a city with Roman rights founded by Agrippina in the reign of Claudius, with an altar for the imperial cult«). Centuries later the word »Colonia« was shortened to Cöln and finally Köln, and is preserved in its English and French version, »Cologne«. A wall, of which significant remains can still be seen, was built to enclose an area of approximately 1 sq km/0.5 sq mi. In about AD 90 Cologne became **capital of the province of Lower Germany**. The Rhine was the eastern border of the empire here.

Soldiers and merchants introduced **Christianity**, possibly in the second century, but at first the new religion had only minor importance alongside the other gods worshipped in the Roman Empire, and Christians were subject to bloody persecution at times. The first known bishop of Cologne, Maternus, is mentioned in records in the year 313. From the 3rd century Franks crossed the Rhine and reached Gaul. In 310 Emperor **Constantine** had the first permanent bridge across the Rhine built in Cologne and constructed the fort

*← Detail of the shrine of the Three Magi. The arrival of their bones in Cologne in 1164 gave the impulse to build the cathedral.*

Divitia, in which the present-day district of Deutz originated, as a bridgehead on the right bank.

**Franks in Cologne** The Roman Empire was not able to hold its frontier against the advance of the Germanic tribes who were collectively known as the Franks. In AD 355 the Franks temporarily occupied Cologne and caused much damage. Around the year 455 the city permanently fell into their hands. Frankish sub-kings made Cologne their capital, and the church of St Gereon, a Roman structure, was used by kings of the Merovingian dynasty, possibly for coronations and burials. Internecine conflicts within the Merovingian royal family allowed the Carolingian dynasty to take power. The most influential Carolingian ruler was **Charlemagne**, who was crowned emperor in Rome on Christmas Day 800. Charlemagne made his chaplain **Hildebold** the first archbishop of Cologne in 795. The archdiocese stretched from Bremen to Liège. Charlemagne's subjugation of the Saxons and extension of his empire eastward gave Cologne, hitherto on the edge of the Frankish lands, a central position.

In the following centuries the archbishops of Cologne were among the most important counsellors of the emperors (later known as Holy Roman emperors). In 881 **Norsemen** occupied Cologne, plundered the city and caused much destruction.

# Rule of the Archbishops · Free Imperial City

| | |
|---|---|
| **1164** | The relics of the Three Magi are brought to Cologne. |
| **1248** | Building of the Gothic cathedral begins. |
| **1259** | Right of staple |
| **1288** | Battle of Worringen |
| **1396** | Craft guilds take over city government. |

**10th–13th century** For over 300 years the city was governed by its archbishops, who were not only prelates but also secular rulers with the status of dukes. They had the powers to dispense justice, hold markets and mint coins, and were obliged to give military support to the emperor in times of war.

In 1156 **Rainald von Dassel** was given the office of chancellor by **Friedrich I (»Barbarossa«)** and was elected archbishop three years later. Rainald's forces supported the emperor in the siege and capture of Milan, and the archbishop was rewarded with a priceless piece of booty: the bones of the Three Magi or Three Wise Men, which, it was believed, had been kept in the church of St Eustorgius in Milan

## *Cologne* Growth of the City

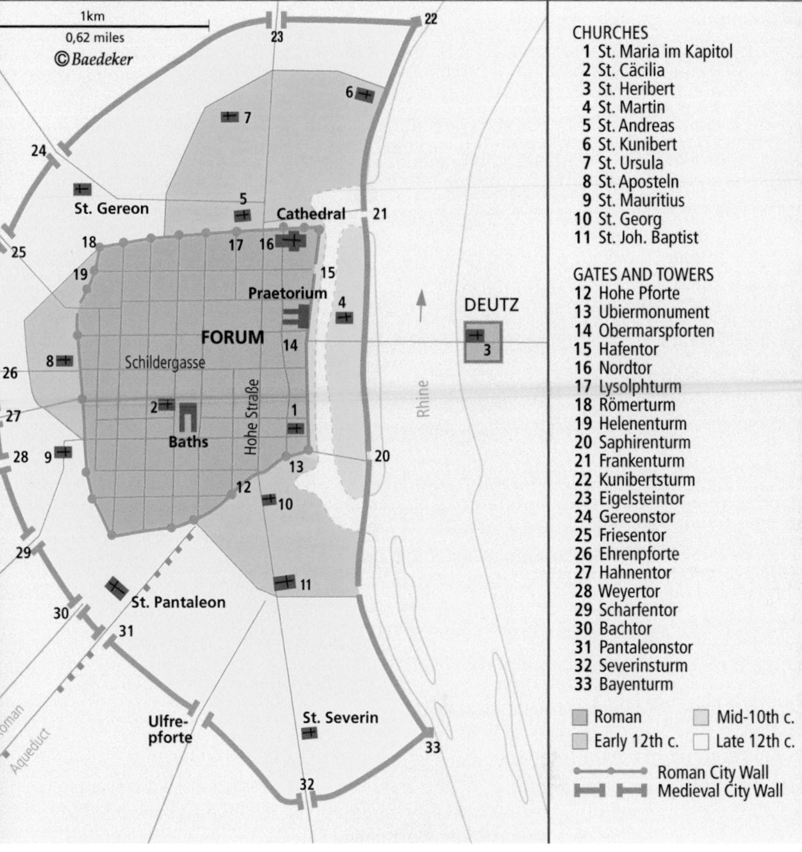


since the 4th century. In 1164 Rainald brought the relics to Cologne, and the shrine of the Three Magi was made to house them. In 1248 **Archbishop Konrad von Hochstaden** laid the foundation stone for a new cathedral, a »reliquary in stone« around the shrine of the Three Magi, which was not completed until 1880. The shrine made Cologne the most important place of pilgrimage in Europe after Rome and Santiago de Compostela.

As the city expanded, new walls were built: in 1106 extensions to the Roman walls in the south, north and west, and between 1180 and 1240 a completely new wall enclosing an area much larger than the original Roman city. Some parts of the medieval wall and its three main gates (Eigelsteintor, Hahnentor and Severinstor) have been preserved.

*When Anton Woensam made this wood-cut of the Rhine panorama in 1532, the tower of Gross St Martin dominated the skyline, and the cathedral was unfinished.*

From the 11th to the 13th century many churches in the Romanesque style were built in the »holy city«, which had been awarded the title »Sancta Colonia« in 1052 by **Pope Leo IX**. Twelve of these churches remain, an ensemble unique in Europe (►Baedeker Special p.38). The first major church building to use the new, Gothic style was the cathedral, which was built on the model of the great cathedrals of northern France.

In 1259 Cologne was granted the **right of staple**: all goods that reached the city had to be unloaded and offered for sale there. This privilege brought great prosperity.

**End of rule by the archbishops**

As the wealth and status of the Cologne merchants increased, they reduced the power of the archbishops step by step. In 1288, after years of conflict, Archbishop Siegfried von Westerburg was defeated in the decisive **Battle of Worringen**. The leading merchant families, known as the patricians, took over the government of Cologne, which was now de facto a free imperial city, i.e. owing allegiance directly to the emperor, even though it officially received this status only in 1475.

In 1349 the bubonic plague broke out. As in many other places, the Jews were accused of having caused the epidemic by poisoning the wells. Almost all members of the substantial Jewish community, which had lived in its own quarter in the city centre since Carolingian times, were massacred. From 1424 until the late 18th century no Jews were allowed to set foot within the city walls.

In 1388 the university was founded and flourished in the late Middle Ages. It was dissolved in 1798 by the French occupying forces, and not re-established until 1919, when Konrad Adenauer was mayor of Cologne.

In the **Hanseatic league of German trading cities** Cologne played a leading role as a centre of long-distance commerce. The merchants of Cologne had especially close links to England, and possessed their own premises in the city of London, known as the steelyard. To this day the city banner flies the colours of the Hanseatic league, red and white.

In the late 14th century the increasingly influential guilds opposed the power of the urban aristocracy, the wealthy merchant families known as patricians. The membership of one or more craft guilds constituted a political representation known as a **Gaffel**. In an agreement of 1396 the guilds proclaimed a new constitution with a democratic character; the members of the city council were chosen from among the 22 Gaffel organizations. Although the patrician families later found ways to reassert their influence, this constitution remained in force until the late 18th century. The guilds were not abolished until 1796, when the French government, according to the principles of the revolution of 1789, replaced compulsory membership of guilds with freedom to practise every trade. This meant that Protestants, who were excluded from guild membership and were thus forced to live and work outside the city, were now able to take part in the economic life of Cologne.

◄ Guilds take power

## Reformation and Thirty Years' War

The teachings of Martin Luther at first found some support in Cologne, but the forces of the Counter-Reformation kept the city a bastion of the Catholic church. In 1520 Luther's writings were burned in public, and in 1529 two »heretics« were burned at the stake. Cologne became a base for the Jesuits directly after the foundation of the order in 1534.

**1520: Luther's writings burned**

In the Thirty Years' War (1618–48) – in contrast to its archbishop, **Ferdinand of Bavaria** – the city declared its neutrality and thus remained largely unaffected by the devastation of this terrible conflict. However, trade and manufacturing diminished during the war years, and the town of Deutz on the right bank of the Rhine, which was not part of Cologne at that time, was occupied by Swedish troops. The later 17th century and the 18th century were a dynamic period in the history of the city.

# French and Prussian Rule

| | |
|---|---|
| **1794** | French troops occupy Cologne. |
| **1815** | Cologne becomes part of the Prussian state. |
| **1880** | Completion of the cathedral. |
| **1881** | Demolition of the city wall |

**French occupation**

In 1794, following the revolution of 1789, French troops occupied Cologne. For 20 years the city and territories west of the Rhine were part of France. The revolutionary ideals of liberty, equality and fraternity that they proclaimed were initially well received by the citizens. However, enthusiasm declined when the city was forced to pay a high level of »contributions« to the French forces, residents had to find billets for French soldiers and their property was confiscated.

After a long period of stagnation, the city was modernized under French rule: in 1797 Protestants gained rights of citizenship, and in 1798 religious freedom allowed Jews to return to Cologne after an absence of almost 400 years. Church property was secularized and the numerous monasteries were dissolved, making land and resources available for economic development.

The French brought in such overdue reforms as street lighting and cleaning, and all the buildings in the city were numbered consecutively – the origin of the brand name »4711« for eau de Cologne, after the number of the house in which it was produced.

The new code of civil law introduced by **Napoleon**, the **Code Civil**, applied in the Rhineland as a département of France, and continued to be in force after 1815. It was not replaced until the new code of law for the German Reich took effect on 1 January 1900.

**Prussia supports completion of the cathedral**

At the Congress of Vienna in 1815 Cologne and the Rhineland were allocated to Prussia. At first this did not find favour with the citizens, as Prussia was a Protestant and largely agrarian state that lay far to the east. The Rhinelanders felt that their relative affluence, modern economy and liberal attitudes were superior to the military mentality of their new Prussian rulers, who lived in Berlin and Potsdam. They were somewhat reconciled to the new state of affairs when **Friedrich Wilhelm IV** ordered that building work on the unfinished cathedral should recommence in 1842; it was completed in 1880, 632 years after the foundation stone was laid.

In Cologne on 1 January 1842 the radical and democratic newspaper *Rheinische Zeitung* was first published. From October 1842 its editor-in-chief was **Karl Marx**. However, due to its opposition to the Prussian government, the newspaper was censored and banned from March 1843. Marx moved to Paris, then Brussels, and did not return to Cologne until 1848, when he and **Friedrich Engels** founded the *Neue Rheinische Zeitung* in support of the March revolution of that year. After the failure of the revolutionary movement, the paper ceased publication in May 1849. Karl Marx and several other journalists of the *Neue Rheinische Zeitung* were exiled from Prussia.

Industrialization ►

Construction of a railway network began in the 1840s. In 1859 the first permanent bridge across the Rhine since Roman times was built to carry rail traffic. Factories for spinning and weaving, flour mills, metal-working enterprises, breweries and engineering companies were established. The banking and insurance sectors grew rapidly, as did the population: from 50,000 in 1815 to 500,000 in 1910.

*For three centuries the unfinished cathedral dominated the cityscape (engraving by Johann Ziegler, 1798).*

**Cologne in imperial Germany**

Soon after the unification of Germany and foundation of the Reich (empire) by **Bismarck** in 1871, the »Kulturkampf«, a conflict between the Catholic church and the Prussian authorities, broke out. The consequences were particularly severe in the strongly Catholic city of Cologne. The archbishop, Cardinal Melchers, was arrested on Bismarck's orders and forced into exile in the Netherlands.

In the 1880s the medieval city wall, which had confined Cologne within its historic boundaries, was demolished and a fine new boulevard, the Ring, built on the site. Beyond this boulevard arose the Neustadt (new town) with spacious squares and streets radiating from them, new churches and areas of housing for both the better-off and the working classes. Industrial areas in the suburbs further out and Deutz on the east bank of the Rhine were incorporated into the city.

The present railway bridge in the city centre, the Hohenzollernbrücke, was built in 1911, and the old horse-drawn trams were replaced with electric trams.

# 20th and 21st Century

| | |
|---|---|
| **1917–33** | Konrad Adenauer is mayor of Cologne. |
| **1945** | At the end of the Second World War 90% of the city centre lies in ruins. |
| **1993 and 1995** | The Rhine floods parts of the old town and suburbs. |
| **2005** | World Youth Day of the Catholic church: Pope Benedict XVI visits Cologne. |

*The Second World War reduced the city to rubble. Only the cathedral rose above the ruins.*

## World Wars and Third Reich

**First World War, between the wars**

With the exception of an English bombing raid at Whitsun 1918, Cologne sustained hardly any damage in the First World War, but the population suffered considerably from food rationing and undernourishment.

In the post-war years a separatist movement, which aimed to make the Rhineland independent of the rest of Germany, met with little support in Cologne. **Konrad Adenauer**, mayor from 1917 until 1933, initiated a number of important projects. He re-established the university in 1919, extended the city limits to include land that was needed for industrial development, attracted a major employer with the Ford automobile plant, founded the trade fair complex in 1924, and ensured that the inner and outer fortifications of the Prussian period were turned into green belts.

The Great Depression was keenly felt in Cologne right into the period of National Socialist rule. After taking power in 1933 the Nazis removed Adenauer from office. Persecution of the Jewish population, which numbered around 20,000 after the First World War, began immediately. In the »Reich pogrom night« of 9 November 1938, in Cologne as all over Germany, synagogues were burned, and the waves of arrests and deportations began. 11,000 individuals were sent to the death camps from the railway station in Deutz.

**Destruction in WWII**

As the large German city that was closest to the western border, Cologne was the target of more bombing raids than any other German city, including the first ever thousand-bomber raid in the night of 30–31 May 1942. All the Rhine bridges were destroyed and only the cathedral, severely damaged, still rose above a field of rubble. The population fell from 800,000 at the start of the war to 40,000. On 6 March 1945, after street fighting in the outskirts and close to the cathedral, the US Army occupied the city centre. In the words of the German military bulletin: »The field of ruins that is Cologne was abandoned to the enemy.«

## Cologne since the Second World War

**Reconstruction**

The people of Cologne returned to their home town and set about the task of rebuilding it. Konrad Adenauer became mayor again, but was removed from the post by the British military authorities after just few months. In December 1945 the university recommenced its work. In May 1946 the first train crossed the Rhine again. Today eight bridges span the river, and since April 1957 the Rheinseilbahn cable car has connected the botanical gardens and zoo with the park on the right bank of the Rhine.

In 1975 the population of Cologne passed the one-million mark, partly as a result of incorporating outlying communities into the city, consolidating its position as the fourth-largest German city after Berlin, Hamburg and Munich. Cultural highlights accompanied the growth of the economy: new museums such as the Römisch-Germanisches Museum next to the cathedral (1974) were opened, and in a decades-long programme the careful reconstruction of twelve major churches culminated in the »Year of the Romanesque Churches« in 1985; in the same year the Cologne author **Heinrich Böll**, winner of the Nobel prize for literature in 1972, died. Meanwhile, in 1980, the centenary of the completion of the cathedral was marked by celebrations, including a visit by Pope John Paul II. 1986 saw the opening of a new cultural complex between the cathedral and the Rhine, to house modern art in the Museum Ludwig and a fine new concert hall, the Philharmonie.

### ? DID YOU KNOW ...?

- ... that a word in Cologne dialect meaning »to steal« derives from the name of an archbishop? Cardinal Joseph Frings, one of the few German bishops who publicly spoke out against the anti-Semitism and reign of terror of the Nazis, preached a sermon on New Year's Eve 1946, in the middle of a severe winter when many Germans were freezing and undernourished, in which he appeared to condone the theft of coal from goods trains. Frings became a local hero, and the word »fringsen« was coined to denote non-serious forms of stealing.

The **1990s**, too, were eventful, not always in a pleasant way. Some valuable items were stolen from the cathedral treasury – but not by local thieves, and the Cologne underworld, its sense of honour offended, helped to return the items to the grateful clergy. In 1993 and

1995 **severe flooding** affected a large part of the historic Old Town, where residents needed boats and walkways to reach their homes. in 1998 the city, always eager to celebrate its famous landmark, commemorated the 750th anniversary of the laying of the foundation stone for the cathedral. In 1999 the **G8 summit of world leaders** was held in Cologne; in the Römisch-Germanisches Museum a transparent covering was laid over the Roman Dionysos Mosaic, so that Bill Clinton, Tony Blair, Gerhard Schröder and their counterparts could dine at a glass table with a view of Roman-style festivities beneath their feet. In terms of local politics, the Social Democrats (SPD) lost power to the conservative CDU for the first time in 43 years.

**21st century** The first decade of the new millennium has been marked by a surge in building activity and inglorious episodes in communal politics. The city government has long been notorious for its caucus politics, its pragmatic policy of muddling through rather than setting long-term goals, and the habit of the two main political parties of dividing between them influential positions, including lucrative positions in city-owned enterprises. When the council twice voted down proposals to reduce the high level of municipal debt by privatizing a housing authority, the ruling coalition of conservatives and liberals

*In August 2005 about a million young people from all over the globe made the pilgrimage to the World Youth Day of the Roman Catholic church in Cologne.*

was succeeded by one of the **conservative CDU and the Green Party,** the first such coalition in a large German city. Both SPD and CDU local politicians were involved in scandals, the former in relation to charges of corruption connected with the building of a huge waste incinerator plant, the latter over questions of contributions to party finances. With a large budget deficit restricting investment and increased competition from other cities, Cologne feared losing its reputation as one of Germany's pre-eminent cultural centres.

◄ Unesco and the cathedral

In 2004 Unesco took exception to plans to construct several tall buildings on the right bank of the Rhine, in line with the cathedral and only about 1000 yards distant from it. The cathedral was placed on the red list of endangered World Cultural Heritage sites for several months, before the city authorities backed down; however, one skyscraper, KölnTriangle, had already been built, with a magnificent view of the »endangered« monument.

◄ Economy

In 2008 the **old exhibition halls, a listed monument** built in 1924–26 by **Adolf Abel** at the prompting of Konrad Adenauer, became the headquarters of the private TV station RTL, after far-reaching construction work that preserved only its Expressionist-style brick façade tower and inner courtyard. The redevelopment of the Rheinau harbour has resulted in some good-quality new architecture in addition to the restoration of old commercial buildings, and the relocation of the regional branch of Microsoft to the harbour has created jobs.

◄ Shopping and architecture

A further architectural highlight was the opening in 2005 of the Weltstadtkaufhaus, a store designed by **Renzo Piano** for the Peek & Cloppenburg fashion group. In 2007 the new diocesan museum Kolumba was opened. A further cultural attraction, housing the ethnological collection of the Rautenstrauch-Joest-Museum and the religious art of the Schnüttgen-Museum, is planned for 2009. New developments for the coming years include the refurbishment of the opera house and an archaeological zone near the city hall that will display the remains of Roman Cologne and the medieval Jewish quarter.

◄ North-south underground line

The biggest construction project of the decade, however, is an underground tram route from the north side of the railway station to the south of the city. Whether or not the planned completion date of 2010 is met, two things have already been achieved: huge disruption to the inner city and a boom in employment for archaeologists, who are removing and investigating the contents of 150,000 tons of earth, and by early 2008 had already found 2 million individual items, including a Roman ship beneath the old marketplace.

◄ Church youth festival

The biggest event of the new millennium, eclipsing even the huge crowds who came to the city for the 2006 World Cup, was the World Youth Day of the Roman Catholic church in August 2005, when about 800,000 young people from all parts of the world came to Cologne for a six-day event crowned by the arrival of **Pope Benedict XVI.**

# Arts and Culture

**In addition to the cathedral, one of the outstanding monuments of Gothic architecture in Europe, the twelve Romanesque churches in the city represent a unique cultural heritage.**

# Art and Architecture

## Roman Period

**City wall**

The remains of a tower known as the Ubiermonument, probably constructed in 5 BC to guard the southern entrance to the harbour, constitute the oldest known stone building in Germany. The Roman city wall is thought to have been built after AD 50. It was almost 4km/2.5mi long, 2.4m/8ft wide and had an estimated height of 7.8m/26ft. There were nine city gates and 19 defensive towers (► plan p.25). The central arch of the north gate has survived and can be seen, along with many other finds from the Roman era, in the Römisch-Germanisches Museum; the letters CCAA inscribed on it as the short form of the full city name (Colonia Claudia Ara Agrippinensium) are still clearly legible on the arch. One tower, the **north-west corner tower** (Römerturm) has survived, in St.-Apern-Strasse. The course of the Roman wall can be traced without difficulty in the modern street pattern because many parts of it remain above and below ground. The main streets of Roman Cologne are still obvious in the city today: the main north-south axis, for example, the cardo maximus, is today the Hohe Strasse.

Between this street and the Rhine stood a row of sizeable public buildings, including imposing temples: the Capitoline temple, in which the three main deities Jupiter, Juno and Minerva were worshipped, was in the southeast corner of the city, the site now occupied by the church of St Maria im Kapitol. The remains of the governor's palace, the **Praetorium**, which can be visited below part of the city hall buildings, testify to the magnificence of Roman Cologne.

**Glass manufacture**

From the mid-1st century potteries and workshops producing glass and metal goods were in operation just outside the city walls. Roman Cologne became an important centre for the production of high-quality glassware and ceramics.

The most remarkable glass vessels made in the city were the so-called **cage cups**, which consisted of clear, thick glass surmounted by a fine network of coloured glass. They were made by coating the base layer with one or more outer layers of coloured glass, which was then painstakingly ground away until only a fragile net remained around the clear core.

The **snake-thread glasses**, carefully formed vessels of clear glass to which coloured glass threads were applied while they were still hot, were a further Cologne speciality. A selection of the finest pieces is on display in the Römisch-Germanisches Museum.

← *Pop Art: an upturned ice-cream cornet by Claes Oldenburg is the distinctive feature of the Neumarkt-Galerie.*

**Dionysos mosaic** Construction work for a bomb shelter next to the cathedral in 1941 brought to light a well-preserved mosaic with an area of 70 sq m/750 sq ft. It is thought to have been the dining room floor of a large villa in the early 3rd century. Its 31 sections, framed in ornamental bands and friezes, depict motifs associated with the cult of the wine god Dionysos, who is depicted in the centre, drunk and leaning for support on a satyr. The quality of the mosaic illustrations is very high, especially the masterly handling of light and shade. The animals and fruit depicted in the trapezium-shaped zones near the edges of the mosaic point to the purpose of the room, but may also refer to the Dionysian fertility cult. The Römisch-Germanisches Museum was built from 1970 to 1974 exactly on the site of the mosaic and marks the approximate size of the villa. Next to the mosaic, the 14.5m/48ft-high Poblicius monument, commissioned by an ex-soldier as a memorial for his family, gives an impression of the grandeur of the funeral monuments that once lined the main roads leading into the city.

**Rhine bridge** Emperor Constantine the Great ordered the building of the first permanent bridge over the Rhine in AD 310. It was 420m/460yd long, with 15 stone piers to support the wooden superstructure. It connected the centre to the **fortress Divitia** (today Deutz) on the right bank. Metal-tipped wooden piles on which the piers rested are on view in the Römisch-Germanisches Museum.

## Romanesque Art and Architecture

**Early Christian tradition** From the 5th century Frankish rulers resided in Cologne. In the early 6th century the Franks under **Clovis I** (»Chlodwig« in German) were converted to Christianity, and in Cologne there are many signs of an unbroken Christian tradition from late Roman times. Three churches were built on the site of Roman cemeteries: St Gereon probably as a memorial or mausoleum that was later used by Frankish kings, St Severin and St Ursula originally as chapels over Christian graves. The history of the cathedral, too, may date back to this period. A Roman house found below the cathedral was possibly used as a place of assembly by early Christians, and the 6th-century buildings on the site, in which two members of a Frankish royal family were interred, were clearly a church. **Charlemagne**, who united the kingdom of the Franks and extended it eastwards, changing the situation of Cologne in his empire from a peripheral to central position, appointed his chaplain **Hildebold** bishop in 787 and elevated the see to the status of an archbishopric in 795. Cologne prospered as a centre of commerce and learning. A new cathedral was completed in 870, and the existence of six other monasteries and collegiate churches for men and women testifies to the importance of the city in Carolingian times. However, with the exception of the 4th-century parts of St Gereon, church architecture before the 10th century survives only in the form of archaeological remains.

Seat of archbishop ►

*View of the decagon and choir of the church of St Gereon.*

A raid by Norsemen in 881 probably caused a great deal of damage, but did not hinder the long-term growth of Cologne, which thanks to its inclusion in the eastern part of the Frankish kingdom became the largest and wealthiest city north of the Alps in the course of the 10th century and a leading centre of western European civilization.

**Sculpture**

The **Gero crucifix** (Gerokreuz), the oldest larger-than-life-size crucifix of Western medieval art, dates from this period. This painted wooden cross, made around 970 for the cathedral and still to be seen there, depicts Christ just after the moment of death in a realistic and expressive manner that marked a new departure in early medieval sculpture and is regarded as a model for later triumphal crosses.

**Churches**

From the mid-10th to the early 13th century many churches were built in Cologne in the Romanesque style. Twelve of them have survived. They represent a unique concentration of Romanesque architecture: nowhere else can all of its phases and styles be seen in such a small area (►Baedeker Special p.38). All twelve were damaged in the Second World War, most of them seriously, but had been carefully reconstructed by the mid-1980s. The churches lie within the medieval area of the city, i.e. inside the Ring boulevard.

This era of ecclesiastical architecture opened with **St Pantaleon**, where Archbishop Bruno initiated a basilica that was completed after his death for Empress Theophanu; both Bruno, brother of Emperor Otto 1, and Theophanu are buried there. Its massive westwork and the clarity of its early Romanesque forms give St Pantaleon great importance in the development of the style.

Construction of the collegiate church of **St Cäcilien** (953–965, completed in 1160) also began under Bruno. This column basilica without transept or tower now accommodates an outstanding collection

*Gross St Martin in the middle of the Old Town is silhouetted against the setting sun.*

# JEWELS OF ROMANESQUE ARCHITECTURE

**Long before the cathedral became the undisputed landmark of the city, Cologne had many other fine churches and a reputation far and wide as a holy city: »Sancta Colonia«. The only other cities that were permitted to use this title in the Middle Ages were Rome, Jerusalem and Trier.**

In a remarkable burst of energy in the 12th and 13th centuries, many churches were built in the Romanesque style in »Holy Cologne«. The sight of the city skyline with its towers must have amazed medieval travellers, whether merchants or pilgrims, many of whom had never seen such monumental buildings before, and their astonishment can only have increased when they stood directly in front of one of these magnificent churches.

Twelve of the great Romanesque churches have survived to the present day – an unrivalled concentration of architecture in this style. With the partial exception of **St Maria Lyskirchen**, which still possesses 13th-century paintings on its vault, all of them suffered severe damage in the Second World War. They were restored in an ambitious programme lasting four decades. Most of the work was completed in time to celebrate the Year of the Romanesque Churches in 1985, 40 years after the end of the war, but some projects took longer: the west tower of St Kunibert was not completed until 1993.

## Towers and Façades

One characteristic of the Romanesque style, which did not fully give way to the Gothic style in Cologne until work began on the cathedral in 1248, is the combination of various architectural elements to form a harmonious whole. On some churches, such as **St Kunibert, St Gereon and St Pantaleon**, two towers flank the apse of the choir to form an east or west façade, while **Gross St Martin** has a single tower, the most beautiful in the city, over the crossing. The »trefoil« choir, a clover-leaf ground plan consisting of three rounded apses in the north, east and south, is a feature of Romanesque architecture in Cologne. The first such choir was built in the 11th century for **St Maria im Kapitol**; it was copied at Gross St Martin and **St Aposteln**. Many of the churches have a triforium (an arcaded wall-passage facing into the church) or a dwarf gallery (a low arcade on the outer wall), features that were developed in this period as a means of structuring the wall elevation. The practice of

covering the church with a stone vault in place of a flat wooden ceiling was also increasingly prevalent in these centuries.

The boom in construction and the precious furnishings of the churches were financed largely by donations from the citizens, especially wealthy merchants and the noble families from whom members of the collegiate foundations were drawn. The twelve great Romanesque buildings were not originally parish churches, but for the most part monastery or collegiate churches. The period of building came to an end in the early 13th century with **St Kunibert**; after that the cathedral was the main building site of the city.

## Cult of Holy Relics

The veneration of saints played an essential role in the status of Cologne as a holy city. Over centuries the number of precious relics continually increased. From the 10th century the cathedral possessed the chains and crozier of St Peter, which took second place after 1164 to the bones of the Three Magi, brought from Milan by Archbishop Rainald von Dassel. However, every church had its treasures. In particular, three of them – St Gereon, St Severin and St Ursula – occupied **the site of Roman cemeteries**, and the remains of Roman citizens were willingly interpreted as the bones of martyrs: the pilgrims who came to the city were an important source of income. It was believed that the possession of the relics of saints and martyrs protected the city from misfortunes.

## Power and Influence

Above all, the power of the relics of the patron saints of the city – St Peter, St Gereon and the Theban Legion, St Ursula and her 11,000 companions, and above all the Three Magi – was thought to make Cologne safe from attack. The wave of building activity on the twelve churches that have been preserved to this day created a worthy setting for these holy treasures; and the construction of a massive city wall, which no enemy ever stormed, surrounded all twelve.

The Roman Catholic Church today seeks to revive the idea of pilgrimage: in 2005 its World Youth Day brought almost one million young Catholics to Cologne, and an annual cathedral pilgrimage is held at the end of September. Most visitors to the city today, however, are tourists. Everyone wants to see the cathedral, but the majestic Romanesque churches, which exemplify all phases of this style, also deserve admiration as a unique architectural ensemble from the Middle Ages.

*The shrine of the Three Magi by Nicholas of Verdun is probably the most famous example of the art of medieval goldsmiths.*

of Christian art from the early Middle Ages to the Baroque period, the Museum Schnütgen.

**St Maria im Kapitol** was built in the mid-11th century on the foundations of a 1st-century Roman temple. It is the first example of a so-called clover-leaf choir, consisting of round apses in the north, south and east. Here it is combined with an axial nave in the west, a plan that was to be copied in many later churches.

The little church of **St Maria Lyskirchen** in the old harbour district by the Rhine, which was built between 1210 and 1220, is the only one of the twelve that suffered relatively little damage in the Second World War. It is outstanding for its well-preserved, excellent 13th-century frescoes.

**St Gereon**, named after a Roman martyr who was adopted as one of the patron saints of the city, has a long history. Its remarkable feature is the fact that an oval Roman building was enclosed within a ten-sided, domed structure in a late Romanesque style that reveals early Gothic elements. A lovely Gothic sacristy later was attached to the Romanesque choir. The design of the east façade is the first example in Cologne of decorative elements that emphasized the storeys of the choir, a feature imitated at St Aposteln, which has a magnificent east façade with dwarf gallery and frieze, as well as at Gross St Martin and St Kunibert. St Kunibert, consecrated in 1247, was the last Romanesque basilica to be built before work began on the Gothic cathedral.

The church of the Benedictine abbey of **Gross St Martin** was consecrated in 1172, but its massive tower was not completed until 1220.

The rich decoration of the east façade, the skilful handling of the enormous bulk of the building and the full repertoire of Romanesque architectural forms characterize this church, which remains to this day the landmark of the Old Town. On the Rhine skyline its unmistakeable tower with four corner turrets is a worthy counterpart to the cathedral.
The »golden centuries« of architecture that produced these wonderful Romanesque churches are still evident in the appearance of »holy Cologne«.

**Illuminated manuscripts**

From the 10th to the 12th century important workshops in Cologne produced illuminated manuscripts. They met the liturgical needs of many churches, and several codices were presented by the archbishops to other dioceses. One particularly fine example, the **gospel of St Pantaleon**, was made in the mid-12th century, probably in the scriptorium of St Pantaleon monastery, and is now held in the city archive, along with a number of other valuable manuscripts. The influence of Byzantine models is characteristic for the manuscripts that were illuminated in Cologne.

**Goldsmiths and jewellers**

The goldsmiths were considered the noblest guild of the city, which ranked alongside Paris as the foremost centre in northern Europe for work in precious metals and jewels in the 12th and 13th centuries. The numerous holy relics held in the churches of Cologne made the city one of the most significant places of pilgrimage of the medieval Christian world after Rome, Jerusalem and Santiago de Compostela.
The veneration of holy relics blossomed as never before when Archbishop **Rainald von Dassel** brought the bones of the Three Magi to Cologne in 1164. In order to house these relics, the goldsmith **Nicholas of Verdun** was commissioned to create the most precious shrine ever made. Between about 1190 and 1220 he and his successors produced one of the most beautiful and famous works of the medieval goldsmith's art.
The reliquary shrine of the Three Magi, which today can be seen behind the high altar of the cathedral, has the form of a basilica, an innovation which was to be influential in the 13th century. In addition to the bones of the Three Magi, it also contains the relics of the martyrs Felix and Nabor and those of St Gregory of Spoleto.
The materials used are gold, silver, copper, bronze and enamel; ancient

### The Three Magi

- Once each year it is possible to catch a glimpse of the relics of the Three Magi: on 6 January, when the cathedral is packed with worshippers, part of the front end of the shrine is opened. When Archbishop Rainald von Dassel brought the relics to Cologne, they attracted a stream of pilgrims and led to the building of the new, Gothic cathedral. It was believed that relics emanated an aura or power, of which pilgrims who passed beneath them could partake. On a few days each year in late September it is still possible to walk beneath the shrine (see www.koelner-dom.de for information).

gems and cameos, and a large number of precious stones decorate it. The shrine is 220cm/7ft long, 150cm/5ft high and 110cm/4ft 6in wide. The figures and scenes represent a carefully thought-out theological programme showing the adoration of the Three Magi as part of the story of salvation from the Old and New Testaments. The dynamism with which the figures are portrayed is a definitive departure from the Byzantine-influenced static appearance of earlier shrines.

Further reliquaries, liturgical items and monstrances from this period can be admired in the cathedral treasury. The diocesan museum Kolumba, which presents religious art from the early Christian period to modern times, has an excellent collection of medieval sculpture and goldsmith work.

## Gothic Art and Architecture

**Cathedral**

Cologne was slow to embrace the Gothic style, probably because Romanesque architecture had attained such a high level of development in the city. The new style made its breakthrough only when construction of the cathedral began in 1248. The reason for building a new cathedral was the flood of pilgrims to the shrine of the Three Magi, which was to be presented in fitting splendour. **Meister Gerhard**, the first cathedral architect, modelled his plans on those of the French royal cathedrals at Amiens and Reims, but further developed the style and aimed to surpass the French cathedrals in size and magnificence. Cologne Cathedral was conceived as the largest in the world in its time, and as a representation on earth of the heavenly Jerusalem. The weight and mass of the Romanesque churches that preceded it gave way to soaring lightness and elaborate ornamentation.

In the first decades, the work proceeded rapidly. In 1265 the choir chapels were completed, in 1277 the sacristy. Around the year 1300 the choir was walled off from the work continuing in the west of the site, furnished with stained glass windows, sculpture, choir stalls and paintings, and consecrated in 1322. In the 14th century work began on the south tower, which would have dwarfed all French cathedrals if it had reached its intended height (now 157m/521ft) in the Middle Ages. However, the pace of work slowed as a result of the enormous costs, even though large sums were donated or raised by the flourishing business of selling indulgences. When building stopped in about 1530, and in 1560 the cathedral chapter formally announced the cessation of work, only the first two storeys of the south tower were finished. All foundations were in place, the nave walls and arcades had reached a height of about 13m/43ft, and the northern aisles had been vaulted. The rest of the church was given a provisional roof. Only the choir was finished for use, and the great building remained a hulk for the next three centuries.

**Secular architecture**

The only house of a patrician family that has survived, the **Overstolzenhaus**, lies to the south of Heumarkt in Rheingasse. It was built to

*The figures of the »Nine Heroes« on the wall of the Hansasaal in the city hall date from 1360.*

impress, between 1220 and 1230, and its façade displays the transition from Romanesque to Gothic style in that it consists almost entirely of rows of windows. The two five-bay lower storeys were probably living accommodation, and the four upper floors, which form a tall stepped gable, were storage space. There were once many such houses, as the wealth of citizens who profited from Rhine trade made its mark on the city between the 13th and 15th centuries.
The rich merchants rebelled against the secular authority of the archbishops, who ruled Cologne, in the 13th century, and achieved the independence of the city through victory at the battle of Worringen in 1288. From the mid-14th century the **city hall (Rathaus)** was built. It is a group of buildings from various periods, much of which was destroyed in the Second World War and rebuilt only in part. The reconstructed parts include the Gothic **Hansasaal**, a hall at the heart of the building that has sculptural decoration in stone. In 1396 serious conflicts between the patrician families and the guilds resulted in a new constitution. The guilds expressed their new-found power by building the massive, 61m/220ft-high **city hall tower** between 1407 and 1414 and adorning it with over 100 figures. The other sign of municipal pride that survives from the 15th century is the Gürzenich, a banqueting hall built from 1441 to entertain high-ranking visitors.

**Painting**

From the early 13th century the art of painting on panels gained in importance alongside the arts of book illumination, stained glass and fresco painting. The spread of the painted altar retable opened up a new field of activity. The painters' workshops were in the street that is still named Schildergasse (»sign-painters' street«), where their guildhall stood.

*»Adoration of the Magi«: the centre part of the »Altar of the City Patron Saints«, the best-known work of Stefan Lochner.*

The art of painting reached its pinnacle in Cologne with the work of **Stefan Lochner** (► Famous People), who stands out as a known name amidst the anonymity of many other painters of the time. Lochner came to Cologne from the area of Lake Constance in about 1430. His most famous work, the *Altar of the City Patron Saints*, was painted around 1440 for the chapel of the city hall and has been in the cathedral since 1809.

Its theme is the adoration of Christ by the Three Magi, whose retinue is formed by the patron saints of Cologne, St Ursula and St Gereon with their followers, an indication that the city council gave the commission. The monumental style of the altarpiece and the magnificence of the contemporary robes of the depicted persons were unprecedented. The natural and lifelike rendering of the figures surpassed all previous work and set new standards.

Lochner's acclaimed representations of the Madonna include the *Madonna with the Violet* (1440, in Kolumba) and the *Madonna in the Rose Bower* (1450, Wallraf-Richartz-Museum), which is probably his last work.

## 16th to 19th Century

**Signs of stagnation**

The period from the 13th to the 15th century was the golden age of Cologne. As economic decline set in from the 16th century, the city lost importance not only as a commercial centre but also as a place of artistic excellence.

**St Peter**

The parish church of St Peter, a basilica with galleries, gained its present appearance in the years 1515–30. Together with St Cäcilien it

is the only remaining ensemble of a collegiate church with its associated parish church, and is one of Cologne's few buildings that date from the early 16th century. Its most interesting features are the fine late medieval stained glass and an altarpiece of the *Crucifixion of St Peter* of 1637 by **Peter Paul Rubens**.
In the last 20 years the church of St Peter has served not only as a parish church but as a place for exhibitions by international contemporary artists.

**Secular architecture**

The major public buildings of the 16th century were heavily indebted to the Renaissance architecture of the Netherlands, for example the **city hall loggia (Rathauslaube)** (1569–73) and the **arsenal (Zeughaus)** (1594–1606) with its wonderful Renaissance entrance. Until 1919 the Zeughaus accommodated the city collection of weapons and is today the home of the Kölnisches Stadtmuseum, which is devoted to the history of the city.

**Private art collections**

Occupation of the city by French forces in 1794 sealed the end of Cologne's status as a free imperial city. The secularization of church property in 1802 meant the dissolution of monasteries and collegiate communities, the closure and demolition of many churches and the sale of valuable libraries and works of art. At the same time keen private collectors were active; citizens with an appreciation of art salvaged works from churches and monasteries, thus establishing the basis for a number of collections that can be admired in Cologne today. The scholar **Ferdinand Franz Wallraf** (1748–1824) laid the basis for the Wallraf-Richartz-Museum. **Alexander Schnütgen** (1843 to 1918), a canon of the cathedral, collected medieval religious art that is now on view in the Museum Schnütgen.

! *Baedeker* TIP

**For a journey through the history of art ...**

... starting with the masters of the Cologne school of Gothic painting, go to the medieval department of the Wallraf-Richartz-Museum. Here you can also see an excellent exhibition of Dutch, Flemish, Italian, Spanish and French painting from the 14th to the 19th century, and finish by admiring the Impressionist works of the Fondation Courboud, which is housed in the same building.

**Completion of the cathedral**

In 1814 Prussian and Russian troops occupied the city, and at the Congress of Vienna in 1815 Cologne was incorporated into the Prussian state. At the same time the medieval plan for the façade of the cathedral came to light again and the idea of completing the building was discussed. After the restoration of the archdiocese of Cologne in 1821, the church also supported this bold scheme. Emergent nationalist sentiment added impetus to the idea, and the project of completing Cologne Cathedral became a symbol for the unification of Germany, the building itself a national monument.

*A railway station in a prominent place: travellers on the concourse have a view of the cathedral.*

From 1841 an **association for building the cathedral, the Zentral-Dombau-Verein**, raised enormous sums of money. The Prussian king **Friedrich Wilhelm IV** promised to share the costs of construction, and in 1842 a foundation stone for the continuation of the work was laid. On 15 October 1880, 632 years after the building was begun, Cologne Cathedral was completed and the skyline of the city, which had changed little in 300 years, now had two more spires.

**Railway station**

Following the linking of Cologne to the railway system in 1839, the main station was built right next to the cathedral and inaugurated in 1859. The present, huge station roof of glass and iron, a monument of 19th-century industrial architecture, dates from 1894. After destruction in the Second World War, the station concourse was rebuilt in the sober style typical of the 1950s, but at the southern end of the building the old waiting room, now a restaurant, gives an impression of former glories.

Demolition of the city wall ▸

The demolition of the city wall from 1881 permitted the development of the Ring boulevard on the site of the old fortifications and the Neustadt (New Town) outside it. The Neustadt was constructed with streets radiating in symmetrical patterns from generously proportioned squares. In the eclectic manner of the late 19th century and early 20th century, a wide variety of historical styles – from neo-Gothic to pseudo-Renaissance and art nouveau – were used, and despite the effects of bombing and insensitive post-war development, many fine house façades and some imposing churches, such as St Agnes on Neusser Strasse and St Michael on Brüsseler Strasse, still testify to this ambitious and era of urban planning.

## 20th and 21st Centuries

**Municipal expansion**

In the late 19th and early 20th centuries Cologne expanded greatly in size through the incorporation of surrounding towns and villages, including the industrial settlements of Deutz and Mülheim on the east (right) bank of the Rhine. Cologne became the fifth-largest German city by area in the 1920s, and benefited from far-sighted planning under Konrad Adenauer, who established an inner and an outer green belt on the site of 19th-century Prussian fortifications.

**Architecture**

New trends in architecture reached the city in the 1920s. The most conspicuous example, built in 1925 to designs by Jakob Koerfer on Hansaring, is the 17-storey steel-frame structure of the **Hansa-Hochhaus**. This brick-clad skyscraper was not only the first in Cologne, with a height of 65m/213ft, but at the time of completion the tallest in Europe. It displays a harmonious combination of traditional architectural vocabulary with the Bauhaus style.

A second significant survival is the **Dischhaus**, built in 1929–30 by **Bruno Paul**. The façade of this elegant office building in Brückenstrasse takes its character from continuous horizontal bands of windows and its rounded shape, which reminded contemporaries of an ocean liner.

In architectural terms, Nazi ideology, with the exception of a broad east-west axis for traffic that cut through the old street pattern from Rudolfplatz to the Deutzer Brücke, has left very few traces in Cologne. The legacy of the National Socialists was that the Second World War reduced the city to rubble. Over 70% of the buildings of the city as a whole, and 90% of those in the centre, were destroyed.

Reconstruction began hesitantly and kept to the historic plan of the city (with the exception of a wide north-south artery for traffic called Nord-Süd-Fahrt, mainly built in the 1960s). The immediate aim was to provide housing and secure the half-ruined medieval buildings. The Griechenmarkt quarter to the south of Neumarkt is a good example of 1950s housing. Even in difficult times the city fathers found the energy and optimism to commission some architecture of high-quality. The outstanding examples in the historic centre are the new wing of the Gürzenich hall

! *Baedeker* TIP

**Models of the city**

Two large-scale models provide an enjoyable overview of the historic and modern city. The model in the Kölnisches Stadtmuseum shows the urban landscape in 157, while that in an inner courtyard of the Spanischer Bau opposite the city hall depicts modern Cologne.

*The Hohenzollernbrücke is the oldest of the eight bridges that span the Rhine in Cologne.*

# ACROSS THE RHINE

**Few cities around the world have so many bridges so close together to span a great river. From the engineering point of view, the Cologne bridges – currently there are eight – are remarkable for the fact that they employ many varying methods of construction.**

The Deutzer Brücke and the Zoobrücke are beam bridges – the least spectacular type to look at, as they have no arches or pylons. Their principal means of support are beams, which have to resist the bending forces that are applied to them. The **Deutzer Brücke** is a hollow-box beam bridge for trams, road vehicles and pedestrians, while the **Zoobrücke**, a box girder bridge, carries road vehicles and pedestrians only.

The **Südbrücke and Hohenzollernbrücke**, great arched constructions, are visually more impressive. The main supports in this type of bridge are the arches, in which the strongest forces are compressive stress. These two railway bridges connect the left bank to the right bank in three mighty arches; the Hohenzollernbrücke, for example, joins the cathedral and railway station to the district of Deutz. For those who are not disturbed by the rumbling of the trains, a walk across the bridge is rewarding, as there is a wonderful view of the Old Town, Museum Ludwig and cathedral.

The **Leverkusener Brücke** in the far north of Cologne, a motorway bridge, and the Severinsbrücke to the south of the Old Town are examples of cable-stayed bridges. In this method of construction, the bridge deck is held by diagonal cables attached to the pylons. The **Severinsbrücke** has just one pylon, a tall pointed structure that reflects the form of the cathedral towers. The cables are stretched between the pylon and the road deck in a fan design.

## Bridges for Road Traffic

The last type of bridge to complete the series is the suspension bridge. Here the full weight is supported by cables, which are suspended between the pylons, and only the tensile strength of the cables is tested. Of this kind of bridge, too, there are two examples in Cologne: the **Rodenkirchener Brücke**, which carries a six-lane motorway in the south of the city, and the **Mülheimer Brücke**, the longest in Cologne with a length of 708m/775yd. From some positions, such as the viewing platform of the

cathedral tower, Konrad-Adenauer-Ufer on the left bank of the river and the roof of the Schokoladenmuseum, it is possible to see five or more of the bridges at the same time.

There was a permanent bridge across the river in Roman times. Emperor Constantine the Great ordered the construction of a bridge to link the city to the fortress in Deutz. It was 420m/460yd long, and consisted of a wooden superstructure supported by stone piers. Some of the iron-tipped piles that were rammed into the bed of the river as foundations for the piers can be seen in the Römisch-Germanisches Museum. In the Middle Ages and in early modern times, the only connection between the two banks of the river was by ferry. Not until 1822 was a pontoon bridge built. It was 400m/440yd long, made of wood and rested on a line of barges. Several times each day it had to be raised to allow ships to pass. The first permanent bridge since ancient times was constructed only in 1855 on the site of the present Hohenzollernbrücke.

## Impulses from Railway Building

The first modern bridge was built for road and rail traffic, but owed its construction above all to the rapid expansion of railway companies that were establishing east-west connections across Germany. It was known locally as the **»mousetrap«** on account of its closed, box-like shape. In 1911 Emperor Wilhelm II personally inaugurated its successor, the Hohenzollernbrücke. The second railway bridge, the Südbrücke, was completed in 1910.

When the **Mülheimer Brücke** opened in 1929 it was the world's longest cable suspension bridge. Until 1920 the people of Cologne had to pay a toll on every bridge, and even after this was abolished, the railway and tram operators were charged two pfennigs for every passenger who made a crossing.

All Cologne bridges were destroyed in the Second World War, the Hohenzollernbrücke blown up by the retreating German army. The first temporary structures to cross the Rhine after the end of the war were built by the Allied occupying forces: first a wooden crossing on the site of the later Deutzer Brücke, and a year later a temporary steel construction, the Patton Bridge. In the following years all the pre-war bridges were rebuilt, and several new ones added. Their varied architecture is one of the defining elements in the appearance of the city.

and the Spanischer Bau, which houses municipal offices. The opera house (1957 by Wilhelm Riphahn), recently considered for demolition, is a respected building that will be restored from 2011.

**Museum architecture**

After the Second World War the **Wallraf-Richartz-Museum**, like almost all others in the city, was homeless, as its buildings had been completely destroyed. In 1957 Rudolf Schwarz and Josef Bernhard built new premises that are now seen as classic examples of »traditional modern« or »alternative modern« style. The gables and façades are a conscious link to traditional Cologne buildings, while the interior displays a new architectural vocabulary, especially in the multi-storeyed central space with its steeply rising staircase. Today the building holds a collection devoted to design and arts and crafts, the **Museum für Angewandte Kunst**.

In 2001 the Wallraf-Richartz-Museum moved into new premises designed by Oswald Mathias Ungers on the square in front of the city hall. Here, in a cube-shaped building which is windowless from some aspects, the city art collection up to the 19th century is exhibited behind a façade of basalt lava and tufa.

*The Römisch-Germanisches Museum and the Museum Ludwig: a first-class complex of museums next to the cathedral*

*Sir Norman Foster's Gerling Ring-Karree is the architectural highlight of Friesenplatz.*

The **Römisch-Germanisches Museum** has a prominent site next to the cathedral. The architects, Heinz Röcke and Klaus Renner, produced an unassuming box shape with horizontal lines that typifies the museum architecture of the 1960s and 1970s.
In 1986 the opening of a cultural complex including the **Museum Ludwig** and the Philharmonie concert hall was well received. Right next to the cathedral and main station, the Cologne architectural practice Busmann & Haberer created a distinctive ensemble that succeeds in terms of both architecture and urban planning. The masses of the building have been carefully arranged so as not to block the view of the cathedral, and the zinc-clad shed-like roofs of the museum form an attractive counterpart to the soaring Gothic architecture.

**New museums**

Further museum projects will consolidate the reputation of Cologne as a city of art and culture. In 2007 **Kolumba**, the art collection of the archdiocese, opened to great acclaim. It is the work of a Swiss architect, Peter Zumthor. The museum occupies the site of the parish church of St Kolumba, which was destroyed in the Second World War, and integrates the chapel named »Madonna in den Trümmern« (Our Lady of the Rubble), built in 1950 around a Madonna figure that survived the bombs and was venerated as a sign of hope. The ground floor, open to the street by means of perforated walls, is a space of true power which presents the archaeological layers of the site, from the tomb vaults of the medieval church back to stonework of Merovingian and Roman times. The carefully designed rooms

above give views of the city and are a worthy setting for a fine exhibition of art.

A new building for the ethnological collection of the **Rautenstrauch-Joest-Museum** and an extension of the Museum Schnütgen are scheduled to open in summer 2009 on Josef-Haubrich-Hof near Neumarkt, and plans are under discussion for a major extension to the Kölnisches Stadtmuseum (history) and a new museum of Jewish culture in association with the archaeological zone next to the city hall.

**Further new architecture**

Several distinguished new buildings have enhanced the cityscape in recent years. In 2001 Sir Norman Foster's **Gerling Ring-Karree** was completed on Friesenplatz for the Gerling insurance company. In the materials used, Foster's building takes its cue from existing Gerling office buildings dating from the 1930s and the post-war period. The design also makes reference to the medieval city gates that once stood (and three of which still stand) where the Ring boulevard now runs.

The most ambitious project of the early 21st century is the redevelopment of the **Rheinauhafen** (►p.224) , in particular the spectacular, projecting »crane buildings« designed by the Hamburg practice Bothe, Richter, Teherani. The former harbour, which covers an area of 235,000 sq m/2.5 million sq ft, is evolving into a new city quarter for residential, cultural and business use, with a row of high-quality new blocks and protected 19th and 20th-century harbour buildings along the Rhine.

After a 16-year process of planning and construction, the **MediaPark** on the edge of the inner city has been completed. The six individual buildings arranged in a semi-circle around an open square are unimpressive – especially considering that the Campo in Siena was allegedly the inspiration for the layout – but the 148m/485ft-high KölnTurm by the French architect Jean Nouvel has become a new architectural landmark of the city. At a tactful distance from the cathedral, it enriches a skyline that had remained unchanged for many years. The conspicuous new feature of the right bank of the Rhine is the **Lanxessarena** (1999, until 2008 known as Kölnarena), Germany's largest indoor sports and event hall with a 76m/250ft-high arch that can be seen from afar.

Deutz on the right bank of the river is a focus of urban planning for the coming years. The trade fair complex with its nimbus of hotels and office buildings is continually developing, and a new station for the high-speed trains heading south to Frankfurt is planned. The newest landmark in Deutz is the 103m/338ft-tall **KölnTriangle**, an office block on Ottoplatz that was opened in 2006.

← *Construction of the MediaPark gave Cologne not just a modern business and entertainment district, but a new feature of the skyline: the 148m/485ft-high KölnTurm.*

**Sculpture** Sculpture, too, followed a new path after the Second World War. Artists who produced representational works took Expressionist figurative sculpture as their starting point. **Ewald Mataré** (1887–1965) took a leading role in the Rhineland. Large-scale projects were few and far between in the period of post-war reconstruction, but for the 700th anniversary of the cathedral in 1948 he was commissioned to renew the doors of the south transept, which had been destroyed. By 1954 he had made four new bronze doors for the cathedral.

The central door, completed in 1948 and known as the **Pope's Door**, displays the coat of arms of Pius XII in addition to the cock and pelican as symbols of vigilance and love. The coat of arms of Cardinal Archbishop Josef Frings can be seen on the **Bishop's Door**, also completed in 1948, along with Cologne saints to personify wisdom, fear of God, strength, science, reason and piety. The **Whitsun Door** of 1953 represents the heavenly Jerusalem; below it are the burning city of Cologne with Noah kneeling and planting the first vine as a symbol of a new beginning for the city. In 1954 Mataré finished the Door of Creation, on which the hand of God represents the creation of the world. The burning bush is a symbol for the appearance of God in the world, and the net represents the church.

A completely different trend in sculpture can be seen on Heinrich-Böll-Platz, part of the Museum Ludwig complex that was completed in 1986. Using granite, cast iron and brick, accompanied by the planting of carefully positioned trees, the Israeli **Dani Karavan** (born 1930) designed it as an environment that relates to its surroundings, including the museum, cathedral, railway bridge and the gardens by the Rhine. In one corner of the square Karavan placed a tall stepped tower, which he named **Ma'alot**. The artist's explanation of the Hebrew title and the design of the square is as follows: »The name derives from the verb ›to ascend‹ and encompasses on the one hand the idea of a step, rung, terrace (...), the upper world. On the other hand it also means, above all, (...) an increase, angle, division of a circle (...). It denotes ›human degrees‹, favourable qualities of humans, strengths, virtues, character.«

Sculpture park ► In 1997 the collectors Eleonore and Michael Stoffels initiated the Skulpturenpark Köln on a green site of 5000 sq m/55,000 sq ft. close to the Zoobrücke between the Rhine and Riehler Strasse. The park now holds about 30 works by internationally renowned artists, some of them on a large scale.

**Painting** After the First World War, in Cologne as in other cities, avant-garde groups of young artists with revolutionary ideas aimed to bury the old casts of mind of the pre-war years. One of the leading figures in this movement was the Dadaist and Surrealist **Max Ernst**, who was born in 1891 in Brühl to the southwest of Cologne and took an active part in the art scene of the city under the name »DADAMAX« until he left for Paris in 1922. With Johannes Baargeld and **Angelika** and **Heinrich Hoerle** he established the Dada movement in Köln.

*Art Cologne is one of Europe's leading fairs for contemporary art.*

Their exhibition in Brauhaus Winter on Schildergasse in 1920 caused a furore.

After Max Ernst's departure a group known as the Progressives formed. Its principal members were Angelika and Heinrich Hoerle and **Franz Wilhelm Seiwert**. The motifs of their paintings reveal their political intent. Workers, the world of labour and its social environment were now seen as worthy subjects for art, and in stylistic terms the group evolved a new figurative Constructivism which, although influenced by Russian and French avant-garde art, retained its own particular characteristics. The movement known as Neue Sachlichkeit (New Objectivity) was also well established in Cologne in the 1920s in the persons of **Anton Räderscheidt** and **Heinrich Maria Davringhausen**. These interesting developments came to an abrupt end in 1933 when the Nazis took power and enforced a rigid policy in cultural matters.

**Galleries**

The private galleries in Cologne today represent an excellent opportunity to keep up with developments in contemporary art. Although the art scene in the city has been affected by the resurgence of Berlin, over 100 commercial galleries, some with international standing, are still based in Cologne. The art boom started in the 1960s with an art fair, now called Art Cologne, that was initiated by the gallery proprietor **Rudolf Zwirner**. Today Art Cologne is one of the leading European art fairs, attracting over 250 exhibitors to the city annually in April.

A flourishing commercial art scene, the presence of many collectors and a favourable attitude on the part of the city authorities have encouraged numerous artists to settle in Cologne, including such prominent names as Gerhard Richter, Sigmar Polke, A. and B. Blum, Jürgen Klauke and Rosemarie Trockel. Gerhard Richter ventured into a new medium with his large stained-glass window for the south façade of Cologne Cathedral, which was unveiled in 2007 and has provoked spirited discussion. Only 200 yards away, in the church of St Andreas, the work of another leading German artist, Markus Lüpertz, can be seen in several glass windows in the south transept.

In the compact city centre it is easy to gain an impression of the contemporary art scene. Most of the galleries can be found either close to the cathedral or in the districts known as Friesenviertel and Belgisches Viertel. In recent years there have been some bold private initiatives such as the cooperation of several gallery owners to open the

**Galerienhaus** (An der Schanz 1 a) in a former electricity transformer plant, and the **Forum für Fotografie und Kunst** in the south of the city (Schönhauser Str. 8, Bayenthal district), which consists of two galleries and three foundations. For art lovers a trip to Cologne is always rewarding: nowhere else in Germany can 2000 years of art be seen in such a small area.

# Music

**Lively music scene**

With a colourful and varied musical life that is continually evolving, Cologne has a music scene to rival that of the capital Berlin; there is something for every taste, from classics to techno. The music scene gets its impulses on the one hand from established orchestras and choirs, from the music school, the opera and concert halls; and one the other hand from a myriad of clubs and pubs, recording studios and small music publishers. There are large halls for touring international rock and pop stars, and small venues catering for special tastes.

*The Philharmonie concert hall stages over 400 performances annually – a wide-ranging programme from classics to jazz, pop and dance.*

*The Stadtgarten is one of the city's main venues for jazz concerts.*

Many visitors come to the city for **musicals**. The most popular are performed in the Musical Dome close to the cathedral, which is scheduled to close by 2011 at the latest and be replaced by a new venue on the right bank of the Rhine that has yet to be built. The four-day annual festival **»c/o pop«** – »Cologne on Pop« – is held each August at sites all over the city to showcase electronic pop music, and includes open-air and club concerts, parties and events with light installations and video art. A forum for presenting and discussing the latest trends in electronic music, multimedia and digitalization, »conference c/o pop«, is held at the same time.

◄ Jazz and MusikTriennale

The centre for jazz in the city is the Kölner Jazzhaus in the Stadtgarten, where a full programme of events includes mainstream and other forms of jazz, and a wide range of other contemporary music with an emphasis on improvisation. The major regional jazz festival, the Leverkusener Jazztage, is held each November in the neighbouring town of Leverkusen. A mixed offering of classics, rock and jazz is the attraction of the **MusikTriennale**, which brings ensembles from all over the world to Cologne every three years between Easter and Whitsun (2010, 2013).

**Westdeutscher Rundfunk**

Westdeutscher Rundfunk (WDR), the largest German public broadcasting company, plays an important role in the musical life of the city by organizing concert series, mainly classics and jazz, many of

*The Bläck Fööss, a local group, are assured of an enthusiastic welcome when they play at the Tanzbrunnen.*

which are held in the concert hall (Grosser Sendesaal) of WDR. An extensive programme of religious music, much of it of high quality, is performed throughout the year in the cathedral and other churches of the city.

**Cologne ensembles**

There is a concert by a local orchestra almost every day of the week: the Gürzenich Orchester, Kölner Philharmoniker, WDR Sinfonieorchester and WDR Rundfunkorchester are the leading ensembles.
At the two music schools, the Hochschule für Musik and the Rheinische Musikhochschule, teachers and students regularly perform. Famous composers have worked at the Kölner Musikhochschule: **Karlheinz Stockhausen** (1928–2007), **Hans Werner Henze** (born 1926) and **Mauricio Kagel** (born 1931). With 1800 students and 440 teachers, the Kölner Musikhochschule is a leading European institution of its kind. It was the first in Germany to offer courses in jazz and popular music, and is one reason why great jazz musicians frequently perform in Cologne.

**Rock and pop**

Countless rock and pop bands are based in Cologne, and the city is known across Germany for its own movement known as **Kölsch rock**, i.e. rock music with lyrics in Kölsch, the local dialect. The Kölsch band BAP, formed by the singer and songwriter **Wolfgang Niedecken** (► Famous People), has been one of the leading German rock bands for almost 30 years.

The locals' love of their home town and its own brand of popular music is expressed loud and clear each year at carnival time, when bands such as the **Bläck Fööss**, De Höhner and BRINGS perform at shows and street events, and dialect songs blare from every pub, where revellers sing along merrily.
One of the most important »Krautrock« groups, Can, formed in Cologne in 1968. Though not commercially successful, their improvised »instant compositions« are cited as an influence by many internationally famous artists.

**Studios, publishers and labels**

Despite a trend for players in the music business to move to Berlin, the German HQ of EMI Electrola is close to Cologne and well-known local labels such as Chlodwig Music and Lipstick, as well as many recording studios, are based in and around the city. Cologne is well provided with stores selling instruments and music, and has what claims to be the world's largest CD shop, Saturn, where the choice is huge and customers with special interests are catered for.

# Famous People

**A Roman empress who gave the city its name, a scholar who initiated the completion of the cathedral and an archbishop who – in special circumstances – condoned theft: read here portraits of some well-known people connected with Cologne.**

## Konrad Adenauer (1876–1967)

**Politician**

Adenauer trained as a lawyer and was mayor of Cologne from 1917 to 1933. The city is indebted to him for the refounding of the university in 1919, the leisure and sports facilities of the inner and outer green belts, the establishment of the trade fair grounds in 1924 and the economic growth of the 1920s, especially the building of the Ford car factory in the north of the city. In 1933 he was removed from office by the Nazis and arrested in 1944. From 1945 Adenauer engaged in politics again as one of the founders of the Christian Democratic Union: he was a leading influence in drawing up the West German constitution in 1948–49 and became the first chancellor of the Federal Republic of Germany in 1949, in addition to holding the office of foreign minister from 1951 to 1955. His chancellorship decisively shaped post-war German history. He achieved the integration of the Federal Republic into the western alliance, e.g. through membership of NATO, established diplomatic relations with the USSR and brought back many prisoners of war from Russian captivity. In 1963 he resigned as chancellor but remained politically active.

### i Cologne characters

- In 1995 the tower of the city hall was adorned with stone statues of people who made a mark in the 2000-year history of the city: saints and emperors, campaigners for women's rights and businessmen, writers and artists, a total of 128 figures from Julia Agrippina to Heinrich Böll. The choice of names was controversial: not everyone was pleased to see Karl Marx on the tower, and the initial inclusion of just five women raised such a storm that the committee of historians was forced to reconsider, eventually finding 18 women worthy of the honour.

## Julia Agrippina (AD 15–59)

Julia Agrippina was the granddaughter of Marcus Vipsanius Agrippa, friend and son-in-law of Emperor Augustus. Agrippa, who campaigned in the Rhineland in 38 BC and 19 BC, brought the Ubii tribe from the right bank to settle the area west of the Rhine and was once considered to have founded the »oppidum ubiorum« that later developed into Cologne.

Julia Agrippina was born in Cologne while her father, Germanicus, was military commander there. She married the Roman senator Gnaeus Domitius Ahenobarbus at the age of 13 and in AD 37 gave a birth to a son, the later Emperor Nero. In AD 48 she married for the third time. Her new husband, Claudius, emperor from 41 to 54, gave her the title »augusta« (empress) in AD 50 and granted full municipal rights to the place of her birth, henceforth named Colonia Clau-

*← Konrad Adenauer, Chancellor of the Federal Republic of Germany, in conversation with Federal President Theodor Heuss in May 1958*

dia Ara Agrippinensium (CCAA). In the Middle Ages the citizens honoured her memory by referring to themselves as »Agrippinians«. In AD 54 Agrippina poisoned her husband Claudius in order to put her son Nero, who was under her influence, on the throne. However, her period of power was short, and in AD 59 the young Nero had his mother murdered.

## Albertus Magnus (*c* 1200–80)

»Albert the Great« was born around the year 1200 in Lauingen on the Danube, the son of an earl, and joined the Dominican order while a student in Padua. After teaching in various German monasteries he took a doctorate in 1247 in Paris and taught theology there. In 1248 the Dominican order sent him to Cologne to establish and head its college (studium generale) there. His most famous pupil was Thomas Aquinas. Albertus Magnus, as he was known within his own lifetime, wrote pioneering commentaries on the works of Aristotle and, in addition to theology, pursued studies on the natural sciences to a degree unusual at that time. His enormous reputation led to his being used as an arbiter in conflicts between the citizens of Cologne and Archbishop Konrad von Hochstaden. He was canonized in 1931 and is revered by the church for his reconciliation of science and religion; his mortal remains rest in the crypt of St Andreas church in Cologne.

*The great philosopher and theologian depicted on a fresco of 1352*

## Sulpiz Boisserée (1783–1851)

**Architect and art collector**

Sulpiz Boisserée, who was born in Cologne, and his brother Melchior devoted themselves to art, literature and philosophy from an early age. In Paris the brothers met Friedrich Schlegel, who aroused their interest in Gothic architecture and in 1804 accompanied them back to Cologne, where they began to collect paintings by early German and Dutch masters, many of them deriving from secularized churches and monasteries. In 1827 King Ludwig I of Bavaria bought their valuable collection, which is now in the Alte Pinakothek in Munich.

From 1808 Sulpiz Boisserée produced drawings of Cologne Cathedral, including views of how it might look if completed, by which means he intended to gain support for continuation of building work on the cathedral. From 1835–36 Sulpiz Boisserée was head of the office for protecting monuments in Bavaria. He travelled in Italy and the south of France in 1838 and was made a Prussian state counsellor in 1845. In his last years he lived in Bonn.

## Heinrich Böll (1917–85)

**Author**

Heinrich Böll was born in Cologne, where he trained to be a bookseller, studied German literature and soon earned his living as an author. Although he lived most of his life in Cologne, his feelings towards his home town were ambivalent. On the one hand he loved and sang the praises of the city: »It is futile to praise Cologne, and yet it must be done, even though it is hard to describe something that is indescribable.« On the other hand he criticized the city and its residents so harshly that many regarded him as a traitor to his own people.

Böll is one of the outstanding figures in post-war German literature. His themes were the material needs and moral anguish of the years after the Second World War, and later the consequences of increasing affluence such as conformity and social injustice. His best-known works are *House without Guardians* (1954), *Billiards at Half-Past Nine* (1959), *The Clown* (1963), *Group Portrait with Lady* (1971) and *The Lost Honour of Katharina Blum* (1974). In 1972 Böll received the Nobel Prize for Literature, and in 1983 – despite objections to his involvement in political and social causes – was awarded the freedom of the city of Cologne.

## Josef Frings (1887–1978)

**Archbishop of Cologne**

Josef Frings was ordained a priest in 1910, became doctor of theology in 1916 in Freiburg, archbishop of Cologne in 1942 and cardinal in 1946. During the Third Reich he publicly criticized anti-Semitism and the Nazi rule of terror. He played an important role in the life of the church in Germany as chairman of the conference of bishops from 1945 to 1965, when he worked for the reconciliation of nations, and during the Second Vatican Council (1962–65), when he was one of the proponents of reform in the church. In the late 1950s and early 1960s he founded two charities, Misereor and Adveniat, that remain important to this day.

Frings was a popular archbishop, who became famous in the post-war years for appearing to condone the theft of coal from goods trains at a time when many people had no money to heat their homes. The word »fringsen« became a local term for stealing. In 1969 Frings retired from office, two years after being awarded the freedom of the city of Cologne.

## Irmgard Keun (1905–82)

**Author** Many of the novels and short stories of Irmgard Keun, including *After Midnight* (1937; English translation: Gollancz 1985), which she wrote in exile, were set in Cologne. Keun was born on 6 February 1905 in Berlin and came to Cologne at the age of eight.

She trained as an actress in the city, but turned to writing, in which she was encouraged by Alfred Döblin, among others. Her first book, *Gilgi, eine von uns* (1931) sold 30,000 copies in the first year. *The Artificial Silk Girl* (Other Press 2002), published a year later, was almost equally successful, and was filmed in 1960.

Her ironic and critical manner of portraying modern young women caused her books to be banned by the Nazis. In 1936 Irmgard Keun went into exile, and travelled around Europe with her partner, the Austrian Jewish poet Joseph Roth. A second work from this period, *Child of All Nations* (1938; Penguin Classics 2008) is available in English translation. It describes 1930s Europe from the point of view of a nine-year-old girl travelling with her parents – the figure of the writer father bears some resemblance to Roth. After Roth's death she returned incognito to Germany and survived the Second World War in hiding. Attempts to take up a literary career in the post-war years had only fitful success. Years of personal and creative crisis led to alcoholism and a six-year spell in a psychiatric clinic in Bonn. Although Keun's work was rediscovered in the 1970s, she lived the last years of her life in modest circumstances in Cologne.

## Stefan Lochner (c 1410–51)

**Painter** Stefan Lochner, the greatest master of the Cologne school of artists, was born around 1410 in Meersburg on Lake Constance and came to Cologne in about 1430. His unmistakable personal style combined the strict religious tradition of medieval art with the »modern« realism of the Low Countries.

In addition to outstanding paintings with a purely religious content such as the *Madonna with the Violet* (1440, in Kolumba) and the *Madonna in the Rose Bower* (1448, now in the Wallraf-Richartz-Museum), Lochner, who was elected to the city council in 1447 and 1451, painted his famous *Altar of the City Patron Saints* for the chapel of the city hall. This work, now in the cathedral, expressed the pride of the citizens of Cologne in a manner that was highly unusual in the context of German art of his time. Stefan Lochner probably died of plague in 1451.

*Stefan Lochner's famous »Altar of the City Patron Saints« (around 1442)*

## Karl Marx (1818–83)

**Philosopher**

After studying law, philosophy and history in Bonn and Berlin and taking his doctorate in Jena, Karl Marx moved to Cologne and worked in 1842 and 1843 as a journalist for the liberal *Rheinische Zeitung* (Rhenish newspaper). His articles, especially his comments on press freedom and the law on stealing wood, resulted in the closure of the paper, which opposed the Prussian government, but set an example for journalism in all Germany. In the following years he changed his abode often; Paris, Brussels and London were his main places of residence. In this period he and Friedrich Engels wrote the *Communist Manifesto*. In 1848 he returned to Cologne, established with Engels the headquarters of the Communist League and founded the *Neue Rheinische Zeitung*. As chief editor he set the revolutionary and democratic tone of the paper. Following the revolutionary events of September 1848, the conservative Prussian government exiled him in 1849. After a short spell in Paris he moved to London and lived there until the end of his life.

## Wolfgang Niedecken (born 1951)

**Musician**

In 1976, when Wolfgang Niedecken started his band BAP, no-one could foresee that they would become one of the most successful groups on the German music scene: at that stage the aim was »to rehearse till there's no more beer in the crate«. However, the very first records that they released made musical history in their home town, and to this day every BAP album has reached one of the top spots in the charts. The band BAP – the word »Bapp« means »father« in the local dialect – evolved around the singer Wolfgang Niedecken, a Bob Dylan fan. BAP became a cult band, with changing personnel over its 30-year history, but whatever their ups and downs, one thing could be relied on: BAP never got stuck in a rut. After 20 album releases and sales running into the millions, the band still goes on tour and gets an enthusiastic reception.

All the lyrics are written and sung in Wolfgang Niedecken's native language: Kölsch. As he wrote in a verse of the song *Für ne Moment*: »As long as I can remember, I have experienced and borne all my thoughts and all my feelings in our own language.«

Niedecken's role as singer and front man of BAP did not exhaust his creative energies. He has made three solo albums and, having studied art in the early 1970s in Cologne, produced paintings and

*Wolfgang Niedecken, leading light of the Kölsch-rock scene in the Kölnarena in 2004.*

graphic art. He has personally designed most of the album covers for BAP and exhibited his work on many occasions. Wolfgang Niedecken is also known for his committed attitude to political and social issues. In 1992 he was one of the organizers of an open-air concert on Chlodwigplatz in the south of the city to protest against racism under the title *Arsch huh – Zäng ussenander* (get off your butt and open your mouth), and in 2004 and 2005 was ambassador for a charity working against poverty in Africa.

## Jacques Offenbach (1819–80)

**Composer** The French-sounding first name is misleading: the composer was born in Cologne as Jakob Offenbach, but changed his name to Jacques after going to Paris, where he spent most of his life. He grew up in a musical family, as his father was cantor of the Cologne synagogue, and many of his works reflect experiences from his youth in the city. He often came back to Cologne, and his ironical and satirical streak, his biting humour and the elements of parody and irreverence in his operettas are attributed to the ready wit typical of the city and its carnival tradition. Offenbach's works, for example *Orpheus in the Underworld*, are considered to have founded the modern operetta genre; to this day he is known for his can-can, which originated as a dance scene in an operetta. His solitary opera, *Tales of Hoffmann*, is still often performed. The square in front of the Cologne opera house, which occupies the site of the old synagogue and the house of his parents, is named Offenbachplatz.

## Rainald von Dassel (c 1120–67)

**Archbishop** By translating the bones of the Three Magi from the conquered city of Milan to his cathedral in 1164, Archbishop Rainald von Dassel laid the foundations for the emergence of Cologne as one of the leading places of pilgrimage in the Christian world, a status that also brought considerable economic benefits. Rainald, the scion of a noble family, was a supporter of imperial power against that of the papacy, which earned him no sympathy from the pope but the favour of Emperor Friedrich I (Barbarossa), who made him imperial chancellor in 1156 and promoted his career in the church. In 1159 the emperor nominated him as archbishop of Cologne; not until six years later was he ordained – in spite of a papal interdict – as a priest and bishop.

## August Sander (1876–1964)

**Photographer** August Sander was born near Siegen, to the south-east of Cologne, and first worked as a miner, before taking up photography in 1897 during his military service in Trier on the Moselle. In 1901 he moved to Linz, on the Danube in Austria, and worked in a photographic studio, of which he became part-owner only a year later. In 1910 Sander moved to Cologne and was associated with the artist circle of »progressives« that had formed around the painters Hoerle and Seiwert. In 1929 he published an outstanding work, portraits of persons and professions of the 1920s, under the title *Antlitz der Zeit* (Face of the Times).

Sander's work met with disapproval during the Nazi period and was appreciated again only after 1945. His photos of Cologne before the Second World War attained a high artistic standard and represent a unique documentation of the city before its destruction. In 1962 Sander received the Bundesverdienstkreuz, the principal honour awarded in the Federal Republic. The main body of his work is held by the August-Sander-Archiv of the Photographischen Sammlung / SK Stiftung Kultur in the MediaPark in Cologne.

## Alice Schwarzer (born 1942)

**Feminist**

Alice Schwarzer is the figurehead of the German feminist movement, a figure known to the majority of Germans. By giving wide publicity to the themes of sexism and the patriarchal society, she has exposed herself to a great deal of malice: all the clichéd terms of abuse that are applied to emancipated women, from »frustrated feminist« to »man-hater« have been hurled at her. Today, after decades of feminist campaigns and publications as a journalist and author of books, she takes a more relaxed attitude: »I have shown that a woman can be critical, and may not always be liked for it, but at the same time is not seen as a candidate for summary execution.«

Alice Schwarzer was born in Wuppertal, 40km/25mi to the northeast of Cologne, and gained her first experience as a journalist in 1966 working for the *Düsseldorfer Nachrichten*. From 1970 to 1974 she lived in Paris, working there as a freelance correspondent for radio, TV and the press while studying psychology and sociology. She was one of the initiators of the feminist movement in Paris (Mouvement de Libération des Femmes), and introduced its ideas to Germany. She first caused a stir in 1971 with books, articles and campaigns against the ban on abortion. In January 1977 the first issue of *EMMA*, an illustrated magazine for women founded by Schwarzer, was published in Cologne. In 1983 she established the FrauenMediaTurm, an information centre about the history of women's emancipation that since 1994 has been based in the Bayenturm, a medieval tower on the Rhine that was part of the Cologne city wall.

Alice Schwarzer has written 21 books, including biographies of the Green Party politicians Petra Kelly and Gert Bastian and of the actress Romy Schneider, and issued a further 16 as publisher. She continues to attract attention, especially through her appearances in TV talk shows, and has received many awards for her political commitment, including the coveted Bundesverdienstkreuz of the Federal Republic of Germany.

SUNNER
HOTEL
PONCHO'S

# Practicalities

WHAT IS THE EASIEST WAY TO GET AROUND IN COLOGNE? WHERE IS THE BEST BEER AND THE MOST COMFORTABLE OVERNIGHT STAY? AND WHAT'S ON IN THE EVENINGS?

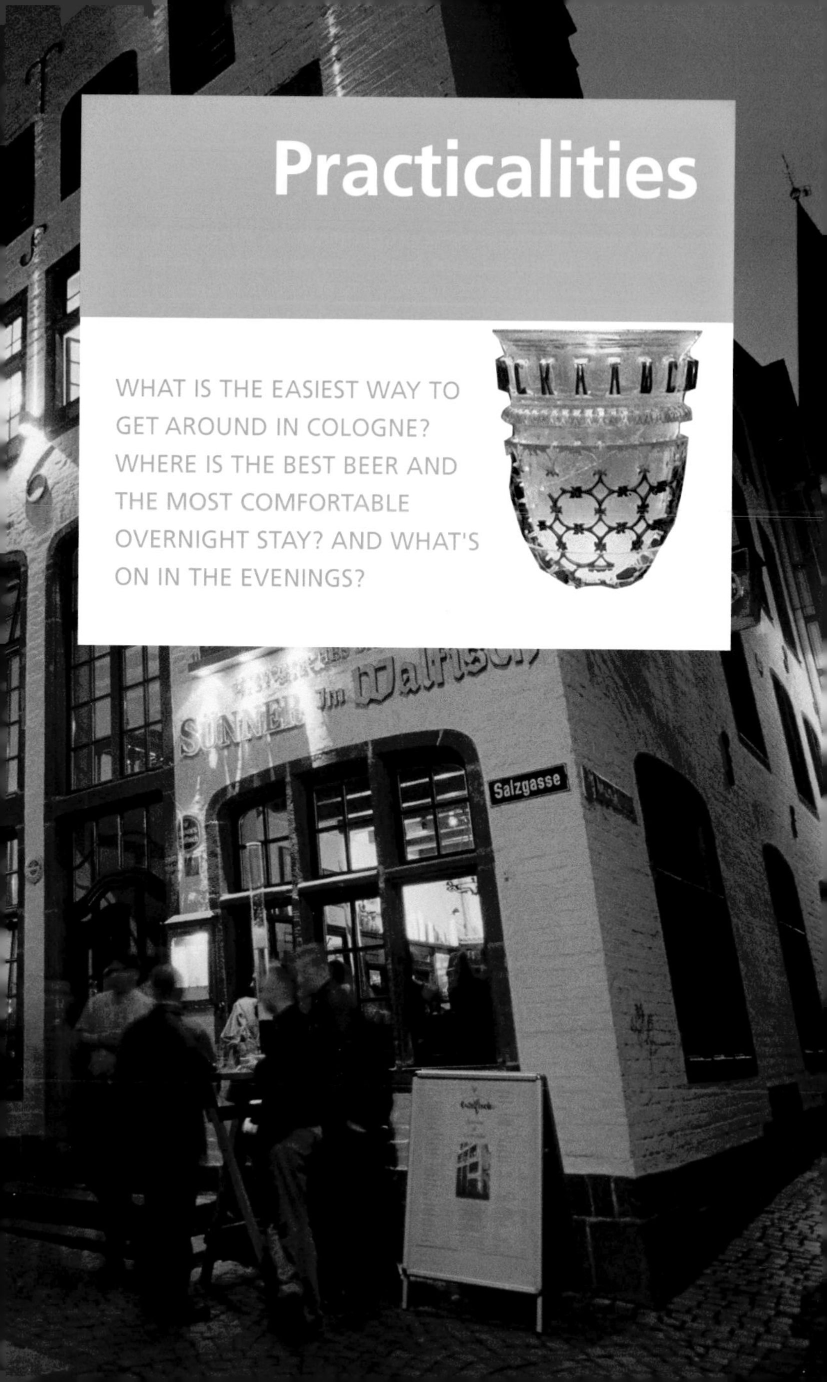

# Accommodation

## Hotels

**Hotel list** The tourist information office (KölnTourismus, ►Information) has a free list of hotels and guest houses. Accommodation can be booked in the office and on the internet site of KölnTourismus. The **Hotel Reservation Service** is also a helpful resource, especially during trade fairs when rooms are scarce in Cologne.

**Hotel prices** It is worth asking whether reductions are available for groups or for a stay longer than one or two days, especially outside the high season. During trade fairs, which are held quite frequently in Cologne, the hotels usually charge substantially more than the standard rates.

## RECOMMENDED HOTELS

▶ ① see plan p. 94/95

▶ **Price categories**
Luxury (cat. I): over 150 €
Mid-range (cat. II): 100 – 150 €
Budget (cat. III): under 100 €
(two persons in a double room)

*Luxurious accommodation in a converted water-tower*

### LUXURY

▶ ① **Dom-Hotel**
Domkloster 2 a
D-50667 Köln
Tel. 202 40
www.koeln.lemeridien.de
124 rooms and suites, sauna, conference facilities, restaurant
Elegant, old-established luxury hotel directly opposite the cathedral.

▶ ② **Excelsior Hotel Ernst**
Trankgasse 1
Domplatz
D-50667 Köln, tel. 27 01
www.excelsiorhotelernst.de
152 rooms and suites, sauna, conference facilities, restaurants
A classic grand hotel, beautifully furnished with excellent service and two gourmet restaurants.

▶ ③ **Hotel im Wasserturm**
Kaygasse 2
D-50676 Köln
Tel. 200 80
www.hotel-im-wasserturm.de
88 rooms and suites, roof-top

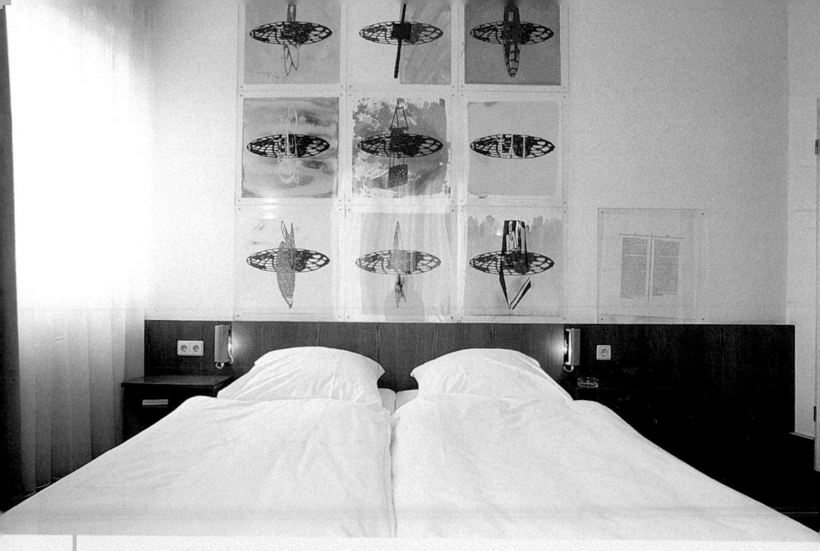

*Artists pay with their works at Hotel Chelsea.*

dining with a wonderful view and bar with garden terrace. The hotel is an impressive conversion of a 19th-century water tower just a few minutes on foot or by tram from the city centre. Chic interior design and excellent food.

## MID-RANGE

### ▶ ④ Ascot

Hohenzollernring 95
D-50672 Köln
Tel. 952 96 50
www.ascot.bestwestern.de
44 rooms
The furnishings in English country-house style match the grand old architecture. The location on the Ring boulevard is ideal for shopping and entertainment within easy reach of the sights.

### ▶ ⑤ Chelsea

Jülicher Str. 1
D-50674 Köln
Tel. 20 71 50
www.hotel-chelsea.de
35 rooms, suites, café-restaurant.
The rooms of this comfortable hotel are decorated with works that contemporary artists donated in lieu of payment. The new rooms on the deconstructivist-style roof, which was added in 2001, are more expensive.

### ▶ ⑥ Classic Hotel Harmonie

Ursulaplatz 13
D-50668 Köln
Tel. 165 70
www.classic-hotel-harmonie.de
72 rooms, cocktail bar
Pleasant hotel in Italian style, entrance in a quiet side street and only 5 minutes` walk from the cathedral.

### ▶ ⑦ Flandrischer Hof

Flandrische Str. 3
D-50674 Köln
Tel. 203 60
www.flandrischerhof.de
195 rooms, restaurant, bar, conference rooms

Surprisingly quiet for its location close to Rudolfplatz. The rooms are well equipped and reasonably large.

▸ ⑧ **Santo**
Dagobertstr. 22
D-50668 Köln
Tel. 913 97 70
www.hotelsanto.de
69 rooms, bar
Modern design hotel with attractive rooms, in an unfashionable area but close to the railway station.

## BUDGET

▸ ⑨ **Coellner Hof**
Hansaring 100
D-50670 Köln
Tel. 16 660
www.coellnerhof.de
78 rooms, restaurant.
This is a reliable mid-standard hotel on the northern edge of the city centre.

▸ ⑩ **Conti**
Brüsseler Str. 40
D-50674 Köln
Tel. 25 87 70
www.conti-hotel.de
49 rooms, restaurant serves Thai food
In the Belgian Quarter, surrounded by pubs and restaurants, and close to the city centre.

▸ ⑪ **Merian Hotel**
Allerheiligenstr. 1
D-50931 Köln
Tel. 166 50
www.merian-hotel-koeln.de
16 singles, 14 doubles, 1 suite
Comfortable rooms, very close to the station and cathedral, though on a busy road.

▸ ⑫ **Rhein-Hotel St. Martin**
Frankenwerft 31
D-50667 Köln
Tel. 257 79 55
www.koeln-altstadt.de/rheinhotel
50 rooms
Unbeatable location on the Rhine promenade and a good standard of comfort.

▸ ⑬ **Gästehaus St. Georg**
Rolandstr. 61
D-50667 Köln
Tel. 937 02 00
www.gaestehaus-st-georg.de
31 rooms, family and group rooms, bistro. The accommodation in this former monastery is simple but good value for money. It lies in the fashionable Südstadt, where there is a lively restaurant and pub scene, and within easy reach of the city centre.

▸ ⑭ **Weber**
Jahnstr. 22
D-50676 Köln
Tel. 27 22 99 50
28 rooms
Small family-run hotel on the edge of the inner city.

## RESERVATIONS

▸ **Hotel Reservation Service**
Drususgasse 7
Tel. 207 76 00, www.hrs.de
Mon–Sat 7am–midnight, Sun 8am–10pm

## YOUTH HOSTELS

▸ **Jugendgästehaus Köln-Riehl**
An der Schanz 14
D-50735 Köln
Tel. 76 70 81
E-mail: koeln-riehl@jugendherberge.de
369 beds in 116 rooms, cafeteria.
Modern hostel 3km/2mi north of

the Old Town, very close to the Rhine between Zoobrücke and Mülheimer Brücke.

► **City Hostel Köln-Deutz**
Siegesstr. 5, D-50679 Köln
Tel. 81 47 11
www.djh.de
506 beds in 157 rooms, bistro, disco. On the right bank of the Rhine and close to the river, just a short walk from the cathedral.

### CAMPING

► **Campingplatz Berger**
Uferstr. 71
D-50996 Köln-Rodenkirchen
Tel. 935 52 40
www.camping-berger-koeln.de
Open all year
Beautifully sited on the banks of the Rhine, 7km/4mi south of the city centre and 1.5km/1mi from the centre of the district of Rodenkirchen. 250 pitches, restaurant, beer garden and shop.

► **Campingplatz der Stadt Köln**
Weidenweg 35, D-51105 Köln-Poll
Tel. 83 19 66
Mid-April–mid-Oct
On the right bank of the Rhine, about 5.5km/3.5mi south of the city centre. 140 pitches, good site for motor homes, restaurant.

# Arrival

By air

Cologne-Bonn airport (officially named Köln-Bonner Flughafen Konrad Adenauer) lies 15km/9mi to the southeast of the city. In 2007 over 50 airlines transported 10 million passengers to and from 127 destinations in Europe, North Africa and the Middle East.

◄ Destinations

There are frequent domestic flights to all parts of Germany and many connections to other European cities. In 2008 the following direct connections existed to airports in the United Kingdom and Ireland: Dublin (Germanwings), East Midlands (BMI), Edinburgh (Germanwings), London Gatwick (easyjet), London Heathrow (Lufthansa), London Stansted (Germanwings) and Manchester (TUIFly). It is also worth considering flights to Düsseldorf airport, which is only 50km/30mi north of Cologne with a direct rail connection, as Düsseldorf has Aer Lingus, British Airways and Lufthansa flights to a wider range of destinations, as well as services to Leeds-Bradford (jet2), and Birmingham, Manchester and Southampton (flybe). The largest German airport, Frankfurt, has a huge number of European and intercontinental connections, and can be reached directly on the ICE high-speed train, with a journey time of just one hour to Cologne and to the station at Cologne-Bonn airport.

◄ Airport to city

From 5am until 1.30am there is a train connection from the airport railway station to Cologne main station (Hauptbahnhof): three trains per hour from 5am until 9pm, two per hour after that. The journey time is 15 minutes.

*Passengers arriving at the main station are greeted with a view of the emblem of the city.*

High-speed **trains** link Cologne to Amsterdam, Berlin, Brussels, Hamburg, London, Paris and Frankfurt. For travellers from the UK who have quick access to a Eurostar station, the train journey to Cologne via Brussels is an attractive alternative to flying, as the fastest connections take under five hours. The main station in Cologne is one of Europe's most important rail hubs with over 1300 arrivals daily. The station lies in the city centre right next to the cathedral. Many long-distance trains also stop across the river at Köln-Deutz station.
There is a good network of local trains serving other stations in the city and regional destinations.

The extensive autobahn network connects Cologne to neighbouring countries and all parts of Germany. For travellers from the United Kingdom coming through northern France and/or Belgium, the best route is the E 42 (Calais/Dunkirk – Lille – Charleroi – Liege – Aachen), or further north the E 40 (Ostend – Bruges – Brussels – Liege – Aachen). The Cologne autobahn ringroad is the meeting point of a number of major routes, such as the A 1 from Aachen, which heads northeast from Cologne to the Ruhr area and eventually Berlin, and the A 3, which leads south to Frankfurt and southern Germany and north to the Netherlands.

**By bus** International and regional buses stop at the bus terminus (Busbahnhof) on Breslauer Platz between the main railway station and the river. There are Eurolines services from Cologne to many destinations all over Europe, including a daily overnight connection from London that arrives at 9am.

## Travel Insurance

**Health insurance** Citizens of EU countries are entitled to treatment in Germany under the local regulations in case of sudden illness or accident on production of their **European health insurance card**. Even with this card, some costs for medical care and prescribed medication must be paid by the patient. Upon presentation of receipts the health insurance at home covers the costs – but not for all treatments. Citizens of non-

EU countries should check whether there are reciprocal agreements between Germany and their country, but must normally pay for medical treatment and medicine themselves and should take out private health insurance. Doctors do not take credit cards: payment in cash will be required.
No vaccinations are required for entry into Germany.

Since some of the costs for medical treatment and medication typically have to be covered by the patient, and the costs for return transportation may not be covered by the normal health insurance, additional travel insurance is recommended.

Private travel insurance

## ARRIVAL INFORMATION

### AIRPORT AND AIRLINES

► **Köln-Bonn Airport**
Information
Tel. 022 03 / 40 40 01
www.koeln-bonn-airport.de

► **BMI**
www.flybmi.com

► **easyjet**
www.easyjet.com

► **Germanwings**
www.germanwings.com

► **Lufthansa**
www.lufthansa.com

► **TUIFly**
www.tuifly.com

### RAIL

► **Eurostar**
Tickets in UK:
Tel. 08705 186 186
www.eurostar.com

► **Deutsche Bahn**
www.bahn.de
Tel. 118 61
(charge for information)
Tel. 08 00 / 150 70 90
(no charge)

### BUS

► **Eurolines**
Bookings online and in UK through National Express
Tel. 087 05 80 80 80
www.eurolines.com and
www.nationalexpress.com

► **Deutsche Touring GmbH**
Eurolines operator in Germany
DTG-Ticket-Center
Breslauer Platz
Tel. 759 86 60

► **Regional buses**
Breslauer Platz bus station
Tel. 12 44 12

### SHARED CAR AGENCIES

A Mitfahrzentrale is an agency that brings together drivers and passengers to share the costs of a trip.

► **Citynetz Mitfahrzentrale**
Krefelder Str. 2
Tel. 194 44
www.citynetz-mitfahrzentrale.de

► **Mc Share**
Maximinenstr. 2
Tel. 92 12 40 20
www.mfz.de

# Children in Cologne

Varied programme

Many of the standard attractions of Cologne are treats for children: the excellent zoo, for example, the cable-car trip across the Rhine from the zoo to the Rheinpark, boat trips and a visit to the Schokoladenmuseum to see how chocolate is made. The views of the city from the tower of the cathedral (over 500 steps) and the KölnTriangle skyscraper on the Deutz side of the river (fast lift to the top) are also diverting. Bicycles are on hire in the Old Town for a car-free trip along the banks of the Rhine, concluding with a ferry ride across the river to the »Groov« (► p.126), where there are pedaloes, a park and an open-air pool. The biggest attraction for children and teenagers in the region is the Phantasialand, 20km/12mi southwest of Cologne in Brühl.

! *Baedeker* TIP

**Get really wet**

A flotilla of little round boats with rubber bumpers sails on the lake in the Mediapark. The fun doesn't stop at bumping, as each boat is fitted with a water pistol for squirting anyone else foolhardy enough to hire one. Minimum age: six. End of April to early Oct, Mon–Fri 3–8pm, Sat and Sun noon–8pm.

*Phantasialand: for strong stomachs of all ages*

## ACTIVITIES FOR CHILDREN

### INFORMATION

▶ **»Äktschen-Telefon«**
Tel. 22 12 55 55
24-hour hotline with details of the latest holiday programmes, trips and festivals for children.

▶ **www.koeln.kinder-stadt.de**
Information on child care and supervised activities, and lots of ideas for leisure time.

### MUSEUMS

▶ **Museumsdienst**
►p.111
The museum service organizes tours, workshops, birthday parties and other events in the municipal museums. Suitable for children who understand German.

▶ **Please Touch**
Glashüttenstr. 20
Tel. 02203 / 59 24 97
www.please-touch.de
Hours: Tue–Fri 9am–3pm
Educational museum with hands-on exhibitions.

### FUN PARK

▶ **Phantasialand**
Berggeiststr. 31
D-50321 Brühl
Ticket hotline: 02232 / 36 600
www.phantasialand.de
Hours: 1 April to 31 Oct daily 9am–6pm
Shuttle bus or bus no. 705 to the park from Brühl railway station. Frequent connections from Cologne to Brühl.

◄ Phantasialand

Phantasialand is **the most-visited fun park in Germany**, with more than 20 different rides, including some white-knuckle roller coasters and high-tech stomach-churners, as well as gentle carousels for smaller children, shows of acrobatics, music and dance, cafés and restaurants and a daily parade.
For children who can speak German there is a huge range of children's events, including theatre and guided tours: see contact details above.

# Christmas Markets

From late November until Christmas the city squares are decked out with seasonal decorations, and the smells of freshly baked waffles, warm sugared almonds and mulled wine fill the air. Visitors come from far and wide to the six or seven markets held each year in the centre of Cologne: on some days the English and Dutch languages are as much in evidence as German. After dark the illuminations, Christmas music and the cathedral as a backdrop create a romantic atmosphere, but be prepared for dense crowds at weekends and watch out for pickpockets.

The number and siting of the markets can change from year to year. The events start before the first Sunday in Advent and normally end on 23 December. Hours: 11am–9pm. See details below, and check www.koeln.de before the journey for the latest information in English.

Apart from the shopping, part of the Christmas experience is to look inside the churches, which have interesting and individual nativity scenes that change week by week from the start of Advent up to 6 January as new figures and scenes are added. The cathedral has the most elaborate model landscape. Nearby the church of St Andreas has two nativity scenes, one sponsored by the guild of brewers with some references to their trade, and St Mariä Himmelfahrt has a charming Italian Annunciation scene with an old clockwork mechanism. St Maria Lyskirchen near the Schokoladenmuseum has a Christmas scene set in a traditional harbourside milieu peopled by local characters. Many of the churches also stage concerts of Christmas music.

## ! *Baedeker* TIP

### An authentic taste of Christmas

On the Christmas market at Alter Markt, or on the adjoining Heumarkt, look out for a stall selling a speciality from Nuremberg, »echte Nürnberger Lebkuchen«. Lebkuchen are flat cakes, sweet and spicy, sometimes coated in chocolate. The genuine original ones are made with no flour, but all the more honey and ground nuts – expensive but irresistible. Fruit bread, and Stollen cake hand-made by a confectioner (go to a traditional café calling itself »Konditorei« to buy this), are also delicious and make high-quality, authentic gifts.

## CHRISTMAS MARKETS

### LOCATIONS

- **Alter Markt**
  On the ancient market place below the tower of the city hall, right next to the pubs and restaurants of the Old Town.

- **Cathedral Christmas market**
  This market in the shadow of the cathedral towers is the showpiece, with an emphasis on high-quality craft products and varied food stalls.

- **Medieval Christmas market**
  The space in front of the Schokoladenmuseum recreates the Middle Ages, with costumed entertainers, old-world products and culinary treats to match.

- **Neumarkt**
  A large Christmas market in the main shopping area.

- **Rudolfplatz**
  One of the smaller markets, pleasantly sited around the medieval city gate.

- **Rhine Christmas market**
  Held on a Rhine boat anchored between the Hohenzollern Brücke and Deutzer Brücke.

# Electricity

The German mains grid generally supplies 230-volt electricity at 50Hz. Visitors who are not from mainland Europe are advised to take an **adapter**.

# Emergency

## IMPORTANT TELEPHONE NUMBERS

- **Police**
  Tel. 110
- **Fire, ambulance, emergency doctor**
  Tel. 112
- **Emergency medical service**
  Tel. 0180 / 504 41 00
- **Emergency dentist**
  Tel. 0180 / 598 67 00
- **Pharmacies**
  Information on night and weekend opening: tel. 01 15 00

# Entertainment

As a city of a million inhabitants, including a large student population and residents from many different countries, Cologne has a diverse and lively nightlife and many alternatives for an evening's entertainment (see also ► Music and Concerts, p.114, ► Theatre, p.125. The pub and nightlife scene is spread across the city, with different quarters catering for different tastes. The **Old Town** is mainly frequented not by locals but by tourists, business visitors and German trippers from the surrounding regions, which means not every pub there offers good value for money; however, the Old Town has genuine charm and plenty of recom-

> **! *Baedeker* TIP**
>
> **A popular beer garden ...**
>
> ... with a fairly central location is on the lake known as the Aachener Weiher, on Aachener Strasse. It is a large and pleasant beer garden in leafy surroundings (tel. 510 55 56, hours noon–midnight). A quieter place to sit, as no music is played, is the café of the Museum für Ostasiatische Kunst on the opposite side of the lake (during museum hours; excellent cakes and light meals).

mendable places to eat and drink. The so-called **Latin Quarter** (»Kwartier Lateng« in the local dialect) between Zülpicher Platz and the university is a young and lively scene; the **Belgisches Viertel** (Belgian Quarter) and Friesenstrasse have a mixture of down-to-earth and trendy places. Nearby on the Ring, between Rudolfplatz and Friesenplatz, there is a buzzing, even raucous atmosphere around the cinemas and nightclubs on Friday and Saturday night.
Many of the best venues for clubbers and the young music scene are outside the city centre. The people of Cologne are attached to their own city districts and meet in their favourite local haunts, for example in suburbs such as Ehrenfeld and Nippes, or in the quarter known as the **Südstadt**, which lies near Chlodwigplatz to the south of the centre.

## Beer Gardens

Street cafés

In the summer months – in fact from March to November, if the weather permits – pubs and cafés set up tables on every available space on pavements and squares, and there are shady beer gardens in parks. The Rhine promenade, the Alter Markt and the shopping areas of the city centre are then crowded with locals and visitors drinking beer and coffee outdoors.

## Cinema

The city has a good mix of big-screen or multiplex cinemas showing the latest box-office hits, on the one hand, and arthouse cinemas on the other. A number of them screen the original English versions of classic films or new releases. In summer there are several venues for open-air cinema.

# ADDRESSES

### BARS

▸ **Capri Lounge**
Benesisstr. 61
Tel. 257 32 26
Tram: Rudolfplatz
A cosy cellar bar with colourful, mosaic-like decorations, and above all creative cocktails. The menu is designed as an LP cover.

▸ **Lotte Haifischbar**
Im Klapperhof 41
Tel. 13 13 35
Tram: Friesenplatz
A refreshingly unpretentious bar. If you don't see your favourite cocktail on the menu, ask the barkeeper – he knows his job.

▸ **Osman 30**
Im Mediapark 8
Tel. 20 80
www.osman30.de
Tram: Christophstr.
Fantastic view from the outdoor terrace and the indoor lounge on the 30th floor of the KölnTower. If you don´t want to leave after

drinks, try the excellent though expensive 3-course set menu.

▶ **Scheinbar**
Brüsseler Str. 10
Tel. 923 20 48
Tram: Rudolfplatz
The velvety-red seating is plush, the lights are low and the cocktail prices reasonable. A student crowd comes to the DJ evenings.

## BEER GARDENS AND OUTDOOR CAFÉS

▶ **Decksteiner Mühle**
Gleueler Str. 371
Tel. 43 38 44
Bus 146 from Neumarkt to Deckstein
Well-frequented at weekends by walkers and cyclists, as it is near the outer green belt. Pleasant garden with view of an old mill wheel.

▶ **Deutzer Bahnhof**
Ottoplatz 7
Tel. 880 06 15
Tram: Bf. Deutz/Messe
This pub and restaurant with a large beer garden is often a venue for live music. Despite its location at a busy traffic junction, the shade of tall trees and the good food make it a deservedly popular port of call.

▶ **Em Ahle Kohberg**
Ostmerheimer Str. 455
Tel. 69 25 25
Rustic timber-framed restaurant with good wines and food, and a lovely garden attached.

▶ **Gasthaus Rennbahn**
Scheibenstr. 40
Tel. 740 83 00
Tram: Scheibenstrasse
1000 seats beneath chestnut trees at the lovely old horse-racing track; wide-ranging menu, popular for Sunday brunch.

! *Baedeker* TIP

**Old Love**

The houseboat *Alte Liebe (Old Love)* on the Rhine at Rodenkirchen, close to the autobahn bridge at the southern end of the city, is a lovely place for sitting and watching the ships go by at close quarters. Ample portions of hearty German food are served to hungry cyclists who pedal here along the river, but guests on the outdoor terrace can simply come for coffee and cake or a glass of beer (tel. 39 23 61, closed Mon).

▶ **Haus am See**
Bachemer Landstr. 420
Tel. 430 92 60
The site with a view of the Decksteiner Weiher lake in the outer green belt makes this old-fashioned restaurant with terrace café ideal for families and walkers. Take in calories with the hearty meals and tempting cakes, or work them off on the pedaloes and crazy golf nearby.

▶ **Herbrand's**
Herbrandstr. 21
Tel. 954 16 26
Tram: Venloer Strasse/Gürtel
A large beer garden on several levels with plenty of shade, much appreciated by locals, including families with children, and thus often crowded. A good place for brunch at weekends.

▶ **Hyatt-Terrasse**
Kennedy-Ufer 2a
Tel. 82 81 17 60

Tram: Bhf Deutz/Messe
This beer garden in front of the Hyatt Hotel has an unsurpassed view across the Rhine to the Old Town and cathedral. Jazz brunch on Sundays.

▶ **Rathenauplatz**
Rathenauplatz
Tel. 801 73 49
Tram: Zülpicher Platz
A pleasant spot beneath the trees on one of the most attractive squares in the city.

▶ **Stadtgarten**
Venloer Str. 40
Tel. 95 29 94 33
Tram: Hans-Böckler-Platz
An inner-city beer garden where the 600 outdoor seats are all required on warm days. Self-service meals.

▶ **Volksgarten**
Volksgartenstr. 27
Tel. 38 26 26
Tram: Eifelplatz
Large beer garden with a view of the lake, in a park in the much-loved Südstadt area.

▶ **Wippenbeck**
Karlstr. 7

*A cooling glass of Kölsch beer on a warm summer day – here on Alter Markt, the old market place*

Tel. 935 31 50
Bus: 130 (Frankstrasse); or boat
The district of Rodenkirchen is best reached by cycling south on the Rhine or taking a boat trip. Wippenbeck is a modern-style café on the Rhine promenade.

## DANCE CLUBS

▶ **Alter Wartesaal**
Hauptbahnhof
Johannisstr. 11
Tel. 912 88 50
www.wartesaal.de
Tram: Dom/Hbf.
A variety of concerts and party evenings, including events for Cologne's large gay and lesbian community.

▶ **Die Halle Tor 2**
Girlitzweg 30
Tel. 94 98 97 98
www.diehalletor2.de
S-Bahn: Technologiepark
Soul and house in a huge factory hall on the western edge of the city.

▶ **Kantine**
Neusser Landstr. 2
Tel. 16 79 16 16
www.kantine.com
Tram: Wilhelm-Sollmann-Str.
Live music, dance nights for the over-30s

▶ **MTC**
Zülpicher Str. 10
Tel. 240 41 88, www.mtcclub.de
Tram: Zülpicher Platz
Rock, punk and soul

▶ **Subway**
Aachener Str. 82
Tel. 51 79 69
Tram: Moltkestr.
Chic basement club with reggae, funk and hip-hop music

▶ **Underground**
Vogelsanger Str. 200
Tel. 54 23 26
Tram: Venloer Str./
Ehrenfeldgürtel
Long-established club, café and beer garden, but the music is up-to-the-minute.

## CINEMAS

▶ **Listings**
www.koeln.de/ausgehen/kino

▶ **Filmhaus**
Maybachstr. 11
Tel. 22 27 10 22
www.koelner-filmhaus.de
Tram: Hansaring
Caters for film buffs with retrospectives, film seasons on special themes; in summer open-air screenings in the park behind the cinema.

▶ **Metropolis**
Ebertplatz 19
Tel. 72 24 36
Tram: Ebertplatz
English-language films every night of the week, including the latest from Hollywood but also arthouse films.

▶ **Off-Broadway**
Zülpicher Str. 24
Tel. 23 24 18
Frequent screenings of non-mainstream films in English and other original-language versions.

▶ **Open-air cinema**
Cinenova, tel. 345 17 20
Tram: Venloer Strasse/Gürtel
In summer in the beer garden at Herbrandstr. 11 in Ehrenfeld district.

# Etiquette and Customs

**Cheerful and straightforward**

Germans in general favour straightforwardness, and are sometimes direct to the point of bluntness. The people of Cologne, too, tend not to waste time with unnecessary niceties when it comes to expressing an opinion or making a request. There is a temptation for outsiders to interpret this as rudeness, but it is better viewed as an endearing local quirk. The Rhinelanders, especially those from Cologne, are seen by other Germans as cheerful and friendly, happy to have a chat or join a party but not particularly hard-working or reliable.

**Rules and regulations**

Germany is a heavily regulated country, and although in this respect the rest of the world may have been catching up in recent times, many people still remark on how Germans tend to follow rules to the letter and often display more deference to those in authority than other nationalities. It is an offence (albeit a minor one) for example to step out into the road at a crossing if the pedestrian signal shows red – visitors may be surprised to see people patiently waiting for the lights to change when there is no vehicle in sight. There are sometimes disapproving looks for those who break this rule (not to mention a fine should a police officer spot the guilty party). The people of Cologne, though, are not particularly disciplined in comparison with those from other regions, and those red lights are often disregarded.

**Efficiency versus bureaucracy**

German efficiency is of course world renowned, and though it will be regularly encountered in banks, hotels, and even government offices, the visitor may at times also come across instances of clanking bureaucracy. Contrary to the expectations of some, this is not in fact a country where everything runs like clockwork. Public transport in Cologne is generally punctual and reliable, but German trains often do not run on time.

**No smoking**

Smoking is now prohibited in all public buildings in Germany, including cafés, bars, restaurants and nightclubs. A smoking zone is permitted in pubs and restaurants if it is closed off from the other public areas, but smokers are only served in non-smoking areas. Individuals breaking this law are liable to a fine of 100 euros; a 2000 euro penalty applies to the proprietor of the offending establishment.

**Tipping**

In restaurants and cafés it is usual to tip about 10% of the amount on the bill. If you pay cash, tell the waiter the amount you wish to pay (normally a rounded up figure) as you hand over the money, or say »Stimmt so« if you don't expect any change at all. If you pay by cheque or credit card, leave the tip in cash on the table or on the plate provided. Taxi drivers, city guides, toilet attendants and room service personnel are also pleased to receive a tip.

History and patriotism

Many Germans do not feel comfortable talking about the events of the Nazi period and the Second World War, which are regarded as a subject for serious discussion and private thought, and the unquestioning patriotism of some other countries is frowned upon by many. Unless you intend to engage in learned discourse, it is best to follow the famous advice – and not mention the war. In recent years, particularly since the football World Cup was held in Germany in 2006 in a happy, harmonious, flag-waving atmosphere, the German flag has been more in evidence than before, and some observers detect a change in the Germans' previously uneasy sense of their identity.

Greetings

The accepted way to greet somebody is to shake hands; men and women who know each other better will kiss each other on both cheeks, like in France; established friends, men included, will even hug one another.

# Festivals, Holidays and Events

The most striking event of the year, which makes its presence felt in every corner of the city, is Carnival, particularly the days of street carnival which end in the early hours of Ash Wednesday and begin the previous Thursday. Depending on the date of Easter, this takes place between early February and early March. Offices and museums do not open during this period, and shops remain closed on the Thursday afternoon and all day Monday.

## CALENDER OF EVENTS

### LISTINGS

▸ **www.koeln.de**
This website has listings in English of many events and venues.

### JANUARY

▸ **Internationale Möbelmesse**
The trade fair of the furniture industry is accompanied by a design event called »Passagen« in the design shops, galleries and showrooms of Cologne.

### FEBRUARY

▸ **Carnival**
Spectacular parades on the Sunday and Monday (►Baedeker Special p.206)

### MARCH

▸ **lit.Cologne**
International literary festival, including readings and discussions in English. Guests in recent years have included Monica Ali, Armistead Maupin and Zadie Smith. (www.litcologne.de)

### APRIL

▸ **MusikTriennale Köln**
A three-week festival held every three years (2010, 2013 ... ). A

large number of concerts from varied genres with a strong international flavour (www.musiktriennalekoeln.de)

▶ **Art Cologne**
Art fair, accompanied by exhibitions and art events all over the city (www.artcologne.de)

## MAY

▶ **Mai-Trödelmarkt**
Flea and antiques market on Neumarkt on the third weekend of the month

▶ **Kölner Weinwoche**
Wine market, end of May or early June on Heumarkt

▶ **Tanzbrunnen season**
Dances, concerts and shows are held at the »dance fountain« in the Rheinpark in Deutz every weekend until September.

## JUNE

▶ **Corpus Christi (Fronleichnam)**
The highlight, known as the »Mülheimer Gottestracht«, is a procession of decorated ships carrying shrines from Mülheim in the north to the cathedral. Start: 11am. Best seen from the bridges: Mülheimer Brücke or Zoobrücke.

▶ **Organ music in the cathedral (Orgelfeierstunden)**
Until early September, every Tuesday at 8pm

*Collectors' heaven: the May flea market on Neumarkt*

## JULY

▶ **Christopher Street Day**
Cologne has a large gay and lesbian population. The colourful and audacious parade with participants from all over Germany is held on the first weekend in July. (www.csd-cologne.de)

▶ **Kölner Lichter**
A spectacular firework display on the Rhine (www.koelner-lichter.de), 2nd or 3rd Saturday in July.

▶ **Summer Jam Festival**
Europe's largest reggae and world beat event takes place over 3 days on a large site by a lake (Fühlinger See) in the north of the city. 25,000 visitors or more camp out for the weekend. (www.summerjam.de)

## AUGUST

▶ **Kölner Sommerfestival**
When its orchestra takes a summer break in July and August, the Philharmonie concert hall is used for dance, musicals and various other events. (www.koelnersommerfestival.de)

▶ **c/o pop**
Five days of club nights, concerts, films and parties. The programme includes electronic music and sometimes jazz. (www.c-o-pop.de)

*Corpus Christi procession of ships from Mülheim to the cathedral*

SEPTEMBER

► **photokina**
The world's leading trade fair for the imaging business; photo exhibitions in various venues (2010, 2012 etc; www.photokina.de).

OCTOBER

► **Köln Marathon**
Half a million spectators line the streets in a carnival atmosphere to watch the 25,000 runners and inline-skaters. (www.koeln-marathon.de).

► **Church processions**
on the Sundays following the days of St Ursula (21 Oct), St Severin (23 Oct) and St Kunibert (12 Nov)

NOVEMBER

► **Cologne Fine Art and Antiques**
A major event for the fine art and antiques business, accompanied by exhibitions in the antique and art galleries.

► **Opening of the carnival season**
on Alter Markt on 11 November at 11.11am

DECEMBER

► **Christmas markets**
see ►Christmas Markets

► **New Year**
Tens of thousands crowd onto the Rhine bridges to watch the midnight fireworks.

# Food and Drink

**Cologne specialities**

Many menus, especially those in Brauhaus restaurants (► Baedeker Special p.90), include dishes typical of Cologne and the Rhineland. They are often listed under their dialect names, which are unfamiliar to people from other parts of Germany, with a brief explanation in High German, and sometimes in English too. Waiters in city-centre restaurants are used to tourists and international business visitors, and most of them speak at least a little English. In case of difficulties, ask for an English menu.

*»Halver Hahn« (»half a chicken«) is in reality a rye-bread roll with cheese.*

The following are specialities of the Cologne region.

**Rheinischer Sauerbraten** (literally »sour roast»): a piece of beef marinated in vinegar, fried with onions, cooked in the marinade and served with potato dumplings and a gravy to which raisins have been added. Horse-meat was once used instead of beef.

Himmel und Ääd (»heaven and earth«):a mixture of mashed potato (from the earth) and pureed apples (heaven), served with fried black pudding.

◄ Himmel und Ääd

Hämcher, also known in High German as Eisbein: boiled shank of salted pork, a substantial piece of meat on the bone, eaten with mustard, mashed potatoes and sauerkraut. Don't order this unless you are really hungry.

◄ Hämcher

Rievkooche are the local version of rösti potatoes: grated potato mixed with a little flour, grated onion and salt, fried until brown and crispy and served with black bread and butter or apple sauce. They are delicious when freshly made with good-quality oil.

◄ Rievkooche

Halver Hahn is a well-worn local joke, but also a tasty snack and the perfect accompaniment to Kölsch beer. It literally means »half a chicken«, but is in fact no more than a rye-bread roll with a piece of mature Gouda cheese and mustard.

◄ Halver Hahn

»Cologne caviar« is black pudding, served with a rye-bread roll and onions – the onions are the »music«.

◄ Kölscher Kaviar met Musik

Other typical dishes in a Brauhaus or German restaurant are Schnitzel (escalope of pork or veal); various forms of sausage such as Bratwurst (fried) or Bockwurst (boiled); and Matjes (pickled herring), delicious when served with potatoes and a cream sauce containing slices of apple and onion (Matjes Hausfrauenart).

Many pubs serve pils or beer from other parts of Germany, but most of the beer drunk in Cologne is the local brew, Kölsch (► Baedeker Special p.154).

◄ Kölsch

## Restaurants and Cafés

From gourmet meals to snacks

As a modern cosmopolitan city, Cologne has a wide range of restaurants serving cuisines from all around the world, as well as traditional German food. In addition to the traditional Brauhaus pubs, there are bistros, gourmet restaurants, cafés and snack bars that serve such favourites as Currywurst with French fries, döner kebabs and gyros. For fast snacking after a few beers or an energetic session on the dance floor, the student quarter around Zülpicher Strasse is the obvious place, but nowhere in Cologne do hungry revellers need to look far for a cheap bite to eat.

Most restaurants in and around the **Old Town**, including Alter Markt and Heumarkt, cater to tourists and business people, especially visitors to trade fairs, which means that prices tend to be higher here. However, it is worth coming here to a Brauhaus, where the customers include locals, and the food is reasonably priced and of reliable,

! *Baedeker* TIP

**Asparagus time**

Between late April and early June, Germans consume great quantities of white asparagus (Spargel), often served with boiled potatoes, cold roast ham and lashings of sauce hollandaise, but also in combination with steak or other meat dishes. If you buy your own at a market, look out for the excellent local Bornheim asparagus.

*A »Köbes« with the main tool of his trade: a round tray to carry glasses of freshly poured Kölsch beer*

# COLOGNE'S TRADITIONAL PUBS

**Every visitor to Cologne, even day-trippers, should take time to sample the local beer in a traditional Brauhaus, a brewery pub where brisk waiters dressed in blue serve the local beer, Kölsch, and hearty Rhineland meals are the perfect accompaniment.**

A Brauhaus is a brewery pub: it is owned by the brewery in many cases, the beer is still brewed on site in others, and some are just the traditional type of pub that originated as a brewery and also had a room for serving customers. These pubs are a popular rendezvous in Cologne, and at weekends or on public holidays it is advisable to book a table in advance, because for many locals an old-established Brauhaus is a second living room, a place to spend a long, jolly evening in accordance with the motto »It is better to drink too much than eat too little«.

## Next to the Brewery

**Päffgen** in Friesenstrasse is a legendary pub, one of the longest-standing and most authentic in the city. The beer has been brewed on the premises since 1883, and is highly prized – not least because the scale of production is modest, and few pubs have the privilege of sourcing Päffgen Kölsch. The atmosphere within the yellowed walls is noisy, and the waiters are known for their no-nonsense manner and ready wit. Päffgen is a large Brauhaus, with 150 seats in the garden at the back. The second traditional Brauhaus with the brewery on site is **Malzmühle** at the south end of Heumarkt, on the edge of the Old Town. The service is swift and the Mühlen-Kölsch beer, darker and maltier than most other kinds, delicious. This is a small pub, so regulars know to arrive early.

## Brauhaus Pubs in the Old Town

In the Old Town it is possible to enjoy a lengthy pub crawl and compare several kinds of Kölsch beer without

having to walk more than a short distance. For visitors coming from the railway station, a half-way stop at **Früh am Dom** is a must. When the brewery moved out in 1988, more space for drinkers was created in the cellar, an atmospheric warren of old stone and brick where barrels were once stored. 160 seats are available outside next to the splashing fountain. From Früh it is a short walk down the slope and right into the street Unter Taschenmacher, where **Brauhaus Sion** occupies a site where brewing was recorded as long ago as the 13th century. Like Früh, Sion is furnished in the rustic style with wooden panelling and scrubbed tables, and customers are greeted upon entering by the sight of a large barrel behind the bar counter. Old prints and photographs of Cologne, and portraits of mayors in one of the rooms, adorn the walls. Sion Kölsch, too, is produced outside the city centre, leaving more space for drinkers, as the on-site brewery was destroyed in the Second World War. A few paces from Sion, in Mühlengasse on the opposite side of Alter Markt, lies **Peters Brauhaus** – not a historic pub, but a well-conceived modern conversion that keeps to the Brauhaus tradition of wooden panelling and heavy tables. Filling Rhenish dishes such as pork shank with sauerkraut are served with the beer. The **Gaffel-Haus** on Alter Markt has an ideal location, with plenty of seating outdoors on the old marketplace in the shadow of the city hall tower, and a handsome interior in a late Renaissance building of 1580. Gaffel is the ancient Cologne word for a guild, and in the room by the entrance the shields of the old city guilds, including that of the brewers, can be seen on the right-hand wall. For thirsty visitors arriving by train,

*Pfaffen Brauhaus at the corner of Heumarkt serves its own brand of beer from a microbrewery.*

the Gaffel brewery has opened a huge new Brauhaus, the largest in Germany, opposite the station: Gaffel am Dom.

A two-minute walk from Alter Markt leads to the wide open space of Heumarkt. Here, in the northeast corner of the square, a lovely old building houses **Zum Pfaffen**, where a member of the Päffgen family serves his own brand of beer. Just a stone's throw away down Salzgasse, a narrow cobbled alley, the original Päffgen Kölsch is served in Bierhaus in der Salzgasse, a large establishment with a fine interior and courtyard seating at the back.

## Veedel: Quarters outside the City Centre

Most Cologne residents identify with their own Veedel (quarter) and prefer to drink their Kölsch close to home, so of course there is no shortage of Brauhaus pubs outside the Old Town. Two of the best, in two of the most traditional quarters, are **Früh em Veedel**, an outlet for the popular Früh Kölsch in the Severinsviertel, and **Em Golde Kappes** in Nippes, conveniently placed by the exit to Florastrasse tram station. The name of the latter pub, a family-run business since 1913 with a stone façade and stained-glass windows, means »the golden cabbage«, and indeed a gilded metal cabbage hangs outside the door. It is a reference to the fact that the Nippes district, north of the city centre, was once a farming area. Here, locals can enjoy good traditional food and beer from the Malzmühle brewery outside or in the atmospheric interior.

Across the Rhine in Siegesstrasse in Deutz lies a Cologne institution, **Lommerzheim**. This pub was famous for its taciturn owner, Hans Lommerzheim, who served pork chops with gigantic dimensions and over decades resolutely refused to repair or renovate the plain room and furnishings. After his death in 2005 the Päffgen brewery took it over, modernized the kitchen – and carefully restored the authentic, neglected appearance of the pub.

though not inspiring, quality. Recommendable restaurants are spread all over the city, with a concentration near the Ring boulevard – between Rudolfplatz, Ehrenstrasse and Friesenstrasse, for example, or in the **Belgian Quarter** (Brüsseler Platz, Bismarckstrasse, Antwerpener, Lütticher and Jülicher Strasse), which has a modern and international flavour. Many of the larger hotels have good restaurants. If you are looking for a change from German, French and Italian food, it is best to avoid the Chinese and Indian restaurants, as Cologne has no large community of residents from these countries to guarantee authenticity. Turkish food, by contrast, is well represented at all levels of quality, for example in the street Weidengasse (Eigelstein quarter), which is just a few minutes' walk north of the station.

Many establishments combine the roles of pub, restaurant and café, with long opening hours and a variety of light dishes or full meals for customers who want more than just a drink. To experience a slice of German life while enjoying a slice of cake, it is worth trying one of the unfashionable **traditional German cafés**, often called Café-Konditorei, which make their own extravagant kinds of gateau with lots of fruit, cream, chocolate or marzipan.

**Curry Cologne**

In Germany Currywurst (fried sausage in a curry-flavoured ketchup) is the equivalent of fish and chips in Britain or a hamburger in America. Most Currywurst is eaten in basic snack bars or on the street, but for those who prefer to sit and savour their sausage, or even wash it down with champagne, Curry Cologne provides good quality and Belgian-style fries at an affordable price (Antwerpener Str. 5, Mon–Thu 11.30am–11pm, Fri and Sat till midnight, Sun 1–10pm).

## RECOMMENDED RESTAURANTS

▶ ① see plan p.94–95

▶ **Price categories**
Expensive (cat. I): over 25 €
Moderate (cat. II): 15–25 €
Inexpensive (cat. III): under 15 €
For a main course

### TOP RESTAURANTS

▶ ① **Graugans in Hyatt Regency Hotel (cat. I)**
Kennedy-Ufer 2 a
Tel. 82 81 17 71
Closed Sun, Mon
Tram: Bf. Deutz/Messe
The attractions of this gourmet restaurant in one of Cologne's finest hotels are both the view across the Rhine to the cathedral and the exquisite, creative cuisine, which combines European and Asian flavours.

▶ ② **La Société (cat. I)**
Kyffhäuserstr. 53
Tel. 23 24 64, www.lasociete.info
Tram: Zülpicher Platz
Truly excellent, modern, French-inspired cuisine – in the middle of the student quarter and without the formal trappings.

## *Cologne* Hotels and Restaurants

**Where to stay**

1. Dom-Hotel
2. Excelsior Hotel Ernst
3. Hotel im Wasserturm
4. Ascot
5. Chelsea
6. Classic Hotel Harmonie
7. Flandrischer Hof
8. Santo
9. Coellner Hof
10. Conti
11. Merian Hotel
12. Rhein-Hotel St. Martin
13. Gästehaus St. Georg
14. Weber

**Where to eat**

1. Graugans im Hyatt Regency
2. La Société
3. Le Moissonier
4. Bieresel
5. Em Krützche

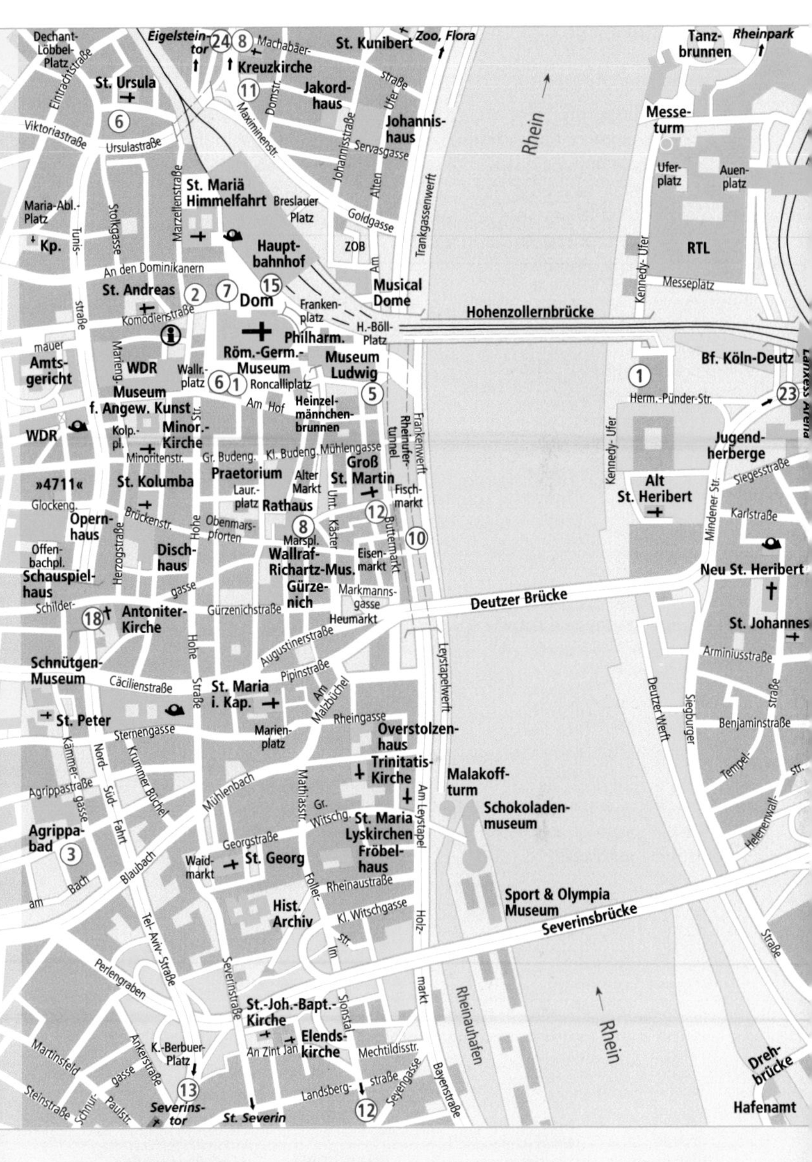


| | | | |
|---|---|---|---|
| ⑥ Früh am Dom | ⑪ Haus Töller | ⑯ Feynsinn | ㉑ 4 Cani della città |
| ⑦ Gaffel am Dom | ⑫ Mainzer Hof | ⑰ Maybach | ㉒ Caminetto |
| ⑧ Gasthaus Brungs | ⑬ Päffgen Brauhaus | ⑱ Stanton | ㉓ HoteLux |
| ⑨ Guten Abend | ⑭ Alcazar | ⑲ Artischocke | ㉔ Konak |
| ⑩ Haxenhaus | ⑮ Alter Wartesaal | ⑳ Plat du Jour | |

▶ ③ **Le Moissonier (cat. I)**
Krefelder Str. 25
Tel. 72 94 79
Closed Sun, Mon
Tram: Hansaring
A long-standing favourite among local lovers of fine French cooking. The interior in the style of a Parisian bistro and an excellent wine list complement the food. Reservations essential!

## BRAUHAUS AND GERMAN FOOD

▶ ④ **Bieresel (cat. III)**
Breite Strasse 114
Tel. 257 60 90
Closed Sun April–Aug
Tram: Appellhofplatz
An unexpected touch of tradition in the shopping district, specializing in mussels during the season (Sept–March).

▶ ⑤ **Em Krützche (cat. II)**
Am Frankenturm 1
Tel. 258 08 39
www.em-kruetzche.de
Tram: Dom/Hbf.
Hearty dishes from Cologne and France in a 400-year-old building. The world leaders dined here at the G8 summit in 1999. Advance booking advisable.

▶ ⑥ **Früh am Dom (cat. III)**
Am Hof 12
Tel. 261 32 11
Tram: Dom/Hbf.
A Cologne institution since 1904 with a cellar that dates from the Middle Ages. Noisy and lively, basic Brauhaus fare and good beer.

▶ ⑦ **Gaffel am Dom (cat. III)**
Trankgasse 7
Tel. 13 74 71
Tram: Dom/Hbf.
Newly opened in 2008, claiming to be the largest Brauhaus in Germany. Rhineland specialities with beer from the Gaffel brewery and an unbeatable location opposite the railway station.

▶ ⑧ **Gasthaus Brungs (cat. II/III)**
Marsplatz 3
Tel. 258 61 66
Tram: Dom/Hbf.
Historic atmosphere, especially in the cellar, and a pleasant outdoor terrace in summer. Try a dish with Spätzle (Swabian noodles).

▶ ⑨ **Guten Abend (cat. II)**
Maternusstr. 18
Tel. 31 25 49
Tram: Rudolfplatz
Currently the only genuine »slow food« organic restaurant in the city. Good meat dishes, carefully prepared salads, tempting desserts. Nothing fancy and well-priced for the quality.

▶ ⑩ **Haxenhaus (cat. III)**
Frankenwerft 19
Tel. 947 24 00
www. haxenhaus.de
Tram: Heumarkt
Lots of old-world atmosphere on the Rhine promenade in the Old Town, friendly service and hearty meals at a reasonable price.

▶ ⑪ **Haus Töller (cat. II/III)**
Weyerstr. 96
Tel. 258 93 16
Tram: Barbarossaplatz
A high-class version of the traditional pub, and just far enough off the tourist route to be authentic.

▶ ⑫ **Mainzer Hof (cat. II/III)**
Maternusstr. 18
Tel. 31 25 49

*The dining area at Alcazar is rarely as empty as this, but always colourful.*

Tram: Chlodwigplatz
A cosy and often crowded »Veedel« (neighbourhood) pub with a menu that changes daily.

▶ ⑬ **Päffgen Brauhaus (cat. III)**
Friesenstr. 64
Tel. 13 54 61
Tram: Friesenplatz
Almost the definitive Cologne Brauhaus, often crowded. Down-to-earth Rhenish food – but it is the beer and the atmosphere that draws the faithful customers.

## MODERN INTERNATIONAL

▶ ⑭ **Alcazar (cat. II/III)**
Bismarckstr. 39 a
Tel. 51 57 33
www.alcazar-koeln.de
Tram: Friesenplatz
This bistro pub with a relaxed atmosphere has kept its popularity over 20 years or more. In the afternoon a fashionable rendezvous, in the evening good for a mixture of German and Mediterranean food.

▶ ⑮ **Alter Wartesaal (cat. II)**
Hauptbahnhof
Johannisstr. 11 (on the cathedral side of the main railway station)
Tel. 912 88 50
Tram: Dom/Hbf.
The name means »old waiting room«, and the stylishly refurbished 1890s interior used to be just that. Celebrities like Mick Jagger have been seen here, often in connection with events in the club next door. Not cheap, but chic, and a good place for Sunday brunch.

▶ ⑯ **Feynsinn (cat. III)**
Rathenauplatz 7
Tel. 240 92 10
Tram: Dasselstr./Bf. Süd
A relaxed pub-bistro-café in the

student quarter, good for all-day breakfast from 10am, an evening meal or just a few beers.

▸ ⑰ **Maybach (cat. II)**
Maybachstr. 111
Tel. 912 35 98
Tram: Hansaring
Mainly Mediterranean food and wines in a nicely converted railway building next to the Mediapark, with a lovely beer garden outside.

▸ ⑱ **Stanton (cat. II/III)**
Schildergasse 57
Tel. 271 07 10

*Pasta, vino and cocktails at 4 Cani della Città.*

Tram: Neumarkt
This oasis in the clamorous shopping zone is on the premises of the Antoniterkirche church and serves imaginative pasta and meat dishes. It is also the ideal place for coffee and a snack when shopping.

## FRENCH

▸ ⑲ **Artischocke (cat. I/II)**
Moltkestr. 50
Tel. 25 28 61
Tram: Moltkestr.
Gourmet cuisine in intimate surroundings.

▸ ⑳ **Plat du Jour (cat. I/II)**
Palmstr. 20
Tel. 257 46 88
www.plat-du-jour.de
(open only evenings, Tue–Sat)
Tram: Friesenplatz
The simple, tasteful interior is just right for the unfussy but excellent French-Moroccan food. Justifiably popular, so book a table in advance.

## ITALIAN

▸ ㉑ **4 Cani della città (cat. II/III)**
Benesisstr. 61
Tel. 257 40 85
Tram: Rudolfplatz
Three in one: the restaurant serves Italian food until late in the evening, the Capri Lounge below has imaginative cocktails and Barista on the first floor is the place to relax over a glass of wine.

▸ ㉒ **Caminetto (cat. III)**
Eifeler Str. 36
Tel. 310 46 64
Tram: Zülpicher Platz
Possibly the best pizza in Cologne – imposing dimensions, hot and fresh from a proper pizza oven. Near the Volksgarten.

### RUSSIAN

▶ ㉓ **HoteLux (cat. II/III)**
Von-Sandt-Platz 10
Tel. 24 11 36
www.hotelux.de
(evenings only)
Tram: Kölnarena
Soviet-themed restaurant in Deutz that serves borshch, blinis and other Russian delicacies. 30 kinds of vodka. Book ahead.

### TURKISH

▶ ㉔ **Konak (cat. III)**
Weidengasse 42
Tel. 12 13 85
Tram: Hansaring
Probably the best restaurant in this street of Turkish shops and eating joints – certainly cheaper than the more famous Bosporus Restaurant nearby.

### CAFÉS AND BREAKFAST

### ... CATHEDRAL AND SIGHTS

▶ **Campi im Funkhaus**
Wallrafplatz 5
Tel. 925 55 55
Tram: Dom/Hbf.
Italian food and good coffee all day, starting with grande or piccolo breakfast.

▶ **Janssen**
Obenmarspforten 7
Tel. 272 73 90
Tram: Dom/Hbf.
A charming old-fashioned café with truly excellent cake and light midday meals, well placed between the busy Hohe Strasse and the Old Town. The manager, Mr Chadwick, has the discreet efficiency of an English butler.

▶ **Reichard**
Unter Fettenhennen 11
Tel. 257 85 42
Tram: Dom/Hbf.
A busy café with good food and snacks all day. Its trump card is the unbeatable location opposite the cathedral façade – on sunny days the terrace fills up quickly.

### ... SHOPPING

▶ **Eigel**
Brückenstr. 1
Tel. 257 58 58
Tram: Dom/Hbf.
An old-style café just off Hohe Strasse that has a good reputation for its cakes and chocolates.

▶ **Fassbender**
Mittelstr. 12
Tel. 925 99 90
Tram: Neumarkt
An up-market café that sells its own tartes, cream cakes, petits fours and quiches to well-heeled shoppers. Excellent quality and prices to match.

▶ **Fromme**
Breite Str. 122
Tel. 257 61 57
Tram: Appellhofplatz
Comfortable seats in which to eat calorie-rich cakes and home-made ice cream; a good location in the pedestrian zone.

### ... NORTH

▶ **Alte Feuerwache**
Melchiorstr. 3, Tel. 973 15 50
Tram: Ebertplatz
Neighbourhood cultural centre in a former fire station with a restaurant that serves snacks and more substantial meals all day and offers an excellent, vegetarian-friendly brunch buffet on Sundays. Seats outside in a large courtyard, where the kids can play while their parents dine.

*A young crowd frequent All Bar One on Friesenplatz.*

### ... SOUTH

**Filos**
Merowinger Str. 42, Tel. 32 91 47
www.filoskoeln.de
Tram: Chlodwigplatz
In the fashionable Südstadt quarter, but not just for a trendy crowd. Good for late breakfasts, snacks all day and low-priced pizza in the evening.

### ... WEST

**Bauturm-Café**
Aachener Str. 24
Tel. 52 89 84
Tram: Rudolfplatz
The café of the Bauturm-Theater attracts an arty crowd who can breakfast here as late as they like or drink cocktails into the early hours.

**Café Central**
Jülicher Str. 1
Tel. 207 15 20
Tram: Rudolfplatz
Extensive breakfast menu until midday. In the afternoons a relaxed café that mutates into a restaurant-bar in the evening.

**Metzgerei Schmitz**
Aachener Str. 30
Tel. 139 55 77
Tram: Rudolfplatz
This former butcher's shop with a delightful interior serves wonderful home-made cake and delicious quiches with salads.

# Health

Medical help

Germany's healthcare system is excellent. Doctors and dentists are listed in the »Gelbe Seiten« (Yellow Pages) under »Ärzte« and »Zahnärzte« respectively. The US and UK consulates can point you in the direction of medical practitioners who speak English.

**i Medical emergency service**

- Tel. 112

**Pharmacies** (Apotheken) are generally open Mon–Fri 9.30am to 6.30pm, Sat 9.30am–2pm, sometimes longer. They are closed on Sundays. Every pharmacy displays in the window or door a list of pharmacies which run an emergency service outside these hours and on holidays.

# Information

## USEFUL ADDRESSES

### INFORMATION IN COLOGNE

▶ **Domforum**
Information and visitor centre of the cathedral
Domkloster 3
(opposite the cathedral)
Tel. 0221 / 92 58 47 30
www.domforum.de
Hours: Mon–Fri 10am–6pm, Sat 10am–5pm, Sun 1pm–5pm.
20-minute audio-visual show about the cathedral, tours in English.

▶ **KölnTourismus**
Unter Fettenhennen 19
(opposite the cathedral towers)
D-50667 Köln
Tel. 0221 / 22 13 04 00
www.koelntourismus.de (English version available)
Hours: July–Sept Mon–Sat 9am–10pm, Sun 10am–6pm; Oct–June Mon–Sat 9am–9pm, Sun 10am–6pm
The city tourist office. Hotel bookings, city tours, souvenirs and all-round information service

▶ **Nordrhein-Westfalen Tourismus e.V.**
Worringer Strasse 2
D-50668 Köln
Tel. 02 21/1 79 45 0
Fax 179 45 17
www.nrw-tourismus.com
The tourist office of the federal state of North Rhine-Westphalia

### INTERNET

▶ **www.koeln.de**
The best portal for city life for visitors and residents. The English version has information about hotels, restaurants, entertainment, sightseeing, events and more.

### EMBASSIES (IN BERLIN)

- **Australian embassy**
  Wallstrasse 76–79, Mitte
  Tel. 880 0880
  www.australian-embassy.de

- **British embassy**
  Wilhelmstrasse 70, Mitte
  Tel. 204 570
  www.britischebotschaft.de

- **Canadian embassy**
  Leipziger Platz 17
  Tiergarten
  Tel. 203 120
  www.kanada-info.de

- **Embassy of the Republic of Ireland**
  Friedrichstrasse 200, Mitte
  Tel. 220 720
  www.botschaft-irland.de

- **New Zealand embassy**
  Friedrichstrasse 60, Mitte
  Tel. 206 210
  www.nzembassy.com

- **United States embassy**
  Neustädtische Kirchstrasse 4–5, Mitte
  Tel. 238 5174
  www.us-botschaft.de

### CONSULATES (IN DÜSSELDORF)

- **British consulate-general**
  Yorckstr. 19
  40476 Düsseldorf
  Tel. 0211 9 44 80

- **Canadian consulate**
  Benrather Strasse 8
  40213 Düsseldorf
  Tel. 0211 17 21 70

- **US consulate-general**
  Willi-Becker-Allee 10
  40227 Düsseldorf
  Tel. 0211 788 89 27

# Language

## GERMAN

### General

| | |
|---|---|
| Yes / No | Ja / Nein |
| Perhaps. / Maybe. | Vielleicht. |
| Please. | Bitte. |
| Thank you. / Thank you very much. | Danke. / Vielen Dank! |
| You're welcome. | Gern geschehen. |
| Excuse me! | Entschuldigung! |
| Pardon? | Wie bitte? |
| I don't understand. | Ich verstehe Sie / Dich nicht. |
| I only speak a bit of ... | Ich spreche nur wenig ... |
| Can you help me, please? | Können Sie mir bitte helfen? |
| I'd like ... | Ich möchte ... |
| I (don't) like this. | Das gefällt mir (nicht). |

| | |
|---|---|
| Do you have ...? | Haben Sie ...? |
| How much is this? | Wieviel kostet es? |
| What time is it? | Wieviel Uhr ist es? |
| What is this called? | Wie heißt dies hier? |

## Getting acquainted

| | |
|---|---|
| Good morning! | Guten Morgen! |
| Good afternoon! | Guten Tag! |
| Good evening! | Guten Abend! |
| Hello! / Hi! | Hallo! / Grüß Dich! |
| My name is ... | Mein Name ist ... |
| What's your name? | Wie ist Ihr / Dein Name? |
| How are you? | Wie geht es Ihnen / Dir? |
| Fine thanks. And you? | Danke. Und Ihnen / Dir? |
| Goodbye! / Bye-bye! | Auf Wiedersehen! |
| Good night! | Gute Nacht! |
| See you! / Bye! | Tschüss! |

## Travelling

| | |
|---|---|
| left / right | links / rechts |
| straight ahead | geradeaus |
| near / far | nah / weit |
| Excuse me, where's ..., please? | Bitte, wo ist ...? |
| ... the train station | ... der Bahnhof |
| ... the bus stop | ... die Bushaltestelle |
| ... the harbour | ... der Hafen |
| ... the airport | ... der Flughafen |
| How far is it? | Wie weit ist das? |
| I'd like to rent a car. | Ich möchte ein Auto mieten. |
| How long? | Wie lange? |

## Traffic

| | |
|---|---|
| My car's broken down. | Ich habe eine Panne. |
| Is there a service station nearby? | Gibt es hier in der Nähe eine Werkstatt? |
| Where's the nearest gas station? | Wo ist die nächste Tankstelle? |
| I want | Ich möchte ... |
| ... liters / gallons of ... | Liter / Gallonen (3,8 l) ... |
| ... regular/premium. | .... Normalbenzin/Super. |
| ... diesel. | ... Diesel. |
| ... unleaded. | ... bleifrei. |
| Full, please. | Volltanken, bitte. |

|  |  |
|---|---|
| Help! | Hilfe! |
| Attention!/Look out! | Achtung!/Vorsicht! |
| Please call ... | Rufen Sie bitte ... |
| ... an ambulance. | ... einen Krankenwagen. |
| ... the police. | ... die Polizei. |
| It was my fault. | Es war meine Schuld. |
| It was your fault. | Es war Ihre Schuld. |
| Please give me your name and address. | Geben Sie mir bitte Namen und Anschrift. |
| Beware of ... | Vorsicht vor ... |
| Bypass (with road number) | Ortsumgehung (mit Straßennummer) |
| Bypass (Byp) | Umgehungsstraße |
| Causeway | Brücke, Pontonbrücke |
| Construction | Bauarbeiten |
| Crossing (Xing) | Kreuzung, Überweg |
| Dead End | Sackgasse |
| Detour | Umleitung |
| Divided Highway | Straße mit Mittelstreifen |
| Do not enter | Einfahrt verboten |
| Exit | Ausfahrt |
| Hill | Steigung / Gefälle/unübersichtlich (Überholverbot) |
| Handicapped Parking | Behindertenparkplatz |
| Junction (Jct) | Kreuzung, Abzweigung, Einmündung |
| Keep off ... | Abstand halten ... |
| Loading Zone | Ladezone |
| Merge (Merging Traffic) | Einmündender Verkehr |
| Narrow Bridge | Schmale Brücke |
| No Parking | Parken verboten |
| No Passing | Überholen verboten |
| No Turn on Red | Rechtsabbiegen bei Rot verboten |
| U Turn | Wenden erlaubt |
| No U Turn | Wenden verboten |
| One Way | Einbahnstraße |
| Passenger Loading Zone | Ein- und Aussteigen erlaubt |
| Ped Xing | Fußgängerüberweg |
| Restricted Parking Zone | Zeitlich begrenztes Parken erlaubt |
| Right of Way | Vorfahrt |
| Road Construction | Straßenbauarbeiten |
| Slippery when wet | Schleudergefahr bei Nässe |
| Slow | Langsam fahren |
| Soft Shoulders | Straßenbankette nicht befestigt |
| Speed Limit | Geschwindigkeitsbegrenzung |
| Toll | Benutzungsgebühr, Maut |
| Tow away Zone | Absolutes Parkverbot, Abschleppzone |
| Xing (Crossing) | Kreuzung, Überweg |
| Yield | Vorfahrt beachten |

## Shopping

| | |
|---|---|
| Where can I find a ...? | Wo finde ich ... eine / ein ..? |
| ... pharmacy | ... Apotheke |
| ... bakery | ... Bäckerei |
| ... department store | ... Kaufhaus |
| ... food store | ... Lebensmittelgeschäft |
| ... supermarket | ... Supermarkt |

## Accommodation

| | |
|---|---|
| Could you recommend ... ? | Können Sie mir ... empfehlen? |
| ... a hotel / motel | ... ein Hotel / Motel |
| ... a bed & breakfast | ... eine Frühstückspension |
| Do you have ...? | Haben Sie noch ...? |
| ... a room for one | ... ein Einzelzimmer |
| ... a room for two | ... ein Doppelzimmer |
| ... with a shower / bath | ... mit Dusche / Bad |
| ... for one night | ... für eine Nacht |
| ... for a week | ... für eine Woche |
| I've reserved a room. | Ich habe ein Zimmer reserviert. |
| How much is the room | Was kostet das Zimmer |
| ... with breakfast? | ... mit Frühstück? |

## Doctor

| | |
|---|---|
| Can you recommend a good doctor? | Können Sie mir einen guten Arzt empfehlen? |
| I need a dentist. | Ich brauche einen Zahnarzt. |
| I feel some pain here. | Ich habe hier Schmerzen. |
| I've got a temperature. | Ich habe Fieber. |
| Prescription | Rezept |
| Injection / shot | Spritze |

## Bank / Post

| | |
|---|---|
| Where's the nearest bank? | Wo ist hier bitte eine Bank? |
| ATM (Automated Teller Machine) | Geldautomat |
| I'd like to change dollars/pounds into euros. | Ich möchte Dollars/Pfund in Euro wechseln. |
| How much is ... | Was kostet ... |
| ... a letter ... | ... ein Brief ... |
| ... a postcard ... | ... eine Postkarte ... |
| to Europe? | nach Europa? |

## Numbers

| | | | |
|---|---|---|---|
| 1 | eins | 2 | zwei |
| 3 | drei | 4 | vier |
| 5 | fünf | 6 | sechs |
| 7 | sieben | 8 | acht |
| 9 | neun | 10 | zehn |
| 11 | elf | 12 | zwölf |
| 13 | dreizehn | 14 | vierzehn |
| 15 | fünfzehn | 16 | sechzehn |
| 17 | siebzehn | 18 | achtzehn |
| 19 | neunzehn | 20 | zwanzig |
| 21 | einundzwanzig | 30 | dreißig |
| 40 | vierzig | 50 | fünfzig |
| 60 | sechzig | 70 | siebzig |
| 80 | achtzig | 90 | neunzig |
| 100 | (ein-)hundert | 1000 | (ein-)tausend |
| 1/2 | ein Halb | 1/3 | ein Drittel |
| 1/4 | ein Viertel | | |

## Restaurant

| | |
|---|---|
| Is there a good restaurant here? | Gibt es hier ein gutes Restaurant? |
| Would you reserve us a table for this evening, please? | Reservieren Sie uns bitte für heute Abend einen Tisch! |
| The menu please! | Die Speisekarte bitte! |
| Cheers! | Auf Ihr Wohl! |
| Could I have the check, please? | Bezahlen, bitte. |
| Where is the restroom, please? | Wo ist bitte die Toilette? |

## Frühstück / Breakfast

| | |
|---|---|
| Kaffee (mit Sahne / Milch) | coffee (with cream / milk) |
| koffeinfreier Kaffee | decaffeinated coffee |
| heiße Schokolade | hot chocolate |
| Tee (mit Milch / Zitrone) | tea (with milk / lemon) |
| Rühreier | scrambled eggs |
| pochierte Eier | poached eggs |
| Eier mit Speck | bacon and eggs |
| Spiegeleier | eggs sunny side up |
| harte / weiche Eier | hard-boiled / soft-boiled eggs |
| (Käse- / Champignon-)Omelett | (cheese / mushroom) omelette |
| Pfannkuchen | pancake |
| Brot / Brötchen / Toast | bread / rolls / toast |
| Butter | butter |
| Zucker | sugar |
| Honig | honey |

| | |
|---|---|
| Marmelade / Orangenmarmelade | jam / marmelade |
| Joghurt | yoghurt |
| Obst | fruit |

## Vorspeisen und Suppen / Starters and Soups

| | |
|---|---|
| Fleischbrühe | broth / consommé |
| Hühnercremesuppe | cream of chicken soup |
| Tomatensuppe | cream of tomato soup |
| gemischter Salat | mixed salad |
| grüner Salat | green salad |
| frittierte Zwiebelringe | onion rings |
| Meeresfrüchtesalat | seafood salad |
| Garnelen- / Krabbencocktail | shrimp / prawn cocktail |
| Räucherlachs | smoked salmon |
| Gemüsesuppe | vegetable soup |

## Fisch und Meeresfrüchte / Fish and Seafood

| | |
|---|---|
| Kabeljau | cod |
| Krebs | crab |
| Aal | eel |
| Schellfisch | haddock |
| Hering | herring |
| Hummer | lobster |
| Muscheln | mussels |
| Austern | oysters |
| Barsch | perch |
| Scholle | plaice |
| Lachs | salmon |
| Jakobsmuscheln | scallops |
| Seezunge | sole |
| Tintenfisch | squid |
| Forelle | trout |
| Tunfisch | tuna |

## Fleisch und Geflügel / Meat and Poultry

| | |
|---|---|
| gegrillte Schweinerippchen | barbecued spare ribs |
| Rindfleisch | beef |
| Hähnchen | chicken |
| Geflügel | poultry |
| Kotelett | chop / cutlet |
| Filetsteak | fillet |
| (junge) Ente | duck(ling) |

| | |
|---|---|
| Schinkensteak | gammon |
| Fleischsoße | gravy |
| Hackfleisch vom Rind | ground beef |
| gekochter Schinken | ham |
| Nieren | kidneys |
| Lamm | lamb |
| Leber | liver |
| Schweinefleisch | pork |
| Würstchen | sausages |
| Lendenstück vom Rind, Steak | sirloin steak |
| Truthahn | turkey |
| Kalbfleisch | veal |
| Reh oder Hirsch | venison |

## Nachspeise und Käse / Dessert and Cheese

| | |
|---|---|
| gedeckter Apfelkuchen | apple pie |
| Hüttenkäse | cottage cheese |
| Vanillesoße | custard |
| Ziegenkäse | goat's cheese |
| Gebäck | pastries |
| Schokoladenplätzchen | brownies |
| Sahne | cream |
| Obstsalat | fruit salad |
| Eiscreme | icecream |

## Gemüse und Salat / Vegetables and Salad

| | |
|---|---|
| gebackene Kartoffeln in der Schale | baked potatoes |
| Pommes frites | french fries |
| Bratkartoffeln | hash browns |
| Kartoffelpüree | mashed potatoes |
| gebackene Bohnen in Tomatensoße | baked beans |
| Kohl | cabbage |
| Karotten | carrots |
| Blumenkohl | cauliflower |
| Tomaten | tomatoes |
| Gurke | cucumber |
| Knoblauch | garlic |
| Lauch | leek |
| Kopfsalat | lettuce |
| Pilze | mushrooms |
| Zwiebeln | onions |
| Erbsen | peas |
| Paprika | peppers |
| Kürbis | pumpkin |
| Spinat | spinach |
| Mais | sweet corn |
| Maiskolben | corn-on-the-cob |

### Obst / Fruit

| | | | |
|---|---|---|---|
| Äpfel | apples | Birnen | pears |
| Aprikosen | apricots | Orange | orange |
| Brombeeren | blackberries | Pfirsiche | peaches |
| Kirschen | cherries | Ananas | pineapple |
| Weintrauben | grapes | Pflaumen | plums |
| Grapefruit | grapefruit | Himbeeren | raspberries |
| Zitrone | lemon | Erdbeeren | strawberries |
| Preiselbeeren | cranberries | | |

### Getränke / Beverages

| | |
|---|---|
| Bier (vom Fass) | beer (on tap) |
| Apfelwein | cider |
| Rotwein / Weißwein | red wine / white wine |
| trocken / lieblich | dry / sweet |
| Sekt, Schaumwein | sparkling wine |
| alkoholfreie Getränke | soft drinks |
| Fruchtsaft | fruit juice |
| gesüßter Zitronensaft | lemonade |
| Milch | milk |
| Mineralwasser | mineral water / spring water |

# Literature

**Chargesheimer/Böll**: *Unter Krahnenbäumen.* Schaden Verlag 2007.
In the post-war years the photographer Chargesheimer recorded the way of life of ordinary people in and around the street Unter Krahnenbäumen. A short text by Heinrich Böll, here with an English translation, complements this outstanding documentation of past times.

**Eric Läufer**: *Via Sanctorum – Ancient Processional Routes to Cologne Saints.* J.P. Bachem Verlag 2005.
A short tour through »Holy Cologne«.

**Franz Mathar**: *The Cologne Brauhaus Trail.* J.P. Bachem Verlag 2003.
A guided pub crawl mixed with some history and all you ever wanted to know about the local beer.

**Barbara Schock-Werner**: *Der Kölner Dom.* Greven Verlag, 2005.
Excellent photos of Cologne Cathedral with a text in English and other languages by the cathedral architect, the first woman to hold this position.

**Eric Taylor**: *Operation Millennium: »Bomber« Harris's Raid on Cologne*, May 1942. Isis Publishing 2007
The story of the first-ever 1000-bomber raid and the damage it did on the night of 30 May 1942.

**Klaus-Jürgen Vetter (ed.)**: *Beautiful Cologne*. Bruckmann Verlag 2005. Photos of the city with short texts in English.

**Gerta Wolff**: *Roman-Germanic Cologne*. J.P. Bachem Verlag 2005.
A detailed guide to the Roman remains of the city, including the exhibits in the Römisch-Germanisches Museum.

# Lost and Found

▶ **Fundbüro der Stadt Köln**
Ottmar-Pohl-Platz 1
Tel. 22 12 63 13
E-mail: fundbuero@stadt-koeln.de
Hours: Mon, Thu 8am–4pm, Tue until 6pm, Wed, Fri until noon

▶ **Deutsche Bahn AG**
Left luggage centre in main station
Tel. 141 31 25
Hotline:
Tel. 01805 / 99 05 99
Hours: 6am–10pm

# Money

**Euro** Since 2002 the euro has been the official currency of Germany.

**Currency regulations** Citizens of EU members countries may import to and export from Germany unlimited amounts in euros.

**Bureaux de change and cash dispensers** The bureau de change in the tourist office opposite the cathedral has long opening hours. Cash dispensers operated by various banks are thick on the ground in the city centre and never far away in the suburbs, so that money can be obtained without problems round the clock by using credit and debit cards with a PIN.

The major international **credit cards** are accepted by banks, most hotels, car rentals and many restaurants and shops. Credit cards have limits.

**i Exchange rates**

- 1 €= 1.35 US$
- 1 US$ = 0.75 €
- 1 £ = 1.27 €
- 1  = 0.79 £

## CONTACT DETAILS FOR CREDIT CARDS

In the event of lost bank or credit cards you can contact the following numbers in UK and USA (phone numbers when dialling from Germany):

- **Eurocard/MasterCard**
  Tel. 001 / 636 7227 111
- **Visa**
  Tel. 001 / 410 581 336
- **American Express UK**
  Tel. 0044 / 1273 696 933
- **American Express USA**
  Tel. 001 / 800 528 4800
- **Diners Club UK**
  Tel. 0044 / 1252 513 500
- **Diners Club USA**
  Tel. 001 / 303 799 9000

Have the bank sort code, account number and card number as well as the expiry date ready.
The following numbers of UK banks (dialling from Germany) can be used to report and stop lost or stolen bank and credit cards issued by those banks:

- **HSBC**
  Tel. 0044 / 1442 422 929
- **Barclaycard**
  Tel. 0044 / 1604 230 230
- **NatWest**
  Tel. 0044 / 142 370 0545
- **Lloyds TSB**
  Tel. 0044 / 1702 278 270

**Loss of bank cards and credit cards**

If bank cards or cheque and credit cards should get lost, you should call your own bank or credit card organization to make sure they are immediately stopped. It is a good idea to make a note of the telephone number on the back of the card.

# Museums

**Museum nights**

Twice a year the Cologne museums and other cultural institutions hold a museum night, the »Lange Nacht der Kölner Museen«, between 7pm and 3am. Shuttle buses run on five routes through the city, connecting the different venues. The price of the ticket includes the shuttle bus, admission to the museums, and to a wide range of special events such as concerts, dance and demonstrations (www.museumsnacht-koeln.de).
The website of the city museums, www.museenkoeln.de, has pages in English.

# MUSEUMS IN COLOGNE

## MUSEUM SERVICE

Richartzstr. 2, tel. 22 12 45 44
www.museenkoeln.de/museumsdienst
Hours: Mon–Thu 9am–1pm and 2–4pm, Fri 9am–1pm
Information and bookings for guided tours, workshops, children's events etc. in the municipal museums

## ART

- **Käthe-Kollwitz-Museum**
►p.198

- **Kölnischer Kunstverein**
Hahnenstrasse 6
Tel. 21 70 21
www.koelnischerkunstverein.de
Hours: Tue–Sun 1–7pm
Cologne's Kunstverein (art society) was founded in 1839 and is the oldest in Germany. In the former British Council building, »Die Brücke«, built in 1949–50 by Wilhelm Riphan, it presents changing exhibitions of contemporary art. The attached cinema has a high-class film programme, including films related to the exhibitions.

- **Museum für Angewandte Kunst**
►p.190

**! *Baedeker* TIP**

**Museum Mondays**

One problem with taking a long weekend in German cities is that almost all museums close on Mondays. In Cologne the exceptions are ►Kolumba, the cathedral treasury and the Photographische Sammlung (see below), which has free admission on Mondays.

- **Museum für Ostasiatische Kunst**
►p.192

- **Keramion (museum for contemporary ceramic art)**
Bonnstr. 12 in Frechen, a small town 10km/6mi west of Cologne
Tel. 022 34 / 69 76 90
www.stiftung-keramion.de
Hours: Tue–Fri 10am–5pm, Sat 2–5pm, Sun 10am–5pm
Tram no. 7 from Neumarkt to Frechen-Bahnhof

- **Museum Ludwig**
►p.193

- **Photographische Sammlung**
Im Mediapark 7
Thu–Tue 2–7pm
High-quality special exhibitions of contemporary and historic photography, and the works of the Cologne photographer August Sander.

- **Skulpturenpark**
Riehler Str./Elsa Brandströmstr.
Elsa-Brandström-Str. 9
Tel. 921 22 83
Hours: March–Oct daily 10.30am–6pm, Nov–Feb until 4.30pm
Next to the Zoobrücke (entrance Riehler Str.), an outdoor exhibition of sculptures and installations by internationally renowned artists. Free admission.

- **Stiftung Kultur**
►p.186

- **Wallraf-Richartz-Museum – Fondation Corboud**
►p.254

## RELIGIOUS ART

► **Domschatzkammer (Cathedral Treasury)**
►p.173

► **Kolumba – Erzbischöfliches Diözesanmuseum**
►p.183

► **Museum Schnütgen**
►p.195

## HISTORY

► **Excavations below St. Severin church**
►p. 228

► **Deutsches Sport & Olympia Museum**
►p.224

► **Deutsches Tanzarchiv (dance)**
►p.186

► **Museum of Eau de Cologne**
►p.212

► **EL-DE-Haus (memorial exhibition on Nazi victims)**
►p.176

► **Geldgeschichtliches Museum**
Neumarkt 18
Tel. 227 23 70
www.ksk-koeln.de
www.geldgeschichte.de
Mon–Fri 9am–6.30pm,
Sat 10am–2pm
The regional savings bank has an exhibition about money: piggy banks, purses, Roman coins etc.

► **Kölner Karnevalsmuseum**
Maarweg 134
Tel. 574 00 74,
www.kk-museum.de
Hours: Thu 10am–8pm,
Fr 10am–5pm, Sat and Sun
11am–5pm
A well-presented exhibition on the history of carnival celebrations since Roman times, worth seeing even for those not specially interested in Carnival as a spotlight on social history and the Cologne mentality.

► **Kölnisches Stadtmuseum**
►p.259

► **Mikwe**
►p.212

► **Praetorium**
►p.202

► **Rautenstrauch-Joest-Museum**
►p.213

► **Rhein-Kreis-Museum Zons**
►p.262

► **Römisch-Germanisches Museum**
►p.218

► **Römische Grabkammer in Köln-Weiden (Roman tomb)**
►p.215

► **Schokoladenmuseum**
►p.223

► **Ubier-Monument**
►p.217

► **Weinmuseum**
Kölner Wein Depot
Amsterdamer Str. 1
Tel. 72 75 70,
www.koelner-wein-depot.de
Hours: Tue–Fri 8am–7pm, Sat until 2pm

# Music · Concerts

Cologne has something for every musical taste, from opera to jazz, rock and musicals (►p.58). See www.koeln.de or call at the office of KölnTicket on Roncalliplatz next to the Römisch-Germanisches Museum to find out what is on.

## CONCERT VENUES

### TICKET OUTLETS

▶ **Lanxessarena Ticket-Shop**
Willy-Brandt-Platz 2
Tel. 80 20

▶ **KölnMusik Event**
Neumarkt-Galerie
in the Mayersche bookshop
Tel. 20 40 83 33
www.koelnticket.de

▶ **KölnMusik Ticket**
Roncalliplatz
Tel. 28 01
www.koelnticket.de

▶ **Box office at Rudolfplatz**
Hohenzollernring 2
Tel. 258 29 57

▶ **www.nrw-ticket.de**
Ticket hotline: tel. 0180 / 500 18 12
Information on events, ticket sales and venues in North Rhine-Westphalia

*Jazz and beer are the staple fare in the Stadtgarten.*

### CLASSICS · OPERA

▶ **KölnKlassik**
www.koelnklassik.de
Portal with daily calendar of events classified by venue.

▶ **Opera: Oper der Stadt Köln**
Offenbachplatz
Tel. 22 12 84 00
www.buehnenkoeln.de
Tram: Appellhofplatz

▶ **Philharmonie**
Bischofsgartenstr. 1
Tel. 20 40 80
www.koelnmusik.de
Tram: Dom/Hbf.
Cologne's main venue for classical

concerts, a beautiful hall with good acoustics.

### JAZZ

▶ **Joe's »Klimperkasten«**
Alter Markt 50, tel. 258 21 32
www.papajoes.de
Piano music daily from 8pm: jazz, swing and blues

▶ **Papa Joe's Jazzlokal »Em Streckstrump«**
Buttermarkt 37
Tel. 257 79 31
Live music every day in the Old Town

▶ **Stadtgarten**
Venloer Str. 40
Tel. 95 29 940
www.stadtgarten.de
Tram: Hans-Böckler-Platz

### MUSICALS

▶ **Musical Dome Köln**
Goldgasse 1/Breslauerplatz
Ticket hotline:
tel. 0180 / 51 52 530
www.musical-dome.de
Tram: Dom/Hbf.

### ROCK

▶ **Alter Wartesaal**
Johannisstr. 11
(Hauptbahnhof)
www.wartesaal.de
Tram: Dom/Hbf.
Tel. 912 88 50
House and techno

▶ **E-Werk**
Schanzenstr. 37
Tel. 96 27 90
www.e-werk-koeln.de
Tram: Von-Sparr-Str.
A mixed bag of concerts and parties.

▶ **Gebäude 9**
Deutz-Mülheimer-Str. 127
Tel. 58 91 94 14
www.gebaeude9.de
Tram: Kölnmesse.
Concerts and events for the young and creative scene, also cinema and theatre.

▶ **Live-Music-Hall**
Lichtstr. 30
Tel. 95 42 990
www.livemusichall.de
Tram: Venloer Str./Gürtel
Concerts, themed party nights.

▶ **Underground**
Vogelsanger Str. 200
Tel. 54 23 26
www.underground-cologne.de
Tram: Venloer Str./Gürtel
Frequent rock and pop concerts.

# Post and Communications

Post offices

Post offices are open from 9am–6pm Mon–Fri, 9am–1pm Sat (closed Sun). There is no longer a post office in the main station, but stamps are sold in the international newsagents there. A conveniently situated large post office offering the full range of services is near the shopping district at Breite Strasse 6 (hours: Mon–Fri 9am–7pm, Sat 9am–1pm).

### DIALLING CODES

▸ **Dialling codes to Cologne**
from Germany 0221
from the UK and Republic of Ireland: tel. 00 49 221
from the USA, Canada and Australia: tel. 00 11 49 221
It is not necessary to dial the 0221 area code for local calls within Cologne.

▸ **Dialling codes from Germany**
to the UK: tel. 00 44
to the Republic of Ireland: Tel. 00 353
to the USA and Canada: tel. 00 1
to Australia: tel. 00 61
The 0 that precedes the subsequent local area code is omitted.

### DIRECTORY ENQUIRIES

▸ **National**
Tel. 11 833

▸ **International**
Tel. 11 834

▸ **Enquiries in English**
Tel. 11 837

Postage stamps

Postage stamps for letters up to 20g/0.7oz within Germany cost €0.55, to other European countries €0.70, and elsewhere €1.70. Sending a postcard home is a little cheaper: €0.65 (Europe) or €1.00 (elsewhere).

Public telephones

Public telephones normally only accept Deutsche Telekom phonecards, available in 5, 10 and 20-euro denominations from post offices and newsagents. International calling cards offer more competitive rates (www.comfi.com). There are a large number of call shops which offer cheap rates for calls abroad.

Mobile phones

The German mobile networks function throughout the country with providers such as T-Mobile, E-Plus, Base and O2. It is worth checking on roaming tariffs, which can be pricey, before you leave.

## Prices · Discounts

WelcomeCard

The Cologne WelcomeCard is an entitlement to **reduced admission to museums and other attractions**, free use of public transport, and discounts for a range of other services, for 1, 2 or 3 days. As the reduction for museums, city tours and boat trips is usually only about €1 per person, check whether it is really worth buying the card based on your individual plans. It is attractive for families, those who use public transport and for visits to the opera and Philharmonie (20% discount). The price of the card (for one day €9 per person, €18 for a family; for two days €14 and €28; for three days €19 and €38. The WelcomeCard is sold at the tourist office (KölnTourismus, ►Information) and in many hotels.

# Shopping

Shopping districts

The main shopping area lies between the cathedral and Neumarkt along two pedestrian streets: **Hohe Strasse** and **Schildergasse**. The large department stores, branches of the major chain stores selling clothes and shoes, shops for sports equipment, toys, perfume and cosmetics, jewellery and household items, leather goods and furnishings, and the three large bookshops are all here.

The upmarket fashion boutiques are in **Mittelstrasse** and the surrounding streets. Stores with a creative and individual character, and those selling young fashions and items that have an esoteric touch or are simply way out, are still to be found around **Ehrenstrasse** and the adjoining Pfeilstrasse and Friesenwall, but this district is gradually being taken over by mainstream stores, and the independent designers are moving to the Belgian Quarter on the other side of the Ring. Here, around Antwerpener Strasse and Brüsseler Strasse, there is a lively shopping district (www.chicbelgique.de for details).

! *Baedeker* TIP

**Hecho a mano**

Cuban »torcedoras« make quality cigars by hand (hecho a mano) at Cologne's only cigar factory. Selected types of tobacco from the Jalapa area in the north of Nicaragua are used. The small-scale production site is open for visitors each Tuesday from 2pm to 7pm (La Galana Zigarrenmanufaktur, Venloer Str. 213, tel. 800 09 23, www.zigarren-manufaktur.de).

## Markets

Markets are held at 38 sites all over the city, often twice weekly, usually between 7am and 1pm. Many of them sell cheap clothing as well as food.

An attractive little market is held on Tuesdays and Fridays next to St. Aposteln church near Neumarkt. The market on Wilhelmplatz (tram: Florastr.) is a colourful mix of German and Turkish stalls (daily except Sun, best on Fri and Sat).

## Souvenirs

Perfume and Kölsch glasses

The small cathedral shop is on the north (railway station) side; the tourist office opposite the cathedral has Cologne T-shirts, bags, etc. There is a concentration of souvenir shops around the cathedral and Alter Markt. There is no shortage of tourist kitsch here, including much that has no connection to Cologne – Bavarian beer mugs, for example, and nut-crackers from Saxony. Two souvenirs that are genuinely local are the glasses for Kölsch beer (slim cylinders holding only 0.2 litres) and eau de Cologne, which is no longer made in the city but has its roots there.

## SHOPPING ADDRESSES

### ANTIQUES

There is a concentration of antique dealers in and around St.-Apern-Str.

▶ **Bernhard von Hünerbein**
Lintgasse 16
Historic musical instruments

▶ **»blaue Galerie« Köln**
Auf dem Berlich 13
Antique jewellery

▶ **Dr. Hampel Antiquitäten**
Neumarkt-Passage
Biedermeier, art déco

▶ **Anne Fidow-Fiddickow**
Herzogstr. 32
Old silver

▶ **Peter Pütz**
Kreishausgalerie
St.-Apern-Str. 17
www.peterpuetz.com
Antique jewellery

### BOOKS

▶ **Kunstbuchhandlung König**
Ehrenstr. 4
Excellent on 20th-century art and architecture. The branch at Breite Str. 79 has many art books at bargain prices, including English and multi-lingual books.

▶ **Mayersche Buchhandlung**
Neumarkt 2 and Schildergasse 31
Two large bookstores with coffee bars and comfortable chairs for browsing. English books also available.

▶ **Thalia**
Neumarkt 18 a
Huge selection on several floors, including books in English

### DEPARTMENT STORES

▶ **Karstadt**
Breite Str. 103
Large department store near Neumarkt: fashion, household items, perfume, jewellery, books, etc. Excellent food department in the basement, convenient restaurant on the top floor.

▶ **Kaufhof**
Hohe Str. 41
Everything under one roof – including the electronics and entertainment media shop Saturn on the top floor.

▶ **Manufactum**
Brückenstr. 23
Well-made old-fashioned products for people who are prepared to pay for quality: food, clothes, furnishings, articles for garden, kitchen and office.

### FASHION AND ACCESSORIES

▶ **Cappelleria**
Richmodstr. 7
Hat-maker with some unusual creations.

! *Baedeker* TIP

**Eau de Cologne**

In 1709 Giovanni Maria Farina began to make perfume in Cologne. He became supplier to crowned heads all over Europe, and the premises where he made his eau de Cologne (Obenmarspforten 21, on the square in front of the city hall, www.farina1709.com), is still a corner shop and still run by the Farina family, who sell perfume made according to the original recipe.

*Hoss an der Oper is one of Cologne's finest delicatessens.*

- **Heller und Vohs**
  Antwerpener Str. 50
  Affordable designer fashion made by Claudia Heller, who shares the premises with jewellery designer Nina Vohs.

- **Gesine Moritz**
  Neumarkt-Passage, Neumarkt 18a
  www.gesine-moritz.de
  Cologne's best-known fashion designer numbers many German celebrities among her customers.

- **NIOVA Schuhe**
  Venloer Str. 31
  High-quality Italian shoes for men and women in the Belgian Quarter

## FLEA MARKETS

Between March and October about 200 flea markets are held in Cologne, usually on Saturday from 9am to 6pm or Sundays from 11am to 6pm. Dates are published in the local newspapers and at www.coelln-konzept.de.

- **Altstadt**
  Last Sunday in the month on the Rhine promenade near the railway bridge

- **Nippes**
  Fourth Sunday in the month on Wilhelmplatz (tram Florastr.)

- **Südstadt**
  First Sunday in the month on Vorgebirgsstr., between Volksgarten and Südstadion

## FLOWERS

- **Blumen Heiko Kalitowitsch**
  Richmodstr. 7

! Baedeker TIP

**»Get well soon, Barbie«**

The »Kölner Puppenklinik« (doll clinic) provides tender loving care for injured dolls. The owner Joyce Merlet replaces the missing eyes in teddy bears and performs major surgery on antique dolls. The shop is a wonderland for young and old (Ehrenstr. 48; tel. 25 46 42)

A wonderful florist with a reputation that extends beyond Cologne.

## FLOWER MARKET

From mid-April to mid-May, daily 9am–6pm on Neumarkt

## FOOD

▶ **Bärenland**
Breite Str. 161
A shop devoted to Germany's favourite sweets: Gummibärchen, bear-shaped wine gums, here made with natural fruit juice.

▶ **English Shop**
An St. Agatha 41
English and American foods, English books and DVDs.

▶ **Honig Müngersdorf**
An St. Agatha 37
A hidden gem among the big retail chains, a family-run shop that sells everything connected with bees and honey: mead, honey biscuits, cakes and sweets, beeswax candles, cosmetic products.

▶ **Hoss an der Oper**
Breite Str. 25
www.hoss-delikatessen.de
Fine foods for a picnic or to take home, e.g. quiches, pastries, salads, desserts.

▶ **Käsehaus Wingenfeld**
Ehrenstr. 90
www.kaesehaus-wingenfeld.de
Cologne's best cheese shop.

▶ **Zimmermann**
Ehrenstr. 75
One of a dying breed: a traditional family-run bakery selling a wide range of home-made bread and cake. Their black bread is particularly good.

## GALLERIES

▶ **Information on gallery exhibitions**
www.koeln-galerien.de
Current programme of the commercial art galleries in Cologne

▶ **Auctions**
*Kunsthaus Lempertz*
Neumarkt 3
Tel. 925 72 90
www.lempertz.de
Contemporary, old and Asian art

*Sotheby's*
St.-Apern-Str.
Tel. 20 71 70
www.sothebys.com

▶ **Galerie Boisserée**
Drususgasse 7
Tel. 257 85 19
www.boisseree.com
Contemporary graphics and painting, bronze sculpture; artists such as Chagall, Corinth, Miró, Liebermann, Kollwitz and Hundertwasser

▶ **Galerie Gmurzynska**
Goethestr. 65 a
Tel. 37 64 40
www.gmurzynska.com
Cubism, Dada, Constructivism, Russian avant-garde, e.g. Arp,

Chagall, Moholy-Nagy, Picasso, Schwitters.

▸ **Galerie Heinz Holtmann**
Obenmarspforten 7
Tel. 257 86 07
www.galerie-holtmann.de
International avant-garde and modern classics, e.g. Beuys, Christo, J. Klauke, Szczesny, Warhol

▸ **Galerie Karsten Greve**
Drususgasse 1
Tel. 257 10 12
www.galerie-karsten-greve.com
International avant-garde since 1945, e.g. Kounellis, Fontana, Knöller, Manzoni, Beuys and Prangenberg

### SPECIALISTS

▸ **Filz Gnoss**
Apostelnstr. 21
Every imaginable product made of felt or wool: slippers, hats, mats ...

▸ **Globetrotter**
Richmodstr. 10
This enormous store has practically everything connected with sports, outdoors and travel: sports and camping equipment, sportswear, travel books and maps, even its own pool for testing kayaks and diving gear.

▸ **Gummi Grün**
Richmodstr. 3
Everything sold here is made of rubber.

▸ **Bruno Wolkenaer**
Ehrenstr. 6
Artists' materials

# Sports and Outdoors

## Sport & Fun

**Spectator sport**

There is no lack of major sporting events in Cologne. The main attractions for spectators are the football team, 1. FC Köln, which has had little success in recent years but plays to a full house in the modern stadium; the ice hockey team, KEC (known as »die Haie«, »the sharks«); the basketball team, RheinEnergie Köln; the horse racing; and the Cologne marathon each October.

**Cycling**

Cologne and its surroundings are ideal for gentle cycling tours, as the city and countryside are flat, and there are many cycle paths.

**Inline skating**

The paved and asphalted paths on the left and right banks of the Rhine are popular among inline skaters.

**Jogging**

Cologne has many parks, some of them large, which provide excellent conditions for joggers. The wooded park on the western edge of the city, the Stadtwald, has many miles of paths suitable for a long or a short run.

# SPORTS VENUES & FACILITIES

## INFORMATION

▶ **Haus des Kölner Sports**
Ulrich-Brisch-Weg 1
Tel. 92 13 00 22
www.sportinkoeln.de
Open: Mon–Thu
9am–5pm. Fri until 1pm
The source of information for all sporting activities in Cologne (not in English).

## AMERICAN FOOTBALL

The Cologne Centurions (www.cologne-centurions.de) play at the RheinEnergieStadion, the Cologne Falcons (www.cologne-falcons.com) at the Südstadion.

## BASEBALL

Baseball is becoming more popular. In the Reit- und Baseballstadion in Müngersdorf (close to the Rheinenergiestadion) up to 2000 spectators watch home games of the Cologne Dodgers and Cologne Cardinals.

## CYCLING

▶ **Cycle routes**
www.radroutenplaner.nrw.de
This website, which exists in an English version, provides suggestions for cycling routes in Cologne, its surroundings and the rest of the federal state of North Rhine-Westphalia.

▶ **Kölner Fahrradverleih**
Markmannsgasse/Deutzer Brücke
Tel. 0171 / 629 87 96
www.koelnerfahrradverleih.de
April–Oct daily 10am–6pm
Cycle hire and guides tours by bike.

*Young inline skaters at the LanxessArena*

▶ **Radstadion Köln**
Aachener Str. (Stadion)
Tel. 94 97 61 20
www.radstadion-koeln.de
The cycling stadium is a venue for top-class international competitions.

## GOLF

▶ **Public golf course in Roggendorf/Thenhofen (northern boundary of Cologne)**
Parallelweg 1
Tel. 78 40 18
www.clarks-golfworld.de

## JOGGING

▶ **Jogging in a group**
www.laufen-in-köln.de

## MARATHON

▶ **Cologne Marathon**
Tel. 33 77 73 11
www.koeln-marathon.de
Every year in early October, for runners and inline skaters. A major event with over 10,000 competitors and hundreds of thousands of spectators.

## HORSE RACING

▶ **Galopprennbahn Weidenpesch**
Scheibenstr.
Tel. 974 50 50
www.koeln-galopp.de
Tram: Scheibenstr.
Races from Easter to early November in leafy surroundings about 4km/2.5mi north of the city centre.

## SPAS

▶ **Claudius Therme**
Sachsenbergstr. 1
Tel. 98 14 40
www.claudius-therme.de
Hours: daily 9am–midnight
The no. 150 bus from Köln-Deutz station; it is pleasanter to walk through the park or take the cable car from the zoo.
A beautiful and lavishly equipped complex built over hot natural mineral springs at the north end of the Rheinpark. Ten indoor and outdoor pools at temperatures between 20°C/68°F and 36°C/97°F, saunas and steam baths, a variety of massage therapies and cosmetic treatments.

▶ **Neptun-Bad**
Neptunplatz 1
Tel. 71 00 71
www.neptunbad.de
Hours: daily 9am–midnight
Tram: Körnerstr.
Tasteful conversion of an art nouveau swimming pool into a Oriental-style spa with saunas and a variety of therapies and massages.

## SPORT STADIUMS

▶ **RheinEnergieStadion**
Aachenerstr.
Tel. 71 61 61 50
www.stadion-koeln.de
Sportpark Müngersdorf
is home to stadiums for football and athletics, tennis courts and hockey pitches, a large swimming pool, arenas for equestrian sport and halls for gymnastics. The largest stadium here is the modern RheinEnergieStadion, which seats 50,000 and is the home of 1. FC Köln football club.

▶ **LanxessArena**
Willy-Brandt-Platz 1
www.koelnarena.de
The largest multi-purpose hall in Germany holds 18,000 spectators for sports, especially ice hockey, and other events such as rock concerts.
Tram: Deutz/Kölnarena

*The Cologne Sharks ice hockey team play at the LanxessArena.*

**Südstadion**
Vorgebirgstr./Höninger Weg
12,000-seater stadium, mainly for Cologne's second football club (Fortuna Köln) and American football.

## SWIMMING POOLS

**Information**
www.koelnbaeder.de
Details of all 16 indoor and outdoor municipal pools, including the Agrippabad and Stadionbad listed below

**Agrippabad**
Kämmergasse 1
Tel. 279 17 30
Tram: Poststr.
Hours:
Mon–Fri 6.30am–10.30pm, Sat–-Sun 9am–9pm
Recently renovated complex that combines pools for serious swimming and diving with a wave machine, slides and play areas, saunas, outdoor terraces for sunbathing and a café. Close to the city centre.

**Aqualand**
Merianstr. 1
Tel. 702 80
www.aqualand.de
Hours: Mon–Thu 9.30am–11pm, Fri until midnight, Sat 9am–midnight, Sun 9am–11pm
An indoor fun pool with slides, sauna, gym and solarium

**Stadionbad**
Aachener Str. next to Rheinenergiestadion
Tel. 279 18 40
Hours: Mon–Fri 10am–8pm, Sat–Sun 9am–8pm
A large complex with eight different pools, play and sunbathing areas, beach volleyball, diving facilities.

# Theatre

Cologne theatres

In addition to the municipal theatres, a wide range of experimental, modern and popular theatre, cabaret and performances of all kinds can be enjoyed in the city. There is no dedicated English-language theatre, but performances in English can sometimes be seen at the Theater am Sachsenring, and occasionally at other venues.

## THEATRES IN COLOGNE

### INFORMATION

www.theaterszene-koeln.de

### BOX OFFICES

►p.114

### MUNICIPAL THEATRES

► **Advance bookings**
Tel. 22 12 84 00
www.buehnenkoeln.de

► **Programme information**
Tel. 22 12 84 60

► **Opera**
Offenbachplatz
Tickets for same evening:
Tel. 22 12 82 48

► **Schauspielhaus**
Offenbachplatz
Tickets for same evening:
Tel. 22 12 82 48

### CABARET

► **atelier-Theater**
Roonstr. 78
Tel. 24 24 85
www.ateliertheater.de
Political cabaret, satire and other performances.
Tram: Zülpicher Platz

► **Senftöpfchen**
Grosse Neugasse 2
Tel. 258 10 58
www.senftoepfchen-theater.de
Tram: Dom/Hbf.
Mixed programme including satire and chansons.

► **Theater am Sachsenring**
Sachsenring 3
Tel. 31 50 15
www.theater-am-sachsenring.de
Tram: Eifelstr.

### PUPPET THEATRE

► **Hänneschen-Theater**
Eisenmarkt 2
Tel. 258 12 01
www.haenneschen.de
The puppets speak Cologne dialect. Usually booked out months in advance.

### CONTEMPORARY THEATRE

► **Theater Der Keller**
Kleingedankstr. 6
Tel. 932 29 59
www.theater-der-keller.de
Modern drama and classics

► **Theater im Bauturm**
Aachener Str. 24
Tel. 52 42 42
www.theaterszene-koeln.de/bauturm
Small theatre with an excellent reputation for high-quality drama

# Time

Germany is in the central European time zone (CET), one hour ahead of Greenwich Mean Time. For the summer months from the end of March to the end of October European summer time is used (CEST = CET+1 hour).

# Tours and Guides

## City Tours

By bus

The tourist offices organizes two-hour tours of the city by bus with commentary in German and English. Hours: Apr–Oct daily 10am, 12.30pm, 3pm, Nov–March daily 11am, 2pm, starting from the tourist office opposite the cathedral. There are also hop-on, hop-off tours in open-top buses, also starting from the tourist office: Wed–Sat every 45 minutes from 10.30am to 4.30pm.

! *Baedeker* TIP

**Tours by rickshaw**

For a personal tour of the city, hire a rickshaw next to the cathedral (tel. 60 47 89 and www.koeln-rikscha.de). If you would prefer to pedal yourself, go to the cycle hire in the Old Town next to the Deutzer Brücke (tel. 0171 / 629 87 96, www.koelnerfahrradverleih.de), which organizes a three-hour tour daily at 1.30pm.

A great range of **guided walks** on historical themes, legends and particular parts of the city, as well as ghost walks and the highly popular tours on Kölsch beer, are offered by the tourist office and a number of private operators. Open tours, which anyone can join with or without booking in advance, are almost all held in German, but English-language tours can be booked privately (► see addresses below). Tours of the cathedral in English take place at 10.30am (daily except Sunday) and 2.30pm (daily), starting inside the main west door.

## Excursions

Island in the Rhine

A few miles south of the city centre on the right bank of the Rhine, in Porz-Zündorf, a little island known as the **Groov** is a popular recreational area, with shady walks, children's playgrounds, cafés, boats for hire on a lake, tennis courts and an open-air swimming pool. Get there on tram no. 7 to Zündorf or by cycling along the left bank of the Rhine to the little ferry at Köln-Weiss.

Rodenkirchen

Rodenkirchen, originally a fishing village on the Rhine, is less than 30 minutes from the city centre on a Rhine boat, tram no. 16, or by

*A rickshaw trip is relaxing – for the passengers, at least.*

bicycle. The old village centre has some charming little lanes with timber-frame houses and the 11th to 17th-century chapel of St Maternus. There are some fine private residences with a view of the Rhine and pleasant riverside cafés.

Some distance from the river in Rodenkirchen lies a large park, the **Forstbotanischer Garten**, where there is a beautiful show of rhododendrons and azaleas in spring, and an extensive collection of trees and shrubs from all around the world, comprising about 4000 different species (Schillingsrotter Str.; hours: daily from 9am, Nov–Feb until 4pm, April–Aug until 8pm, March, Sept and Oct until 6pm, bus no. 135 or half a mile on foot from Rodenkirchen tram stop).

**Rheinisches Freilichtmuseum**

About 45km/30mi southwest of Cologne at Mechernich-Kommern, historic villages and rural life have been recreated at the Rheinisches Freilichtmuseum. The old timber-frame houses, barns and farm buildings are beautifully set, and demonstrations of rural crafts complement the exhibits. By car: autobahn A 1 towards Euskirchen, exit at Wisskirchen, from where the museum is signposted (hours: April –Oct daily 9am–6pm, Nov–March daily 10am–4pm). The museum is not easily reached by public transport (two bus services daily on summer weekends from Mechernich railway station).

**Wildlife park**

About 10km/6mi northeast of the city centre in the district of Dünnwald there is a 20-hectare/50-acre wildlife park with red and roe deer, moufflons, wild boar and European bison (tram no. 4 to Höhenhaus, then bus 154 or 155 to Wildpark; hours: daily until dusk).

## Boat Trips

Köln-Düsseldorfer

The old-established Köln-Düsseldorfer shipping line operates a variety of services on the Rhine and Moselle from April to October. In addition to the one-hour round trips with a view of the city panorama between the Zoobrücke and Rodenkirchen, there are excursions to Zons, evening tours, and longer-distance journeys south to Bonn, Königswinter and beyond.

## SIGHTSEEING & EXCURSIONS

### BOATS AND FERRIES

► **Ferry to Deutz**
Tel. 38 47 38
April–Oct 10am–5.30pm, during trade fairs from 7.30am
Every 10 minutes, ferry from Hohenzollernbrücke to trade fair in Deutz.

► **Weiss-Zündorf Ferry**
Tel. 022 36 / 683 34
www.faehre-koelnkrokodil.de
April–Oct Mon–Fri 11am–7pm, Sat and Sun 10am–8pm

► **KD Köln-Düsseldorfer**
Frankenwerft 35
Tel. 258 30 11
www.k-d.com

► **Dampfschifffahrt Colonia**
Pier: Hohenzollernbrücke
Tel. 257 42 25
One-hour Rhine trips from 10am; June–Sept evening trips with live music

► **KölnTourist – Personenschifffahrt am Dom GmbH**
Konrad-Adenauer-Ufer
Tel. 12 16 00
www.koelntourist.net
Round trips from Hohenzollernbrücke to Rodenkirchen; in summer day trips to Königswinter, Rolandseck and Linz.

### TOURS AND GUIDED WALKS

► **CCS-Cologne Coach Service Busreisen GmbH**
Marienstr. 67
Tel. 979 25 70
www.ccs-busreisen.de
Start: tourist office (KölnTourismus) opposite cathedral (corner of Unter Fettenhennen and Burgmauer); buy ticket in bus

► **Inside Cologne**
Bismarckstr. 70
Tel. 52 19 77
www.insidecologne.de
Tours in German open to all; private bookings for English tours

► **KoelnTourismus**
►Information

► **Spurenlese**
Tel. 977 10 56
www.spurenlese.de
Tours in German open to all; private bookings for English tours.

# Transport

Cologne has a dense transport network of bus and tram lines. In the city centre and on some suburban lines, the trams (Strassenbahnen) run underground, and are then called U-Bahn. Trams run every 10 minutes on most routes in the daytime, reducing to every 15 minutes in the evening or less frequently late at night. Traffic on most lines starts before 5am and goes on until 1am, with a very limited service between 1am and 5am.

City transport authority: KVB

## ADDRESSES

### PUBLIC TRANSPORT

▶ **Information on timetables**
Tel. 01803 / 50 40 30 (24 hours)
www.kvb-koeln.de

▶ **Ehrenfeld customer centre**
Ehrenfeldgürtel 15

▶ **Neumarkt customer centre**
HUGO Passage (subway to U-Bahn station)

▶ **Kunden-Center Westforum**
KVB-Hauptverwaltung Braunsfeld
Scheidtweilerstr. 38

### AUTOMOBILE CLUBS · BREAKDOWN SERVICE

▶ **ADAC**
Luxemburger Str. 169
Tel. 47 27 47
Breakdowns: Tel. 01802 / 22 22 22
www.adac.de

▶ **Automobil-Club Verkehr (ACV)**
Goldgasse 2
Tel. 912 69 10
www.acv.de

▶ **ACE Autoclub Europa**
Tel. 018 02 / 34 35 36
www.ace-online.de

### CAR HIRE

All leading international car hire firms are represented at Cologne-Bonn airport.

▶ **Avis**
Hauptbahnhof
(main railway station)
Tel. 913 00 63
www.avis.de

▶ **Europcar**
Christophstr. 26
Tel. 912 60 10
www.europcar.de

▶ **Hertz**
Bismarckstr. 19
Tel. 51 50 84
www.hertz.de

### TAXI

▶ **Taxiruf Köln**
Tel. 28 82 or 194 10
www.taxiruf.de

▶ **Kugel Köln Taxi**
Tel. 760 28 29
Standard-size taxis and minibuses; English-speaking drivers available on request

## Cologne Rail Services

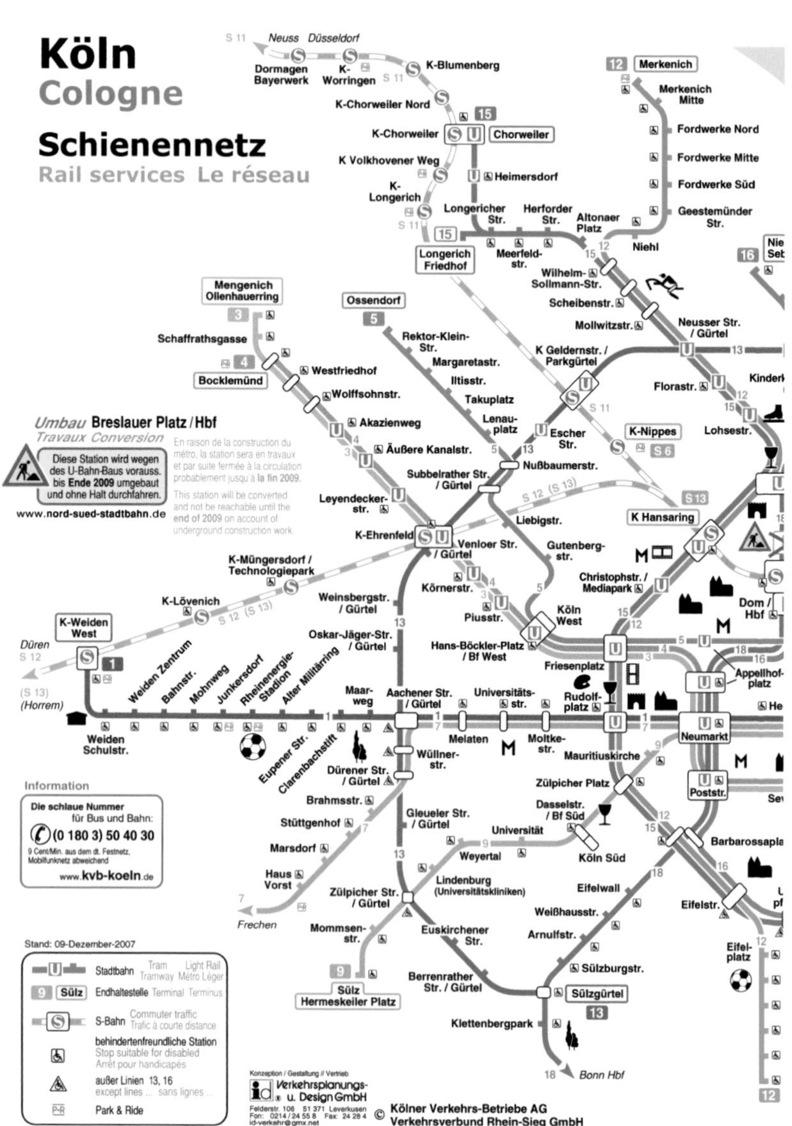

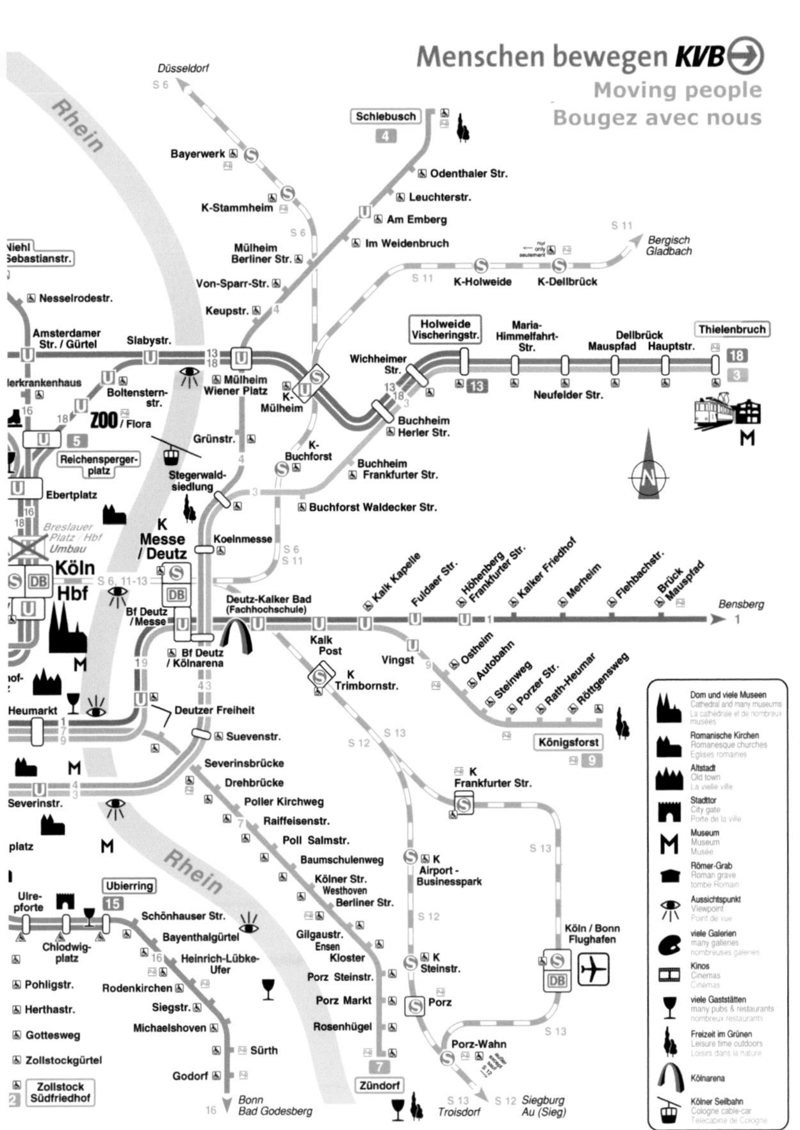
Menschen bewegen KVB
Moving people
Bougez avec nous
Rhein
Düsseldorf
Schlebusch
Bayerwerk
K-Stammheim
Odenthaler Str.
Leuchterstr.
Am Emberg
Im Weidenbruch
Mülheim Berliner Str.
Von-Sparr-Str.
Keupstr.
Bergisch Gladbach
K-Holweide
K-Dellbrück
Niehl Sebastianstr.
Nesselrodestr.
Amsterdamer Str. / Gürtel
Slabystr.
Holweide Vischeringstr.
Maria-Himmelfahrt-Str.
Dellbrück Mauspfad
Dellbrück Hauptstr.
Thielenbruch
Wichheimer Str.
Mülheim Wiener Platz
K-Mülheim
Boltensternstr.
ZOO / Flora
Neufelder Str.
Buchheim Herler Str.
Grünstr.
Reichenspergerplatz
K-Buchforst
Buchheim Frankfurter Str.
Stegerwaldsiedlung
Ebertplatz
Buchforst Waldecker Str.
Breslauer Platz / Hbf Umbau
K Messe / Deutz
Koelnmesse
Köln Hbf
Kalk Kapelle
Fuldaer Str.
Höhenberg Frankfurter Str.
Kalker Friedhof
Merheim
Flehbachstr.
Brück Mauspfad
Bensberg
Deutz-Kalker Bad (Fachhochschule)
Bf Deutz / Messe
Kalk Post
Vingst
Bf Deutz / Kölnarena
K Trimbornstr.
Ostheim
Autobahn
Steinweg
Porzer Str.
Rath-Heumar
Röttgensweg
Heumarkt
Deutzer Freiheit
Suevenstr.
Königsforst
Severinsbrücke
Drehbrücke
K Frankfurter Str.
Severinstr.
Poller Kirchweg
Raiffeisenstr.
Poll Salmstr.
Baumschulenweg
K Airport-Businesspark
Kölner Str. Westhoven
Berliner Str.
Ubierring
Ulrepforte
Schönhauser Str.
Bayenthalgürtel
Chlodwigplatz
Gilgaustr. Ensen
Kloster
Heinrich-Lübke-Ufer
Köln / Bonn Flughafen
K Steinstr.
Porz Steinstr.
Pohligstr.
Rodenkirchen
Porz Markt
Porz
Herthastr.
Siegstr.
Rosenhügel
Gottesweg
Michaelshoven
Porz-Wahn
Sürth
Zollstockgürtel
Godorf
Zündorf
Zollstock Südfriedhof
Bonn Bad Godesberg
Troisdorf
Siegburg Au (Sieg)
Dom und viele Museen
Cathedral and many museums
La cathédrale et de nombreux musées
Romanische Kirchen
Romanesque churches
Eglises romaines
Altstadt
Old town
La vieille ville
Stadttor
City gate
Porte de la ville
Museum
Museum
Musée
Römer-Grab
Roman grave
tombe Romain
Aussichtspunkt
Viewpoint
Point de vue
viele Galerien
many galleries
nombreuses galeries
Kinos
Cinemas
Cinémas
viele Gaststätten
many pubs & restaurants
nombreux restaurants
Freizeit im Grünen
Leisure time outdoors
Loisirs dans la nature
Kölnarena
Kölner Seilbahn
Cologne cable-car
Telécabine de Cologne

**Verkehrsverbund Rhein-Sieg** The city transport system is part of an integrated regional network (Verkehrsverbund Rhein-Sieg, VRS). Tickets bought in Cologne are valid for the whole network, including regional trains. Two trams, no. 16 and no. 18, connect Cologne and Bonn. A tram ticket bought in Cologne for a journey to the railway station can also be used for the onward journey by rail, e.g. to Bonn or Schloss Augustusburg in Brühl.

**Prices** The price depends on the distance travelled. For a journey of maximum four stops (Kurzstrecke, marked K), the cheapest rate applies. For longer journeys within Cologne, and to the airport, tariff 1b applies. Longer journeys outside the city cost more; at each U-Bahn station and overground tram stop there is a list of destinations with the appropriate price category. In addition to single tickets there are cost-saving multiple tickets, e.g. a strip with four fields to be stamped for four journeys, day tickets and group tickets, all of which are available from the ticket machines.

**WelcomeCard** For visitors on a short break who want to use public transport, the Welcome-Card (►Prices · Discounts) is attractive, as it permits free use of all trams, trains and buses on the regional network (Verkehrsverbund Rhein-Sieg), which covers not only the city of Cologne but an extensive surrounding area, including Bonn.

**Ticket sales** Tickets are sold in the customer centres, at some kiosks and from machines on the platforms and in the trams. Single tickets bought from machines are already stamped with the time and date; multiple tickets must be validated by stamping them in the machine inside the tram next to the door.

**Taxis** Taxis can be hailed from the kerbside, ordered by phone or found at taxi ranks, which are never far away in the inner city.

# Travellers with Disabilities

Germany is a relatively wheelchair-friendly country. Thanks to lowered kerbs and installation of lifts, it is possible for wheelchair-users to get around in the central shopping and sightseeing areas of Cologne and to cross the main Rhine bridges, although the slopes and cobblestones make things more difficult in some alleys of the Old Town. Museums and the cathedral have good wheelchair access. Almost all city-centre underground tram stations and many local sta-

**i Online Guide**

- www.rolliguide-koeln.de
- Details on accessibility of sights and hotels – website in German, no English version available.

tions have lifts down from street level, and the city is carrying out a programme to make access to trams easier by raising the level of platforms.

## Weights and Measures

### IMPERIAL/ METRIC MEASURES

1 inch = 2.54 centimetres
1 centimetre = 0.39 inches
1 foot = 0.3 metres
1 metre = 3.3 feet
1 mile = 1.61 kilometres
1 kilometre = 0.62 miles
1 kilogram = 2.2 pounds
1 pound = 0.45 kilograms
1 gallon = 4.54 litres
1 litre = 0.22 gallons

The metric system is used in Germany. Visitors should keep in mind that a comma is used for decimals (2,5 not 2.5) and a point indicates thousands (2.500 instead of 2,500).

## When to Go

Climate

Cologne is close enough to the North Sea to be influenced by the temperate maritime climate. The winters are milder than in most parts of Germany, and the low altitude of the city in the Rhine basin means that little snow falls.

A second result of the protected, low-lying situation is the tendency for summers to be humid. This means that the best times of year for visiting Cologne are April to June and September to October.

# Tours

FROM THE CATHEDRAL TO THE CHOCOLATE MUSEUM; ACROSS THE RIVER TO SEE THE RHINE PANORAMA; THROUGH THE ALLEYWAYS OF THE OLD TOWN AND ALONG THE MOST ATTRACTIVE SHOPPING STREETS – THE BEST WAY TO EXPLORE COLOGNE IS ON FOOT.

# TOURS THROUGH COLOGNE

**These three tours can be used as a quick introduction to the city and its main sights. But if you take your time and stop at the shops, cafés, churches and museums along the way, each tour is a rewarding full day.**

**TOUR 1** **A First Impression**
If you are only stopping over in Cologne, take a look at the cathedral and then spend a couple of hours on the Rhine and in the Old Town. ▶ **page 138**

**TOUR 2** **Art, History and Shopping**
Combine a stroll through Cologne's most interesting shopping district with a visit to impressive churches and museums. ▶ **page 141**

**TOUR 3** **From the Cathedral to the Harbour**
This walk starts at Germany's most-visited sight, the cathedral, and passes many historic monuments on the way to the new harbour development, where an extremely popular museum tells the story of chocolate. ▶ **page 143**

*A fast way to tour Cologne on foot*

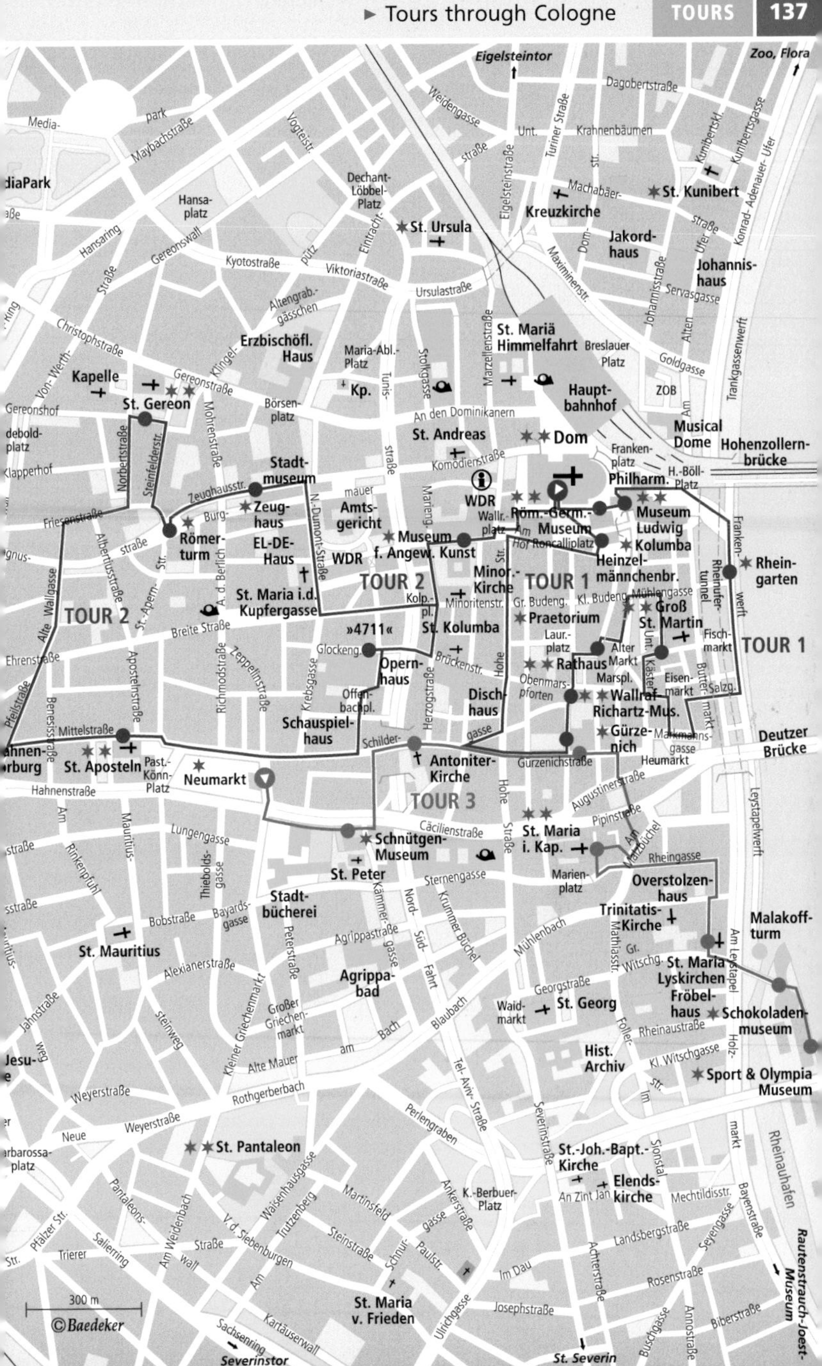
Eigelsteintor
Zoo, Flora
Dagobertstraße
Weidengasse
Unt. Krahnenbäumen
Turiner Straße
Kunibertskl.
Kunibertsgasse
Konrad-Adenauer-Ufer
Media-park
Maybachstraße
Vogteistr.
Straße
Eigelsteinstraße
Machabäer-
St. Kunibert
diaPark
Hansa-platz
Dechant-Löbbel-Platz
Kreuzkirche
Jakord-haus
Hansaring
Gereonswall
St. Ursula
Eintracht-
Dom-
Ufer-straße
Johannis-haus
Kyotostraße
pütz
Viktoriastraße
Maximinenstr.
Johannisstraße
Servasgasse
Christophstraße
Altengrab.-gässchen
Ursulastraße
Marzellenstraße
Alten
Trankgassenwerft
Von-Werth-
Erzbischöfl. Haus
Maria-Abl.-Platz
St. Mariä Himmelfahrt
Breslauer Platz
Goldgasse
Kapelle
Klingel-
Gereonstraße
Tunis-
Stolkgasse
Kp.
Haupt-bahnhof
ZOB
Gereonshof
St. Gereon
Mohrenstraße
Börsen-platz
An den Dominikanern
Am
Musical Dome
debold-platz
Norbertstraße
Steinfelderstr.
St. Andreas
Dom
Hohenzollern-brücke
Klapperhof
Stadt-museum
straße
Komödienstraße
Franken-platz
H.-Böll-Platz
Philharm.
Zeughausstr.
mauer
WDR
Friesenstraße
Burg-
Zeug-haus
Amts-gericht
Marieng.
Röm.-Germ.-Museum
Museum Ludwig
Römer-turm
Museum f. Angew. Kunst
Wallr.-platz
Am Hof
Roncalliplatz
Kolumba
Franken-
Rhein-garten
gnus-
straße
EL-DE-Haus
N.-Dumont-Straße
WDR
Heinzel-männchenbr.
Albertusstraße
Alte Wallgasse
TOUR 2
St.-Apern-Str.
A. d. Berlich
St. Maria i.d. Kupfergasse
TOUR 2
Kolp.-pl.
Minor.-Kirche
TOUR 1
Gr. Budeng.
Kl. Budeng.
Mühlengasse
Groß St. Martin
Rheinufer-tunnel
werft
Minoritenstr.
Praetorium
Breite Straße
»4711«
St. Kolumba
Laur.-platz
Fisch-markt
TOUR 1
Ehrenstraße
Glockeng.
Alter Markt
Unt.
Richmodstraße
Zeppelinstraße
Opern-haus
Brückenstr.
Hohe
Rathaus
Marspl.
Käster
Pfeilstraße
Benesisstraße
Apostelnstraße
Krebsgasse
Herzogstraße
Obenmars-pforten
Eisen-markt
Butter-markt
Salzg.
Offen-bachpl.
Disch-haus
Wallraf-Richartz-Mus.
Mittelstraße
Schauspiel-haus
gasse
Gürze-nich
Markmanns-gasse
Deutzer Brücke
Hahnen-burg
St. Aposteln
Past.-Könn-Platz
Schilder-
Antoniter-Kirche
Gürzenichstraße
Heumarkt
Neumarkt
Hahnenstraße
TOUR 3
Hohe Straße
Augustinerstraße
Am
Mauritius-
Lungengasse
Cäcilienstraße
Pipinstraße
Leystapelwerft
Rinkenpfuhl
Schnütgen-Museum
St. Maria i. Kap.
Am Malzbüchel
Thiebolds-gasse
St. Peter
Sternengasse
Rheingasse
Marien-platz
Overstolzen-haus
Stadt-bücherei
Kämmer-gasse
Krummer Büchel
Bayards-gasse
Peterstraße
Nord-Süd-Fahrt
Trinitatis-Kirche
Malakoff-turm
Bobstraße
Agrippastraße
Mühlenbach
St. Mauritius
Mathiasstr.
Gr. Witschg.
Am Leystapel
Alexianerstraße
Agrippa-bad
St. Maria Lyskirchen
Georgstraße
Fröbel-haus
Jahnstraße
Großer Griechen-markt
Waid-markt
St. Georg
Schokoladen-museum
Kleiner Griechenmarkt
Steinweg
Bach
Blaubach
Foller-str.
Rheinaustraße
Holz-
weg
Jesu-
am
Hist. Archiv
Kl. Witschgasse
Alte Mauer
Sport & Olympia Museum
Weyerstraße
Rothgerberbach
Tel-Aviv-Straße
Im
Severinstraße
markt
Rheinauhafen
Neue
Weyerstraße
Perlengraben
barossa-platz
St. Pantaleon
St.-Joh.-Bapt.-Kirche
Sionstal
Waisenhausgasse
Elends-kirche
Pantaleons-
Martinsfeld
K.-Berbuer-Platz
An Zint Jan
Mechtildisstr.
Bayenstraße
Pfälzer Str.
Am Weidenbach
Trutzenberg
Ankerstraße
Landsbergstraße
Severgasse
Rautenstrauch-Joest-Museum
Str.
Trierer
Salierring
Straße
V. d. Siebenburgen
Steinstraße
gasse
Paulstr.
Im Dau
Achterstraße
Rosenstraße
wall
Am
Schnur-
Josephstraße
300 m
Kartäuserwall
St. Maria v. Frieden
Ulrichgasse
Biberstraße
Buschgasse
Annostraße
©Baedeker
Sachsenring
Severinstor
St. Severin

# Getting Around in Cologne

**! Baedeker TIP**

**Thought-provoking architecture**

In a part of the city known as the Gereon quarter, the Gerling insurance company built a remarkable group of office blocks in the 1930s, 1950s and later years (see Tour 2). The tallest of them was designed by Erich Hennes, an assistant of Albert Speer during the Nazi years, and the overall design of the square on Gereonshof with its fountains, sculptural decorations and lamps was the work of Arno Breker, Hitler's favourite sculptor. The quarter, a unique ensemble that is due for redevelopment from 2009, expresses the highly conservative spirit of the company in the post-war decades.

Cologne has a compact city centre that can be explored on foot. Most of the outlying sights can be reached quickly from the cathedral by underground tram. If you want to see more than the immediate area of the cathedral and Old Town but have little time, a city tour by bus is recommended (► Practicalities, City Tours). The alternatives are to be driven around in a rickshaw, rent a bicycle or board the miniature »train« to the Schokoladenmuseum. The obvious and unmissable starting point for a day in Cologne is the cathedral, from where it is only a stone's throw to the Römisch-Germanisches Museum and the modern art in the Museum Ludwig. The busiest shopping streets are the Hohe Strasse, which starts at the cathedral, and Schildergasse, just a few minutes further away.

## Tour 1 A First Impression

**Start and end:** Cathedral **Duration:** approx. 2 hours

**This tour includes the city's most famous sight, the cathedral, its charming Old Town and a wonderful panoramic view from the opposite bank of the Rhine. You can walk the route without stopping within one hour, but make sure you give the cathedral the time it deserves by viewing its breathtaking Gothic architecture from inside, admiring the stained-glass windows and other works of art, and by taking a close look at the precious shrine of the Three Magi. If you visit one of the museums, have a leisurely drink or meal in the Old Town and see the other sights along the route, the tour amounts to a well-filled day.**

Start at the ❶ ** **cathedral**, the most-visited sight in the whole of Germany. Directly to the south of it, the ❷ * **Römisch-Germanisches Museum** obligingly displays its two finest exhibits, the funeral

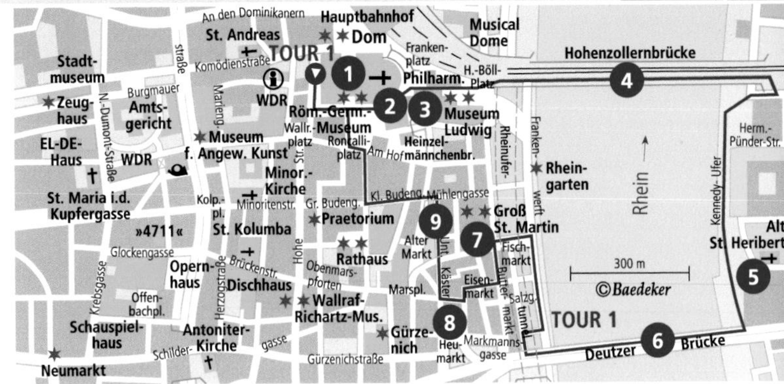


monument of Poblicius and the Dionysos mosaic, free of charge to anyone who looks through the window. If you are interested in the Romans, it is worth going inside.

Head towards the Rhine and the ❸ ✶✶ **Museum Ludwig**, which has a high-quality collection of 20th-century painting and sculpture. The metal-clad arches of the roof are intended to represent the waves of the river. Below the paving of Heinrich-Böll-Platz lies the Philharmonie, an impressive concert hall with wonderful acoustics. Steps lead down to the bank of the Rhine, but this tour keeps left, where a walkway on the railway bridge leads past the equestrian statue of Emperor Wilhelm II and over to the right bank of the river. As you cross there is a view straight ahead to the Hyatt Hotel and behind it the curved glass tower called KölnTriangle. The arch visible to the right on the skyline supports the roof of the KölnArena. Look north through the arches of the bridge to see the three-towered church of St Kunibert on the left bank and the brick tower of Köln-Messe, the trade fair complex, on the right bank.

The bridge, ❹ **Hohenzollernbrücke**, takes its name from the royal family of Prussia. It was opened in 1911, blown up by the retreating German army in 1945, restored, and widened in the 1980s. Its predecessor of 1859, the first permanent bridge to be built across the Rhine since the Roman bridge in Cologne, was built in the axis of the cathedral at the express wish of King Friedrich Wilhelm IV, who regarded both cathedral and bridge as symbols of German unity.

! *Baedeker* TIP

**By »train« or rickshaw**

In the summer months a rickshaw trip is a pleasant way to see the sights. The drivers can pedal through narrow alleys not open to motor traffic. Pick one up on the square in front of the cathedral or at Neumarkt. They also run sightseeing trips (ask for an English-speaking driver) and special tours across the bridges or at night (tel. 60 47 89). Next to the cathedral green-and-yellow miniature »trains« depart every half hour for the world of chocolate in the Schokoladenmuseum (»Schoko-Express«) and the animal kingdom in Cologne Zoo (»Zoo-Express«).

For a short detour, on the far side of the bridge continue straight ahead to the KölnTriangle and take the lift to the lookout terrace on the top floor. To continue this tour, descend to the river bank next to the second equestrian statue (of Wilhelm I), and walk south to the next bridge. You pass the café terrace of the Hyatt Hotel, a monument to the cuirassiers who were stationed here from 1850 and the white-painted church of ❺ **Alt-St Heribert**, a 17th-century building on the site of an abbey founded in 1002, which in turn occupied the site of a Roman fort. Remains of the Roman gate can be seen to the east of the church. Re-cross the Rhine on the ❻ **Deutzer Brücke** for the best view of the Old Town and Cologne skyline, and descend the spiral steps to the gardens on the left bank between the Old Town and the river. The gardens were built in the 1980s when the riverbank road was put into a tunnel. Note the walls that serve as flood defences and the little round tower with a dial that marks the level of the Rhine.

The little houses of the Old Town and the restaurant tables by the Rhine gardens are a pleasant scene. To get an impression of the district – taking detours through the little alleys and squares on the way

*The glass pyramid on the square in front of the city hall gives a view into the mikvah, a medieval Jewish bath.*

– walk back north for the impressive view of the tower of ❼ ✶✶ **Gross St Martin**, one of Cologne's twelve major Romanesque churches, then double back along Buttermarkt and turn right into Salzgasse to reach ❽ **Heumarkt** (Haymarket), which the English traveller Captain Coryate in the early 17th century – when the bridgehead of Deutzer Brücke and Second World War bombs had not yet marred its appearance – described as the most beautiful square in Europe after St Mark's Square in Venice.

The short street Unter Käster leads to the old market place, ❾ **Alter Markt**, the heart of old Cologne in the shadow of the city hall tower. This is the centre of the carnival festivities before Lent. From here the way back to the cathedral is obvious: left up the hill and right towards the famous spires.

# Tour 2 Art, History and Shopping

**Start:** Neumarkt **End:** Cathedral
**Duration:** ½ to 1 day

**This walk leads to quieter parts of the city centre as well as some of the most attractive streets for shopping and nightlife. There are plenty of sights on the way, including two fine churches, a number of museums and Roman remains.**

The tour starts at ❶ **Neumarkt**, a large square in the shopping district. At its west end, the towers, dome and apses of the Romanesque church of ❷ ✶✶ **St Aposteln** are a wonderful sight.

Go to the right of the church past the statue of Konrad Adenauer and along Mittelstrasse, a street of elegant boutiques, to the western city gate, ❸ ✶ **Hahnentor**, a survival of the medieval fortifications through which kings once entered the city. Go back a few steps and

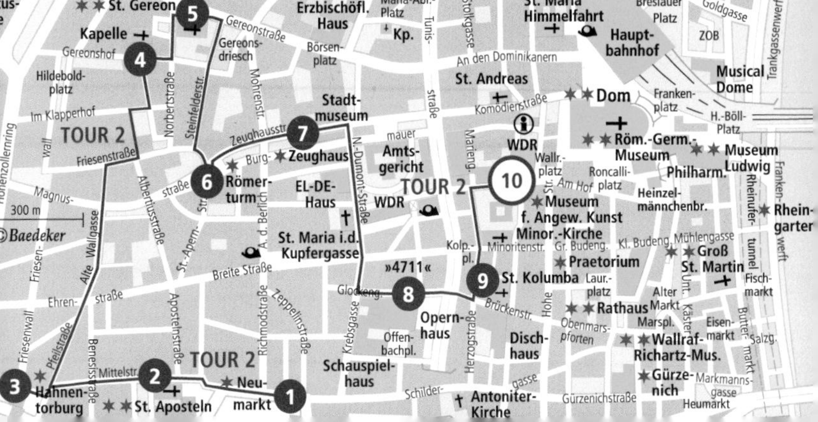

## ? DID YOU KNOW ...?

- ... that »4711«, a well-known brand of Cologne perfume, owes its name to a French invasion? In 1794, at the beginning of the 20-year French occupation, the city council decided to number all the houses in Cologne. A building in Glockengasse, where Wilhelm Mülhens made his eau de Cologne and sold it as a medicine, got the number 4711. In 1810 the French government decreed that the recipes for all medicinal products should be made public, but Mülhens evaded the regulation by declaring his product to be perfume, and later chose the house number as the brand name.

into Pfeilstrasse, where there is a colourful mix of little shops, galleries and cafés, cross **Breite Strasse**, also an interesting shopping street that is worth a detour to left or right, and head north along Alte Wallgasse to the narrow Friesenstrasse, a lively scene at night and site of Brauhaus Päffgen, one of Cologne's last traditional pubs with a brewery attached, a place with a genuine Kölsch atmosphere. At Friesenstrasse turn left to Päffgen, but right to continue the tour: after 50 metres, opposite Albertstrasse, go left on a path between the buildings, past the gravestone of a Roman soldier, to the ❹**Gerling office buildings**, a harmonized ensemble of varying dates from the 1930s to 1960s. Spiesergasse and Gereonshof lead to ❺✱✱ **St Gereon**, one of the finest and most interesting churches of the city. From the little green square east of the church walk along Steinfelderstrasse to Zeughausstrasse to see the ❻✱ **Römerturm**, a corner tower of the Roman city wall.

Head east on Zeughausstrasse to the 400-year-old ❼✱ **Zeughaus**, conspicuous for its red-and-white shutters and a golden Ford car on the tower. It houses the **Stadtmuseum**, which presents the history of the city.

*»Four tons of vanilla, please.« That's how much the ice cream on the roof of Neumarkt-Galerie weighs.*

From here cross Burgmauer and walk via Appellhofplatz along Neven-DuMont-Strasse, past the **EL-DE-Haus** and the church of St Maria in der Kupfergasse on the right, and the tall greenish building of the broadcaster WDR, known as the »four-slab house«, on the left. Turn left into Glockengasse, where the opera house occupies the site of the former synagogue, and the perfumery in the ❽**4711-Haus** sells eau de Cologne and provides entertainment each hour on the hour with a glockenspiel. On the opposite side of the six-lane main road ❾✱ **Kolumba** is a new highlight of the Cologne museum scene. It displays religious art in an ingenious architectural setting. Between Kolumba and the cathedral (take Kolumbastrasse and Drususgasse) it is worth stopping at the **Minoritenkirche**, a church of Franciscan friars that contains the grave of the Scottish-born medieval philosopher Duns Scotus, or to see design and crafts from the Middle Ages to the present day in the ⑩ ✶ **Museum für Angewandte Kunst**.

# Tour 3 From the Cathedral to the Harbour

**Start:** Cathedral
**End:** Museums at the harbour
**Duration:** ½ day

**This walk, a trip through 2000 years of history, first leads through Roman Cologne to the city hall and a beautiful church, then goes down to the harbour (Rheinauhafen), site of museums devoted to chocolate and sports and some spectacular new buildings.**

From the south side of the ❶ ✶✶ **cathedral** walk across Roncalliplatz past the Dom-Hotel and look out for a stone-carved fountain

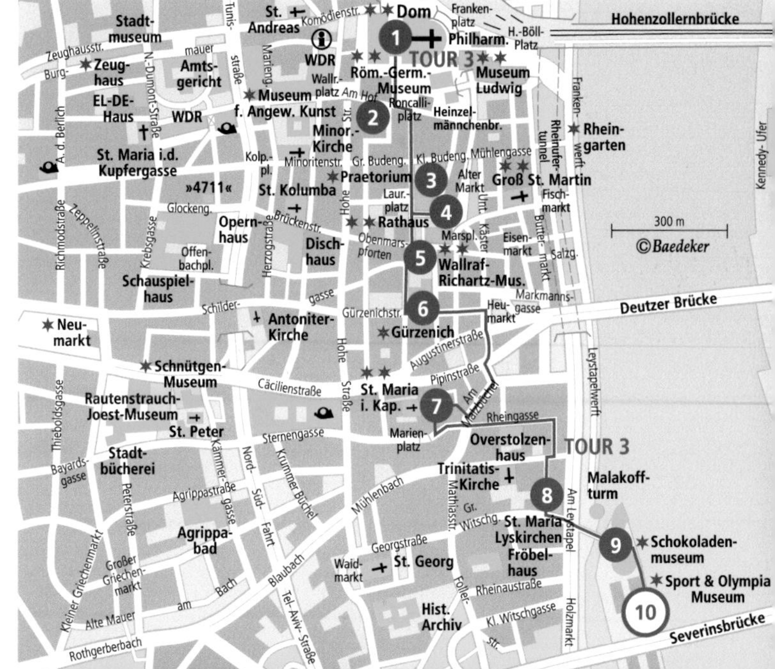

! Baedeker TIP

**The Cologne Riviera**

The cycle path along the left bank of the Rhine is deservedly popular. From the city centre head south to the autobahn bridge at Rodenkirchen, where there are cafés on boats and on the riverbank; of these the boat *Alte Liebe* (old love) and the café Zum Treppchen in Kirchstrasse are long-established Cologne institutions. Continue south along the »Cologne Riviera«, where there are little sandy beaches and meadows as far as the campsite. The next stretch follows a bend in the Rhine under trees. Then take the charming old-fashioned ferry over to the village of Zündorf, where there is a wooded area, a lake with rowing boats and pedaloes, a row of cafés and, a few minutes further south, an outdoor swimming pool.

on the right. It is the ❷ **Heinzelmännchenbrunnen** and tells the story of the elves (Heinzelmännchen) who once did the work of the Cologne craftsmen at night, until the tailor's wife saw them and they disappeared. From here go downhill and right into Unter Goldschmied. At the next corner a small tunnel-like structure, a slice out of a Roman sewer that still runs below the road here, is an invitation to turn left down Budengasse to the ❸ ✶ **Praetorium**, the remains of the Roman governor's palace with an exhibition on Roman Cologne. Continue straight on, passing a monument to Cardinal Josef Frings on the right, to reach the square in front of the ❹ ✶✶ **Rathaus** (city hall).This is also the site of the **mikwe**, a medieval Jewish bath, which from 2011 will be part of a new archaeological zone showing Roman remains and those of the Jewish quarter. On the right at the corner of Obenmarspforten note the shop with a red tulip logo in its window. Here the Italian inventor of eau de Cologne, Giovanni Maria Farina, had his perfumery in the 18th century; the Farina family still own this perfume shop. Diagonally opposite stands the ❺ ✶✶ **Wallraf-Richartz-Museum**, an outstanding collection of art from the Middle Ages to the 19th century.

Go on past the ruins of the church of St Alban to the ❻ ✶ **Gürzenich**, a 15th-century banqueting hall that is still a high-class venue for celebrations, especially at carnival time. Turn left here down Gürzenichstrasse, right at Heumarkt, cross the tramlines and two roads and bear right to the church of ❼ ✶✶ **St Maria im Kapitol**, which occupies the site of the Roman Capitoline temple. Its east end on a »clover-leaf« ground plan is impressive both outside and inside.

From Königstrasse cross the road to see the 13th-century **Overstolzenhaus** in Rheingasse. It is Cologne's only surviving house of a patrician family from the Romanesque period. The **Trinitatiskirche** on Filzgraben, the next street to the south, was the first purpose-built Protestant church in the city (1860). From here it is not far to ❽ **St Maria Lyskirchen**, the only one of the twelve Romanesque churches in Cologne where ceiling frescoes have survived.

Cross the road on the Rhine bank to the Rheinauhafen (harbour), where the ❾ ✶ **Schokoladenmuseum**, a ship-like structure incorporating older harbour buildings, proves year for year that an exhibition on the 3000-year history of chocolate and its manufacture, as

*The gardens next to the Rhine in the Old Town are a pleasant place to relax on a sunny day.*

well as the chance to buy some in the museum shop, attracts more visitors than museums of Roman history or religious art.

Directly south the ⑩ ✶ **Deutsches Sport & Olympia Museum** is dedicated to national, international and Olympic sport. There are interactive exhibits for the energetic. To see the progress of the new harbour development, including the eye-catching »crane buildings«, walk south from here to the **Bayenturm**, part of the medieval fortifications, and return to the centre by tram from Ubierring.

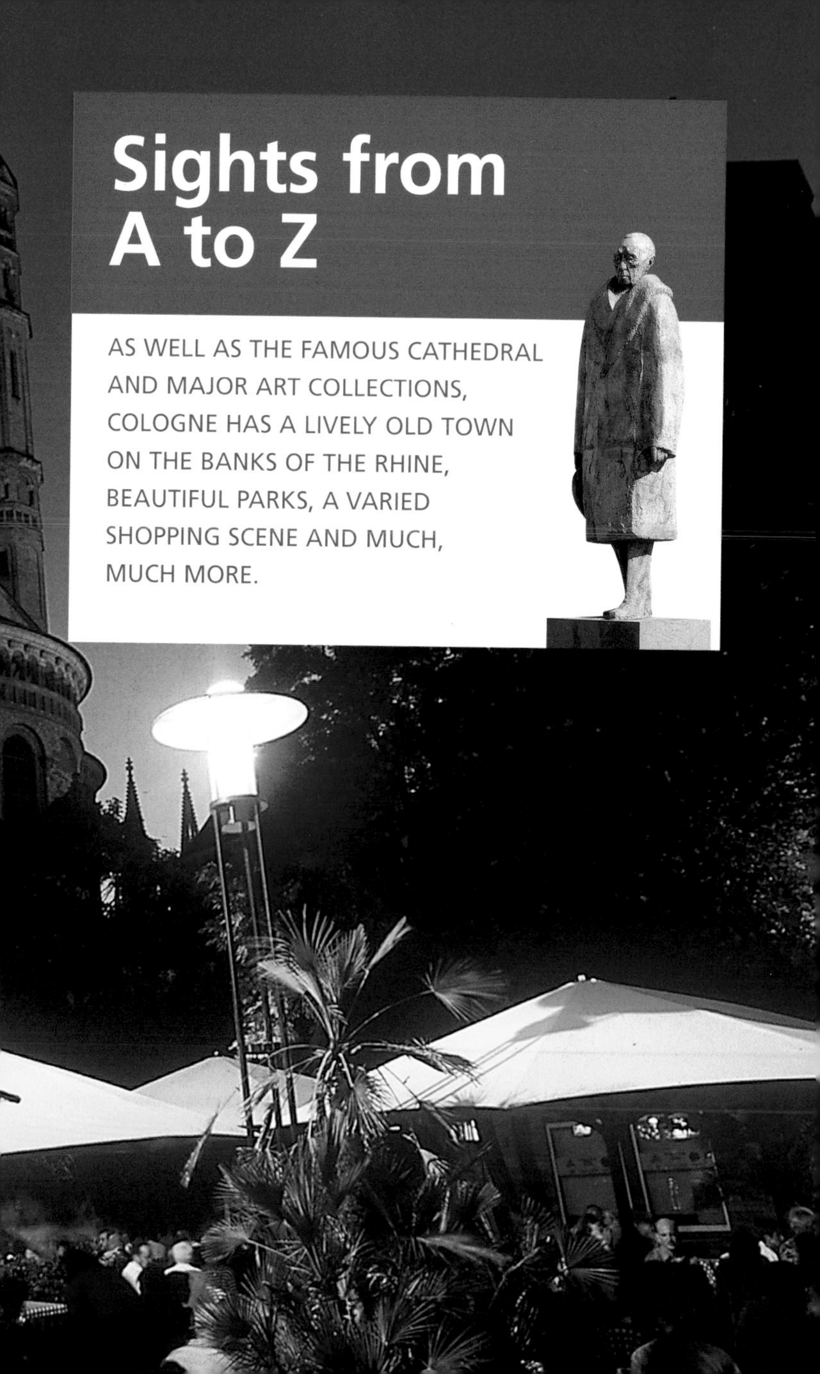

# Sights from A to Z

AS WELL AS THE FAMOUS CATHEDRAL AND MAJOR ART COLLECTIONS, COLOGNE HAS A LIVELY OLD TOWN ON THE BANKS OF THE RHINE, BEAUTIFUL PARKS, A VARIED SHOPPING SCENE AND MUCH, MUCH MORE.

# Altenberg

Excursion

**Location:** 20km/12mi northeast of Köln
**Bus:** 212 from Leverkusen-Mitte (train to Leverkusen)
**Internet:** www.altenberger-dom.de

**Altenberg lies in the Bergisches Land, a hilly and wooded area to the east of Cologne. Its main attraction, the Cistercian church known as the Altenberger Dom, has an attractive setting in the valley of the river Dhünn. The surrounding woods are good for walking, and children enjoy the picturesque Märchenwald (Fairy-tale Forest).**

**Former Cistercian abbey**

Altenberg was originally the name of an abbey that the earls of Berg founded in 1133 next to their old family seat (on the »alten Berg«, the »old hill«), before they themselves moved further east to a new castle on the river Wupper. **Altenberg Abbey**, a house of the strict Cistercian order, existed until 1803, when it was secularized. Following the sale of the buildings, the establishment of a dye factory on the site and a devastating fire in 1815, the former monastery buildings were reconstructed only in the second half of the 19th century.

## Altenberger Dom

Guided tours: March–Dec Sat 11am, Sun 1pm, 3.30pm (German); in English by arrangement: tel. 02174 / 45 33

The Altenberger Dom, which took more than a century to complete, is particularly admired for its impressive, eight-part west window, the **largest church window in Germany**, which contains fine stained glass.

The present Gothic basilica was built on the site of the original Romanesque abbey church between 1259 and 1379. Its aisled transept is almost as wide as the nave; the south transept is shortened, as monastery buildings once abutted onto it.

In accordance with the strict regulations of the Cistercian order, the church is a plain building, its beauty based entirely on clear proportions and the functionality of the Gothic architecture. The absence of decoration makes the principles the Gothic system easily recognizable: as far as possible all the walls are opened up as window surfaces, and the weight of the stone is directed and supported by the regular row of flying buttresses. In place of a tower, a modest spirelet crowns the roof. Around the choir there is an ambulatory, from which seven six-sided chapels radiate. A severe fire in 1815 destroyed the

! *Baedeker* TIP

**Church music**

The Altenberger Dom is famous for its concerts of church music, most of which take place between May and October on Sundays at 11.45am and 2.30pm. In the summer months there are also organ concerts on Thursdays at 8pm.

roofs of the church, and in 1830 the vault of the crossing collapsed. During rebuilding (1835–47) the choir chapels were given hipped roofs like those of Cologne Cathedral. Since 1857 the church has been used for both Protestant and Catholic services, as decreed by the king of Prussia.

*The Cistercian church at Altenberg attracts pilgrims and concert-goers.*

The **interior decoration** of the church is a subdued red and green framework for the famous windows, whose purpose in Gothic architecture was to admit the light of the heavenly Jerusalem. The most impressive windows are the eight-part **west window**, which measures 8 × 18m/25 × 60ft and has gold-coloured glass dating from around 1400, and the **north window**, 6 × 19m/20 × 62ft in size with mainly grey ornamental glass dating from before 1300. As the Cistercians were not allowed to use coloured glass, the windows of the late 13th century were produced in shades of grey. To the right of the beautiful wrought-iron screen stands a figure of the founder of the order, **St Bernard of Clairvaux**, and to the left a figure of Moses (both 17th century). Stone sculptures depicting the Annunciation (about 1380) that adorned the west door have been placed by the east wall of the north aisle of the choir. In the axis of the choir there is a 15th-century altar cross, and to the north a late Gothic tabernacle of 1490. The tombstones of various abbots can be seen in the choir chapels, and the heart of Archbishop Engelbert von Berg, who was murdered in 1225, is kept in a reliquary in the axial chapel. The 15th-century altar of the Virgin Mary in the south aisle of the choir depicts the Coronation of the Virgin.

◄ Transept

The tombs of eight dukes of Berg have given the north transept the name **Dukes' Choir**. The tomb nearest to the crossing is that of the founder of the abbey, Adolf II. The bronze sculpture of *Bernard of Clairvaux as a Mystic* was made by W. Franzen in 1985; Franzen also sculpted a bronze in the Von-Steinen-Kapelle of the north transept: *The Crucified Christ Embraces Bernard of Clairvaux and Martin Luther* (1986–87). Tombstones have been set into the wall of the south aisle, in which there are no windows as the cloister lay behind it. The most notable is the first, that of Abbot Johann Blanckenberg († 1662).

## Remains of Monastery Buildings

**Baroque gate**

The old way of entering the abbey was to cross the bridge over the river Dhünn to the west of the church and pass through the surviving Baroque gate (18th century). The central niche of the gate arch contains a figure of Bernard of Clairvaux on the outside, a Madonna on the inside.

To the left of the bridge, on the foundations of the former porter's lodge and the hostel for pilgrims, is the **Altenberger Hof**, an inn with a lovely garden terrace. To the right of the gate stood a chapel dedicated to the Virgin, the remains of which are incorporated into the brewery building of 1715. The monastery itself lay further south, divided into several courts by buildings on a north-south axis, of which only the lay brothers' wing remains.

To the north lay the farm buildings and the hospital, of which the **Chapel of St Mark** (1222) has survived with noteworthy paintings: the ornamentation on the central window behind the altar and the Coronation of the Virgin on the west wall date from 1300. The windows were made around 1900.

! *Baedeker* TIP

**Refreshments**

When visiting Altenberg, do not fail to try Bergische Waffeln (waffles with warm sour cherries and whipped cream) in one of the cafés. The local equivalent of afternoon tea is the Bergische Kaffeetafel, including currant bread with sugar-beet syrup, and bread with ham and sausage. The Altenberger Hof is an upscale inn, the Küchenhof a more rustic café.

**Märchenwald**

Opening hours:
Daily 9am–6pm

The Märchenwald (Fairytale Forest) is a ten-minute walk north of the abbey. It is an ideal combination of a pleasant walk with an attraction for children. Under a thick canopy of trees little houses contain scenes of the best-known characters from the fairy tales of the Brothers Grimm.

# ★★ Altstadt · Old Town

G/H 7

**Location:** Between Hohenzollernbrücke and Deutzer Brücke
**Bus:** 132 (Rathaus), 133 (Gürzenichstr.)
**Tram:** 5, 16, 18 (Dom/Hbf) or 1, 7, 9 (Heumarkt)

**Even a short visit to Cologne should include a walk along the Rhine promenade and through the narrow alleys and picturesque courtyards of the Old Town, where there is a pub, restaurant, café or nightspot in almost every building.**

**History of the Old Town**

The district that Cologne residents normally call the Altstadt (Old Town) is not identical to the Roman or medieval town, which were

considerably larger. It is an area also known as the Martinsviertel (St Martin's quarter), which was once a **trading quarter on the Rhine** and originally an island in the river. The probable reason why the Romans chose this site was that an arm of the Rhine behind the elongated island was a natural harbour directly adjacent to higher, flood-free land to the west. They built warehouses on the island, and this district remained a commercial quarter even after the first harbour silted up in the 2nd century AD.
Archbishop **Bruno I** raised the level of the old Rhine arm in the 10th century and established the Benedictine abbey of ►Gross St Martin on the former island. The area prospered in the Middle Ages, as ships with a deep draught coming up from the North Sea had to unload their goods onto flat-bottomed boats suitable for the middle reaches of the Rhine; from 1259, when the Right of Staple was introduced, all ships were obliged to stop in Cologne and offer their goods for sale. In the 19th century the advent of rail transport and the construction of modern harbours to the north and south brought the commercial role of the quarter to an end. It became a poor and unsavoury district, prompting the city authorities to redevelop the area in the 1930s. At that time the worst back-to-back slum housing was demolished, some historic buildings were even relocated, and new open spaces were created. The work had scarcely been completed when bombing reduced the whole area to rubble in the Second World War. The dates on the buildings – 1930s and 1950s in some cases – reveal the eventful history of the Old Town, but with cobbled lanes and little gabled houses, its old Rhenish character has survived all the destruction and reconstruction, and street names such as Buttermarkt and Salzgasse (Salt Alley) still betray its origin as a place of trade.

## Tour of the Old Town

**Famous Rhine panorama**

The Old Town is bordered by the Hohenzollernbrücke to the north and the Deutzer Brücke to the south, by the Rhine to the east and the line of the original harbour in an arm of the Rhine (Bechergasse – Alter Markt – Heumarkt) to the west. It is an entertainment and residential district, and largely free of cars. The network of streets is basically that of the Middle Ages, and newer developments such as the apartments to the north and west of Gross St Martin church, designed by Joachim Schürmann and built from 1975 to 1978, have been built with the intention of preserving the character of the quarter, for example by retaining gable fronts.

## The Rhine Bank (Frankenwerft)

**Heinrich-Böll-Platz**

From the cathedral walk east past the ►Römisch-Germanisches Museum and ► Museum Ludwig, across and down the steps to the Rhine promenade, here called Frankenwerft.

*Today more cake than fish is sold on Fischmarkt.*

Rheingarten ▶

In the gardens (Rheingarten) there is a sculptural water installation by the Scottish artist **Eduardo Paolozzi**. Its forms have associations with river and road traffic, a reference to the site and to the tunnel for cars beneath the gardens. On hot days when water flows through its basins and channels, the sculpture becomes an adventure playground for children.

Stapelhaus ▶

The long building a little further south is the Stapelhaus, constructed in the 16th century as a store for fish and rebuilt after the Second World War. It takes its name from the Right of Staple, as in the early 19th century goods that had to be unloaded for sale in Cologne were stored here.

Fischmarkt ▶

On Fischmarkt, with pretty gabled houses and the tower of Gross St Martin as a backdrop, beer and coffee are now on sale in place of fish. A little further, past the moorings of the Köln-Düsseldorfer shipping line, turn right next to the Haxenhaus restaurant.

## Salzgasse and Eisenmarkt

**Grinkopf and Walfisch**

At Salzgasse no. 2 look out for the Grinkopf, a grotesque head. There were once many of these in the Old Town; they had iron »fangs«, between which a beam was wedged so that a rope pulley could load goods into the cellar. No. 13, called Walfisch (whale), dates from 1626.

Hänneschen-Theater ▶

Near the top of Salzgasse turn left into an alley leading to Eisenmarkt, home of the famous Hänneschen-Theater, a **puppet theatre** that is not just for children. It was founded in 1802 and has a gallery of traditional characters who speak the Kölsch dialect, including the irrepressible Hänneschen (diminutive form of Johannes) and his

quick-witted girlfriend Bärbelchen. This traditional form is combined with topical themes, and the performances (about 275 per year) are usually sold out. The puppets are on display in a window at the back of the theatre in Markmannsgasse.
In front of the theatre the bench with a bronze monument to the city's best-loved actor, **Willy Millowitsch** (1909–99), provides an unmissable photo opportunity for his fans.

## Heumarkt

**Divided square**

Heumarkt (Haymarket) was once a long and imposing square surrounded by the magnificent houses of rich merchant families. However, the construction of the bridge (1913–15) with the consequent flow of traffic across the square has robbed Heumarkt of its coherence. The northern part of the square retains some of its character, although it is obvious that most of the buildings are recent, but the southern end in front of Hotel Maritim and the Malzmühle pub is now entirely dominated by traffic.

**Buildings**

Heumarkt no. 77, named Zum St Peter, is a fine 16th-century building at the northwest corner of the square; at the northeast corner, no. 62, a pub named Zum Pfaffen, has an attractive Rococo façade of 1776. Beyond the roads and the tramlines at the south end of Heumarkt, the Malzmühle, a popular brewery and pub, also has some historic character in contrast to the large Hotel Maritim, a modern complex with a glass-roofed atrium and several restaurants.

**Equestrian statue**

The equestrian statue of **Friedrich Wilhelm III**, now close to the road and tramlines that cut the square into two parts, was once the focal point of Heumarkt and in the early 20th century a rendezvous for young people, who arranged to meet »under the tail« of the horse. The statue was unveiled in 1878 in honour of the Prussian king who was officially regarded as the liberator of the Rhineland from French rule in 1815. However, the citizens of Cologne had mixed feelings about being ruled by Protestant Prussians from distant Berlin, and over 20 years of wrangling about the design and siting of the monument preceded its inauguration. The king by no means shared the views of all the reformers, scholars and generals whose figures adorn the base of his statue. The monument was badly damaged in 1943. Its parts were dispersed, some melted down, and cast again in 1990. When the horse and rider were removed for safety reasons in 2007 restoration of the monument had still not been completed. A campaign is under way to raise money to put the king back on his pedestal.

## Ostermannplatz

**Ostermann Fountain**

At the north end of Heumarkt, the street Unter Käster leads to Alter Markt. On the way there make a detour to the right through a little

# JOIN US FOR A DRINK ...

**»Drink doch eine met« (»have one with us«): when spoken in Cologne dialect, these words have the force of one of the Ten Commandments, and are also the title of a popular song that everyone knows and can roar out in the pub at Carnival time. The local beer, Kölsch, is a symbol of the city. The same word, which means simply »from Cologne«, is used to denote the dialect and the people of Cologne. Kölsch, they will tell you, is the only language that you can drink, and the word stands for their way of life.**

A Brauhaus, a traditional brew-pub, is the best place to taste a fresh, cool glass of **Kölsch**. And the best place in the pub, for many regulars, is at the bar, where drinkers stand two deep at any time of the day or evening and engage in lively conversation. To be accepted here, there is no question about which beer to drink: Kölsch, a light-coloured brew which according to court ruling of 1963 may only be produced in Cologne and its surroundings, and is served in special glasses known as **Stangen** – slender, cylindrical glasses holding 0.2 litres (about one third of a pint).

As part of the cultural heritage of Cologne, this traditional beer is prized and lauded as highly as the cathedral. It is the product of centuries of history: a **tax on beer** was raised decades before the foundation stone of the cathedral was laid in 1248, and the earliest records of breweries in Cologne date back to the 11th century.

However, just as the appearance of the cathedral was altered over the centuries, so too did the methods of brewing beer develop. Until the 15th century it was flavoured with a mixture of ground herbs and could not be kept for long. The addition of hops replaced the herbs, giving beer its bitter taste and allowing it to be stored and transported better.

## Laws on Purity

In 1396 the Cologne brewers were organized as a guild with trade and

*The waiter in a Cologne Brauhaus, known as a Köbes, carries a specially made tray for glasses of Kölsch beer.*

political functions. The guild monitored the activities and production of individual breweries, and its political arm chose representatives on the city council. The brewers also formed a religious brotherhood, the Brotherhood of St Peter of Milan, which exists to this day, meeting twice yearly for a service in St Andreas church. Their patron saint, St Peter the Martyr of Milan, was a 13th-century inquisitor who was waylaid and killed by heretics; a stone bust of him can be seen above the entrance to the Brauhaus Früh am Dom.

From the 15th century the brewers made efforts, with mixed success, to regulate the production methods and ingredients of beer. They had difficulties enforcing their regulations inside the city, and little chance of doing so beyond the city limits. The Bavarian purity laws of 1516, which state that only water, hops and malted barley should be used, applied to bottom-fermented beer. Kölsch, by contrast, is top-fermented, i.e. the kinds of yeast that are used rise to the top of the vat during the fermentation process.

In 1986 the 24 members of the association of Cologne brewers signed the **Kölsch Convention**, an agreement about the production process, place of production and manner of serving the beer. It specifies the cylindrical »Stange« as the only glass that may be used and stipulates that Kölsch must not be brewed outside the city, except in several specified old-established breweries. This agreement has been approved by the European authorities, which gives Kölsch beer the status of a »protected geographical indication«, i.e. like champagne and many food products, it may only come from a defined region.

Only two long-standing Brauhaus pubs still exist in the strict sense that the beer is brewed and served on the same premises: Malzmühle on Heumarkt and Päffgen in Friesenstrasse. Most old breweries have moved production out to the suburbs. However, almost every Brauhaus retains a fitting that is colloquially called the **»confessional«**: a wooden cubicle with a window and two seats, sometimes elaborately carved. Originally it stood next to the wall so that the owner

could keep an eye on both the pub inside and the passage outside, where beer was tapped from the barrel and deliveries were made to the brewery at the back.

Despite closures and mergers, there are still twelve Kölsch breweries making over 20 kinds of Kölsch – a greater variety of beers than in any other city of the world, it is claimed. **Defying globalization** and industrial concentration, the beer-drinkers of Cologne largely ignore well-known international brands and maintain three local beers brewed by small family companies, Früh, Reissdorf and Gaffel, in their position of market leaders.

## How to Drink Kölsch

Old habits die hard in the innumerable pubs of the city. One of them is to speak the Kölsch dialect and to address fellow-customers and waiters as »du« (»you«), rather than the more formal »Sie«. The waiter in a Brauhaus is known for obscure reasons as a Köbes, the local version of the name »Jakob«. The **Köbes** traditionally wears a blue apron and shirt, and the tools of his trade are a leather purse and a round tray specially made to take the Kölsch glasses. A good Köbes is expected to demonstrate rough-and-ready wit, and can be relied upon to make disparaging comments to guests who order any drink other than Kölsch.

Seated guests do not order from the bar. The Köbes moves swiftly through the pub and brings a fresh Kölsch unasked to anyone whose glass is empty. Marks on the beer mat act as a tally for the bill, and customers who have drunk enough signal this by taking the mat from beneath their glass and placing it on the top. The small size of the glass means that the waiter is kept busy all evening, but this is a necessary inconvenience as Kölsch, which is low on CO2, soon goes flat if it is left standing. Only a freshly-tapped glass tastes good, which explains the popularity of the ten-litre barrels often seen at Carnival time, when groups of clowns and other costumed revellers parade through the streets pulling their own barrel on a little cart. And so, when they sing »Join us for a drink«, you can do just that.

passage that leads to Ostermannplatz, a space created during redevelopment in the 1930s. The fountain was made in 1938 in memory of **Willi Ostermann** (1876–1936), a musician whose songs were hits at Carnival time. Some of them are still well known, and characters from his songs are depicted on the fountain.

## Alter Markt

**Heart of old Cologne**

Alter Markt, the old marketplace, has more historic atmosphere than any other square in the city even though little remains of its medieval buildings. The highlight, apart from the view of the ►Rathaus (city hall) tower, is a pair of late Renaissance houses dating from 1580, Zur Brezel and Zum Dorn (no. 20–22). With their tall gables they are the only old buildings that have survived on the east side of the marketplace. The Gaffel brewery now has a Brauhaus-style pub here. Until the 2nd century AD an arm of the Rhine flowed on this site, which was used as a harbour in early Roman times. In 2007 a large section of a Roman ship was discovered on the west side of the square, 14m/46ft below the modern street level.

◄ Jan von Werth

A fountain with a statue of the cavalry general Jan von Werth was erected in the middle of the square in 1884. The story of Jan von Werth, subject of a popular poem by **Karl Cramer**, is illustrated on the base of the statue. Jan, a poor stable boy, fell in love with a farmer's daughter named Griet, who rejected him in the hope of marrying a richer man (scene on the side facing the city hall). Disappointed, Jan left and enlisted to fight in the Thirty Years' War, becoming rich and famous – and gaining the nickname Black Hans for his ruthless methods of waging war. Years later, when Jan returned to Cologne, a proud general on his charger, he passed through the city gate and saw Griet, now a poor market woman (scene on the east side, towards the Rhine). This scene is played out every year at the southern city gate, Severinstorburg, at Carnival time with the following dialogue, an example of the pragmatic attitude to life that is typical of Cologne:

*Jan: »Griet, if only you had done it!« (married me).*
*Griet: »Jan, if only I'd known!«*

Alter Markt is the centre of the Carnival celebrations. The Carnival season begins here each year on 11 November at 11.11am – eleven is considered the »crazy number« – and Alter Markt is also the scene of the opening of the days of the street carnival on the Thursday before Ash Wednesday (►Baedeker Special, p.200).

A figure below the roof of house no. 24 illustrates the coarser side of the local sense of humour. The **»Kallendresser«** (»gutter shitter«, a crouching man with his trousers down) is a post-war replacement by the sculptor Ewald Mataré of a figure that was once attached to a neighbouring house. A number of different stories relate the origin of the Kallendresser: some say it represents a resident who was too lazy to go down to the privy in the backyard, while others see it as a political statement, expressing disrespect to the authorities in the city hall opposite. The answer to this gesture can be seen every hour on the tower of the city hall, when the **Platzjabbek** – the grim-looking face below the clock – sticks out his tongue at the citizens below as the hour is chimed.

### Mühlengasse

**Brügelmann-haus** At the north end of Alter Markt, Mühlengasse leads down to the Rhine. The name of the street (»Mill Lane«) refers to the mills that were anchored in the Rhine and powered by the river current in the Middle Ages. On the left near Alter Markt the classical Brügelmann-haus, built in 1895, is the only remaining historic factory building in the Old Town. From 1820 the yarn merchant Friedrich Wilhelm Brügelmann established a factory here using Arkwright spinning machines. Shortly before the First World War over 1000 people worked here. The building is now occupied by Peters Brauhaus and a small cabaret theatre called Senftöpfchen (»the mustard pot«, entrance in Grosse Neugasse 2).

## Belgisches Viertel · Belgian Quarter

G/H 6

**Location:** Around Brüsseler Platz **Tram:** 3, 4, 5, 12, 15 (Friesenplatz)
**Bus:** 142 (Bismarckstrasse)

**The Belgian quarter is so called because the streets are named after towns in Belgium. It is a lively area with many pubs, restaurants, little independent shops and an art scene.**

**Brüsseler Platz** The quarter is bounded to the south and north by Aachener Strasse and Venloer Strasse respectively, to the east by Hohenzollernring and to the west by the inner green belt. Its centre, Brüsseler Platz, is surrounded by cafés and imposing townhouses built around 1900. On its west side, half hidden behind trees, stands the Catholic parish church of **St Michael**, built with two towers in neo-Romanesque style with Byzantine influence between 1902 and 1906.

**Friesenplatz** Friesenplatz, an attractive square created in the late 19th century when the Ring boulevard was built, was neglected after the Second World War to the extent that it became little more than a road junction, but was improved in the 1990s and has partly regained its function as an urban space. It is close to the shopping streets around Ehrenstrasse and the nightlife of Friesenstrasse and the Ring. Its architectural highlight is the **Ring-Karree** (2001) by **Sir Norman Foster**.

The three towers of differing heights, built for the offices of an insurance company, are a reference to the city gates on the Ring. Two lower wings accommodate shops and cafés.

# Brauweiler

Excursion

**Location:** 13km/8mi west **Bus:** 961, 962 (Breslauer Platz)

**The little town of Brauweiler and its beautiful medieval Benedictine abbey are attractively set close to a low range of hills.**

**Former Benedictine abbey**

The large abbey that dominates the town was founded in 1024 by Mathilde, a daughter of Emperor **Otto II**, on the site of previous buildings that can be traced back to the 6th century. The church displays a mixture of Romanesque styles from various periods between 1050 and the 13th century, including Gothic elements, and its towers can be seen rising above the plain from far away. The impressive westwork (around 1140) with its tower (1515) is 69m/226ft high. Above the nave and the 13th-century Romanesque choir in the mature Rhenish style are an octagonal crossing tower and smaller flanking towers (13th and 19th centuries). The entrance to the church is at the northwest corner of the Baroque abbey buildings, which date from the 18th century. The west door with its relief sculpture inside the porch dates from the 12th century. Inside the church the Romanesque forms of the wall elevation in the nave, crossing and choir, which is raised to accommodate a crypt beneath, harmonize well with the late Gothic vaulting of the nave and its painted floral decoration. The remains of medieval painting on the piers of the choir and nave are worthy of note. The outstanding items in the richly furnished interior are a Renaissance altar of St Anthony in the south transept, a lovely altar of 1180 dedicated to the Virgin in the south choir aisle, and a figure of the abbey founder, Mathilde (about 1200) over the door that leads to the south.

The entrance to the **crypt** is next to the steps leading up to the crossing. It was altered in about 1200 and based on the crypt of ►St Maria im Kapitol, but the oldest parts date from around 1050.

*The wall paintings in the chapterhouse date from the 12th century.*

It is also worth viewing the cloister to the south of the church (entrance from the south aisle), which was built before 1200 but lost its west and north wings in 1810; the chapter house in the east wing of the cloister, where the beautiful Romanesque vault is adorned with 12th-century paintings; and the lapidarium with its unique 11th-century slabs decorated in relief showing depictions of Christ, the apostles and the signs of the zodiac.

# Deutz

F–J 8–9

**Location:** Right bank of the Rhine between Zoobrücke and Südbrücke
**Bus:** 150, 250, 260 (Bf. Deutz/Messe) or 153, 156 (Deutz/Kölnarena)

**Tram:** 1, 7, 9 (Deutzer Freiheit) or 1, 3, 4, 9 (Deutz/Kölnarena)

**There is no better place than Kennedy-Ufer in Deutz to admire Cologne's famous Rhine panorama with the majestic cathedral, the towers of Gross St Martin and the narrow-fronted little houses of the Old Town. The Rheinpark, the trade fair complex (Messe) and the church Alt St Heribert are all worth a visit, as is the shopping street Deutzer Freiheit and – to the south of the Deutzer Brücke – the harbour and the riverbank meadows known as the Poller Wiesen.**

**»The wrong side«** Deutz, situated on the right bank of the Rhine and incorporated into Cologne in 1888, has always been viewed with suspicion by the residents of the left bank and given derogatory names: »land of the barbarians« (inscription on a Roman gravestone of the 4th century, when the Rhine was the border of the Roman Empire) or »heathen territory« (St Boniface in the 8th century). According to the city council of Cologne in 1596, anyone who stayed on the Deutz side for an extended period was in danger of losing »his wits, sense and health«. To this day »true« Cologne citizens enjoy nurturing the prejudice that the other bank of the river is beyond the pale, and that, as Konrad Adenauer said, »Siberia starts just beyond Deutz«. The right bank is known in Kölsch dialect as the »Schäl Sick« (literally »the squinty side«), a term that is said to derive from the blinkered, and thus squinting, horses that pulled boats against the current on the right-bank towpath.

**History** Deutz originated as the **Roman fort Divitia**, which Emperor Constantine founded around AD 310. It had an area of 141 sq m/1520 sq ft and accommodated a garrison of up to 900 men. At the same time the first permanent Rhine bridge was built to link the fort to the left bank, i.e. the Roman side of the river. Soon after the end of Roman

*From the Rheinterrassen there is a superb view across to the left bank.*

rule the barracks seem to have fallen into decay and been demolished, as Frankish houses were then built within the walls of the fort. Around the year 1000 Emperor **Otto III** donated the land to **Archbishop Heribert**, who began to build the Benedictine monastery that was later named after him. A small settlement of craftsmen and merchants grew up around the monastery, and the walls of the old fort were pulled down in 1242. Deutz, which was not well defended, had a turbulent existence up to the 18th century: again and again passing armies that were unable to capture the rich and strongly fortified city of Cologne on the other bank plundered and devastated Deutz. Whoever ruled Deutz controlled Cologne's trade routes to the east, and the city itself invaded Deutz several times to prevent other powers from taking this strategically important site. In 1856 Deutz was given municipal rights, and was incorporated into the city of Cologne in 1888. It became an industrial area in the 19th century and the site of trade fairs in the 20th century, an economic base that was re-established after the Second World War.

**Future plans**

The »wrong side« of the river has considerable potential for further development. The large areas that were once used by industry became free for other uses in recent decades, and much has been done to transform the district, for example with the construction of the Lanxessarena, a large indoor hall for sports, concerts and other events with a conspicuous arch that supports the roof. The Hyatt Hotel on the banks of the Rhine and the skyscraper named KölnTriangle a short distance beyond it are further signs of change. There are plans to expand Deutz railway station into a hub for the high-speed ICE trains and, in the long term, to use parts of Deutz harbour for residential and leisure purposes. Further east, the site of a chemical factory established in 1858 in the Kalk district is now occupied by the new police headquarters and a huge shopping centre called Köln Arcaden.

## Messe · Trade Fair

History

The tradition of trading and trade fairs in Cologne goes back to the Middle Ages. From 1922 the construction of the trade fair halls by the banks of the Rhine to the north of the Hohenzollernbrücke revived this tradition. Mayor Konrad Adenauer opened the first fair on the site in 1924. Three years later Adolf Abel added the tower on the Rhine front, the **Messeturm**, and gave the halls an austerely designed brick façade. The complex has continually been enlarged, and now consists of eleven large halls with an exhibition space of 284,000 sq m/3 million sq ft, extending far east of the river to Deutz-Mülheimer Strasse. The completion of four new halls at the north of the site in 2006 made it the world's fourth-largest trade fair complex. The 1920s buildings, now protected monuments, have been rebuilt inside to serve as offices and TV studios, while the façades have been preserved.

To the west of the tower on the Rhine a **memorial plaque** refers to the darkest days of the site during the »Third Reich«: »From 1942 to 1944 the exhibition halls were used as a prison camp. A branch of Buchenwald concentration camp was established here from late 1942 ...« Almost 12,000 Jews were deported to the death camps from here, and political prisoners, including Konrad Adenauer, were interned in the so-called Educational Labour Camp.

! *Baedeker* TIP

**High above the river**

Anyone who enjoys a ride in a cable car with an unbeatable view of the city from a height of 50m/165ft above the Rhine should take a trip in the Rheinseilbahn, which runs between the zoo (on Riehler Strasse; cross the tramlines from the zoo entrance) and the Rheinpark (Auenweg). It operates from late March to the end of October daily from 10am to 6pm; the journey time is about six minutes. On a few days each year there are trips after dark. Information: www.koelner-seilbahn.de.

## ✶ Rheinpark

Charming park

The Rheinpark, which lies on the Rhine directly north of the trade fair complex and extends as far as the next bridge, the Zoobrücke, is the perfect place to tke a walk and recover from the bustle of the city. The area to the north of the Zoobrücke is the **Jugendpark**. The varied attractions of the Rheinpark include a large children's playground, flower beds, ponds, cafés, a chair lift, miniature railway, thermal baths with spa facilities and a cable car that crosses the Rhine to the zoo.

The park was originally created for the Budesgartenschau (federal flower and garden show) of 1957. Since then it has been adorned with **sculptures** by modern artists: female figures of the 1950s such as Kurt Lehmann's *Sitzende* (*Seated Woman*) and Gerhard Marcks' *Eva* were complemented in the 1970s by abstract works, including ***Windrose*** by the Baschet brothers, an installation of wind, sound and water close to the Tanzbrunnen. Its 14 sculptures make music as they move in the wind.

The **Tanzbrunnen** (dance fountain, 1957) is an extremely popular venue for open-air events. Its stage or dance floor is suspended over a pond beneath a star-shaped canopy designed by **Frei Otto**. In 1971 six umbrella-like structures were added to provide further shelter. In the summer months the Tanzbrunnen is the venue for well-attended talent contests and many types of concert. The semicircular building around the Tanzbrunnen to the north of the trade fair tower (Messeturm) is part of the old trade fair complex and is known as the Staatenhaus.

! *Baedeker* TIP

**Climbing in the park**

The Jugendpark, immediately to the north of the Rheinpark, has facilities for climbers, who can move across swaying bridges 10m/33ft above the ground or tackle rope courses – all under the supervision of qualified climbing instructors. Information in English at www.insight-out.de.

From here a little chair lift sways across the park to the Zoobrücke. ◄ Chair lift

## ★ Kennedy-Ufer

Panoramic view

Kennedy-Ufer, the bank of the Rhine between the Deutzer Brücke and Hohenzollernbrücke bridges, is the best place from which to enjoy at leisure the wonderful view of the Old Town and the famous city skyline, of which the cathedral, the tower of Gross St Martin and the city hall tower are the most prominent features. To the south of the railway bridge (Hohenzollernbrücke) is the Hyatt Regency Hotel, a large complex of polished granite and glass. Further along is a **monument to the cuirassiers**, erected in 1928 to commemorate the Prussian cavalrymen who were stationed here from the mid-19th century and the cuirassiers who fell in the First World War.

## Alt St Heribert

Former Benedictine monastery

The former Benedictine abbey and its once-magnificent church were founded in 1002 by **Heribert, imperial chancellor and archbishop of Cologne**, on the site of the Roman fort. On the foundations of the original church, which was destroyed and rebuilt many times, a 17th-century Baroque church now stands. A few remains of the fort can be seen to the southeast of the church. The 18th-century monastery buildings were destroyed in the Second World War and reconstructed as a home for senior citizens. The church itself also lost most of its Baroque interior in the war, and was restored with its two towers flanking the choir. It has been used since 1994 by a Greek Orthodox congregation.

The greatest treasure of the church, the shrine of St Heribert, is today in church of Neu St Heribert (► p.164). Today the ensemble of church and monastery buildings lies in the shadow of the 1970s Lufthansa office building.

## Deutz Town Centre

**Deutzer Freiheit** From the Deutzer Brücke the long shopping street called Deutzer Freiheit leads through the centre of old Deutz. The name Freiheit (freedom) harks back to the time when Deutz was a town independent of Cologne and was granted certain liberties by its lord, in early days the archbishop.

**Neu St Heribert** At the corner of Deutzer Freiheit and Tempelstrasse it is worth visiting the 19th-century parish church of Neu St Heribert, which was built in neo-Romanesque style and reconstructed after severe damage in the Second World War. The original church had a tower over the crossing and higher roofs. During restoration ornamental choir windows were added and the interior painted in a restrained manner.

Shrine of St Heribert ► The most precious item in the church is the golden shrine in the choir that contains the bones of Heribert, archbishop of Cologne and founder of the monastery in Deutz. The figures on the 12th-century shrine, the work of Cologne goldsmiths, are the twelve apostles, kings and prophets on the sides, Christ above Archbishop Heribert at the front end, and the Virgin and Child at the back. Twelve medallions on the top narrate the life of St Heribert.

**St Johannes** The Lutheran church of St Johannes, in Tempelstrasse diagonally opposite Neu St Heribert, is situated in a residential quarter typical of a 19th-century garrison town. The 18th-century church was rebuilt after 1945.

**! *Baedeker* TIP**

**Superb panorama**

In 2006 Cologne gained a new landmark: KölnTriangle, a 103m/338ft-tall office tower close to the Rhine in Deutz (Ottoplatz 1). The lifts take less than 30 seconds to ascend to the viewing terrace on the 29th floor, which is glazed all round. The view across the river to the cathedral and the Old Town is superb.

At the east end of Deutzer Freiheit on the right is Reischplatz, where a memorial plaque on house no. 6 marks the site of a **synagogue** that was completely destroyed in the Reich pogrom night (9–10 November 1938) and not rebuilt. The Jewish community in Deutz became prominent after 1424, when Jews were expelled from Cologne; they were not permitted to live in the city until 1798. Some Jews thus settled on the opposite bank of the Rhine in Deutz.

**Jewish cemetery** The Jewish cemetery lies to the south of Deutzer Ring outside the area of old Deutz. It was used from 1699 until 1918 and now belongs to the Jewish congregation in Cologne. Some gravestones, such as those of the families Löw, Hirsch and Rindskopf, have Hebrew inscriptions and symbolic ornamentation. Many of them were laid on the ground, as the Prussian army decreed that the line of fire from the nearby fortifications should not be blocked by upright stones.

*The Poller Wiesen, meadows on the right bank of the Rhine, are well used for sports and relaxation.*

At Ottoplatz on the north side of the historic part of Deutz, the railway station of 1914, **Bahnhof Deutz**, is conspicuous for its domed roof. An original four-stroke engine has been placed in front of the station to commemorate the inventor **Nicolaus August Otto**. In 1864 Otto founded an engine factory in Cologne, moving to more spacious premises in Deutz five years later. The successor of Otto's company, Deutz AG, still produces engines.

The left bank of the Rhine has Cologne Cathedral, the right bank the largest indoor arena in Germany, the multi-functional **LanxessArena**, which was opened in 1998. With the 76m/250ft-high steel arch from which the roof is suspended and the adjacent buildings, which were constructed at the same time to accommodate the city administration, it is a dominant feature of the urban scene in Deutz and a highly visible element on the skyline. The 8000 sq m/85,000 sq ft of glass that constitute the walls of the foyer provide an open view of the network of staircases, bridges and supports inside. Thanks to its roof construction the arena is popularly known as the **Henkelmännche** (the »pot with handle« that once held a worker's lunch). It has a seating capacity of 18,000 and is used primarily for concerts, shows and ice hockey matches of the »Kölner Haie« (»Cologne Sharks«), for which an ice rink is raised from beneath the floor of the hall.

## Deutzer Hafen and Poller Wiesen

**Green river bank**

For a walk along the river, the banks of the Rhine south of Deutz – from the harbour, Deutzer Hafen, to the district of Westhoven – is an alternative to the more frequented left bank. Deutzer Hafen was inaugurated in 1908. The entrance to it is below the Severinsbrücke, the bridge to the south of the Deutzer Brücke. Further south a swing bridge crosses to Alfred-Schütte-Allee, which leads along the river to the meadows called Poller Wiesen. There is an impressive view to the new harbour development on the left bank, the Rheinauhafen, including interesting new buildings and the huge old warehouse known as the Siebengebirge (►p.225).

# ★★ Dom · Cologne Cathedral

G 7

**Location:** City centre
**S-Bahn:** S 6, S 11, S 12, S 13 (Hbf)
**Internet:** www.koelner-dom.de
**Bus:** 132
**Tram:** 5, 16, 18 (Dom/Hbf)

**Cologne Cathedral, planned in the Middle Ages to be the largest cathedral in existence, is one of the most important buildings of the Christian world and has been a UNESCO World Heritage site since 1996. It is the symbol and landmark of the city, its geographical centre and, with six million visitors each year, deservedly the most popular attraction for tourists in all Germany.**

## History of the Cathedral

**A crowning achievement of Gothic architecture**

Although the cathedral was built over a number of centuries and is the product of varying aesthetic philosophies, it is regarded by many as the pinnacle of Gothic architecture. Political events lay behind the plan to build a new cathedral: in 1164 Archbishop **Rainald von Dassel**, chancellor to **Emperor Friedrich Barbarossa**, brought the relics of the Three Magi to Cologne from Milan as booty after a military campaign. In the Middle Ages the Three Magi were regarded as the first Christian kings, and thus as models for kingship and examples to Christian rulers. Possession of these relics, especially at a time when Barbarossa was engaged in conflict with the papacy, represented the ultimate legitimation of his rule. The relics were at first placed in the 9th-century predecessor to the present cathedral, which itself occupied the site of previous buildings dating back to the 4th century. A Roman house, remains of which have been excavated below the floor of the cathedral, may have been the first place of Christian worship here. 6th-century buildings on this site have been identified with greater certainty as an early church. 6th-century graves of a young woman and a boy, thought to be members of a Frankish royal house, were excavated here.

1248: foundation stone laid ►

The fame and importance of the relics of the Three Magi drew such a flood of pilgrims that the decision was taken to build a larger and more prestigious cathedral to surpass the other churches of the city in grandeur. In 1248 Archbishop **Konrad von Hochstaden** laid the foundation stone for the Gothic cathedral. It was modelled on the royal cathedrals of northern France rather than on existing buildings in the Romanesque style that was characteristic of the Rhineland. The first architect was **Gerhard von Rile**, who may have originated from the Moselle valley, and was certainly well acquainted with French Gothic cathedrals.

Construction until about 1530 ►

In the following three centuries the cathedral was a major building site that caused an expansion of manual trades, which were forced to specialize and meet higher demands than ever before. In this period the guilds developed in Cologne.

*The west front of Cologne Cathedral is probably the world's largest church façade.*

The chapels of the choir were finished by 1261, the sacristy (now the Chapel of the Sacrament) by 1277, the choir by 1322. The immense costs, which had to be met from donations and the sale of indulgences, meant that the work proceeded ever more slowly, and came to a standstill sometime before 1535. By then all the foundations had been built and the whole area of the nave had a provisional roof. The north tower was barely begun, and the crane on the south tower, which had attained a height of 58m/190ft, was the landmark of the city for more than 300 years.

◀ Completion in the 19th century

In 1842 work began again. The impulses for the completion of the work came from the appreciation of the Middle Ages in the Romantic period; national sentiment, which came to see the cathedral as a symbol for the unification of Germany, also payed a part, as did the rediscovery in 1814 of the original plan of the west façade, which probably dates from around 1300. **King Friedrich Wilhelm IV** of Prussia laid the foundation stone for the continuation, and the completion was celebrated in 1880 in the presence of the German emperor, **Wilhelm I**.

◀ Restoration

However, work on the cathedral will never truly come to a stop. The cathedral workshop is permanently engaged in restoration work, as the effects of weathering and atmospheric pollution continually erode the stone.

## Exterior

**Heavenly Jerusalem**

In the 13th century a Gothic cathedral was regarded as an image of the heavenly Jerusalem, its towers and pinnacles forming the silhouette of the city of God. Large window surfaces – at Cologne Cathedral covering an area of about 10,000 sq m/110,000 sq ft – break up the massiveness of the building.

West façade ► In the same way, the 7000 sq m/75,000 sq ft west façade has few flat wall surfaces: it consists of three portals, windows, tracery and buttresses, and the towers rise to a height of 157m/515ft in a forest of pinnacles.

Petersportal ► The **oldest doorway of the cathedral**, the Petersportal, is on the west façade to the right of the central door. Five figures of the apostles on this entrance date from the late 14th century. Those now in place are copies; the originals, done by members of the Parler family of architects and sculptors, are in the possession of the Diocesan Museum (►Kolumba). The tympanum is the only original sculpture on the Petersportal. It depicts the martyrdom of St Peter, who was crucified head downwards, and St Paul, who was beheaded.

South façade ► The skeleton structure of Gothic architecture is even clearer on the sides of the cathedral, where the flying buttresses and a host of piers and pinnacles make the masses of stone appear to dissolve into lightness. The façade of the south transept dates from the 19th, the choir to its right from the 13th century. The four bronze doors on the south side were made in the mid-20th century by **Ewald Mataré**.

North façade ► The façade of the north transept was badly damaged in the Second World War, and restoration work was not completed until 1982. At the northwest corner of the cathedral, where the stone still clearly looks newer than that of the surrounding areas, repair work was completed in 2005, covering red brickwork that was hastily put in place in 1943 when a bomb blew out a large amount of masonry.

## Interior

**Perfect harmony** Inside the cathedral the spirit of Gothic architecture is revealed. The space has a mystical quality. The dissolution of wall surfaces makes it difficult to discern boundaries, and the interior is illuminated by colourful stained-glass windows that seem not of this world. The vaulted roof is supported by over 100 piers, which attain a height of 43.35m/142ft in the nave. The proportions of this image of the heavenly Jerusalem reveal perfect harmony: all measurements are based on the dimensions of the crossing, a square measuring 14.45m/47ft 5in: the height of the nave and the width of the church are three times this measure, and the distance between the piers is one half of it.

! *Baedeker* TIP

### Tours in English

The inner choir of the cathedral, where the shrine of the Three Magi rests, is normally closed to visitors, but can be entered as part of a tour: 10.30am (daily except Sunday) and 2.30pm (daily) in English.

**North aisle** The five colourful Renaissance windows of the north aisle date from 1507–09. The second and fourth from the west were donated by archbishops, who are shown at the bottom with the coats of arms of their families. The third (central) window, donated by the city council, depicts the birth of Christ, with the heraldic emblems of the city and four martial saints. The altar at the east end of the north aisle, the **Clarenaltar**, was used for many years as the main altar of the cathedral after being taken from the convent of the Poor Clares, which was destroyed in 1807. It dates from 1350–60; the rear side was painted in 1905 by Wilhelm Mengenberg.

North transept

A Baroque **Madonna of Mercy** is the conspicuous feature of the east side of the north transept. This statue of the Virgin and Child is clad in a dress of white silk, to which are attached jewellery and other precious items donated by believers to thank the Virgin or ask for her intercession.

Choir

The crossing at the centre of the cathedral, which was originally intended for the shrine of the Three Magi, is occupied by a modern bronze altar. Behind it are the **choir stalls**, consisting of 104 seats made in 1310, one of the largest such ensembles to survive from the Middle Ages. It seated the 24 members of the cathedral chapter, their 27 deputies and visitors to the chapter; two seats were reserved for the emperor and the pope. The 14th-century choir screens behind the stalls depict scenes from the lives of the saints associated with the cathedral. The 13th-century figures on the piers of the choir, fine work by the sculptors of the cathedral workshop, represent Christ, the Virgin and the apostles.

The windows of the clerestory, which are almost 18m/60ft high and date from about 1300, display a monumental cycle of royal figures: on the sides the 24 kings of Juda and the 24 kings of the apocalypse, at the east end the Adoration of the Magi.

◄ North side of choir

The **Kreuzkapelle** (Chapel of the Cross) is on the north side of the choir. Here a doorway leads into the **Sakramentskapelle** (Chapel of the Sacrament), one of the oldest parts of the cathedral. It was used as a chapterhouse, for example when the cathedral chapter elected a new archbishop.

A stone tablet to the left of the doorway to the chapel is the »Judenprivileg« (Jews' Privilege) of 1266, in which the archbishop guaranteed to the Jews of Cologne rights of burial, equality with Christians in respect of customs duties and a monopoly of credit transactions.

✶

◄ Chapel of the Cross and Gero Crucifix

The Gero Crucifix hangs on the east wall of the Kreuzkapelle (Chapel of the Cross) . This cross with a larger-than-life figure of Christ was donated by Archbishop Gero († 976) and numbers among the very few such monumental figures from this period. It was one of the great treasures of the old, 9th-century cathedral. Around 1270 it was placed in the newly completed St Stephen's Chapel of the present building, and was brought to the Chapel of the Cross in 1350. The golden sunburst was added in the 17th century.

◄ Mosaic floor

The floor of the choir is a precious late 19th-century ceramic mosaic, designed by August von Essenwein and produced by Villeroy und Boch. The part in the crossing (covered) represents the cosmos; the

# COLOGNE CATHEDRAL

**★★ It took over 600 years, including a break lasting 300 years, to complete Cologne Cathedral. However, the result, an exceptional work of Gothic architecture, was worth waiting for.**

Hours:
daily 6am–7.30pm
Tours in English: 10.30am (daily except Sunday) and 2.30pm (daily)
Tel. 92 58 47 30

### ① South tower

The south tower has a height of exactly 157.31m/516ft 2in. From ground level there are 509 steps to the viewing platform at the base of the openwork spire. Eight bells, including »Big Peter«, hang in the belfry.

### ② North tower

With a height of 157.38m/516ft 4in, the north tower is just taller than its neighbour.

### ③ Crossing spire

The smaller tower with spire over the crossing contains three more bells. Its tip is 109m/358ft high.

### ④ Windows

The windows have a total surface of about 10,000 sq m/11,000 sq ft.

### ⑤ Gero Crucifix

The 2.88m/9ft 6in-high crucifix is the oldest surviving example of its size in northern Europe. It was made in the late 10th century.

### ⑥ Choir stalls

The early 14th-century choir stalls have 104 seats and are the largest in Germany. Two seats are normally unoccupied, as they are reserved for the pope and emperor.

## *Cologne Cathedral* Plan

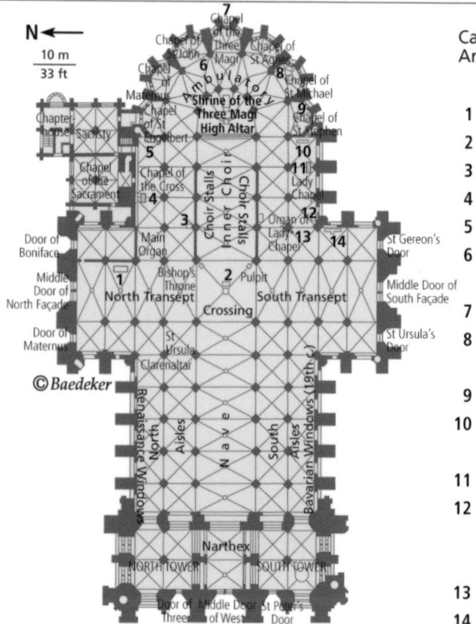


Cathedral Church of the Archdiocese of Cologne

1 Madonna of Mercy
2 Bronze altar
3 Entrance to crypt
4 Judenprivileg
5 Gero Crucifix
6 Tomb of Archbishop Konrad von Hochstaden
7 Old Bible Window
8 Crucifixion (1548) by B. Bruyn the Elder
9 New Bible Window
10 Altarpiece by Stefan Lochner
11 Madonna of Milan
12 Tomb of Archbishop Rainald von Dassel
13 St Christopher
14 Agilolphus Altar

*100 pillars, some decorated saints and apostles, support the vault of the cathedral.*

*The Shrine of the Three Magi, which is considered the finest example of medieval goldsmith work in Europe, holds the relics of the Three Magi.*

*ker*

*St Peter's Bell, the largest free-swinging bell in the world, weighs 24 tons and was cast in Apolda in Thuringia in 1923. »Dicker Pitter« (»Big Peter«), as the bell is known, is tolled only on special occasions.*

*In 1999 Barbara Schock-Werner became the first woman to hold the post of cathedral architect. She is responsible for all the work on maintaining the World Cultural Heritage site. The cathedral workshop employs almost 90 people, including stonemasons, sculptors, goldsmiths and art restorers.*

floor of the inner choir has mankind and the Christian world as its theme; and the floor of the ambulatory depicts the history of the archdiocese and cathedral of Cologne.

Apse and choir chapels ► Seven chapels radiate from the apse. All except the middle one contain the tombs of archbishops. The third chapel (counting clockwise from north to south) also holds the tomb of Richeza († 1063), queen of Poland, the fifth chapel the sarcophagus (1280) of St Irmgardis.

Old Bible Window ► The **oldest window in the cathedral**, dating from about 1260, is the Älteres Bibelfenster (Old Bible Window) in the middle chapel, the Chapel of the Three Magi. It is divided vertically into two parts, showing on the left scenes from the Old Testament that were believed to prefigure the New Testament scenes shown on the right. The two other windows in this chapel are dated *c*1320. This chapel once housed the shrine of the Three Magi, and was remodelled in neo-Gothic style in 1892. The Jüngeres Bibelfenster (Newer Bible Window) of about 1280 in the 7th chapel (St Stephen's Chapel) was made for the church of a Dominican monastery that was demolished in 1804.

✶ ✶ [Sh]rine of the Three Magi ► The inner choir is the clearest representation of the religious and political message of the cathedral. At the east end is the shrine of the Three Magi, one of the most magnificent examples of medieval goldsmith work. It was made from about 1190 by **Nicholas of Verdun** and his workshop, and was probably completed around 1220. The lower section of the sides, depicting prophets, priests and kings, was probably the work of Nicholas himself. The front end (facing west) was made from pure gold donated by King Otto IV, who ensured that Cologne supported his position in the empire in this way. It shows the Adoration of the Kings (Three Magi), with Otto IV behind them as a fourth king, the baptism of Christ, and Christ in majesty above. On the opposite end of the shrine the bishop with mitre is a depiction of **Rainald von Dassel**. Below this are the scenes of the Flagellation and Crucifixion of Christ.

The shrine contains relics that are traditionally believed to be the bones of the Three Magi. The cloth in which they are wrapped dates from the 2nd century.

On 6 January, the day of the Three Magi, a panel at the front of the shrine is opened to reveal a partial view of three skulls.

Marienkapelle ► The most famous painting in the cathedral, known as the **Altar of the City Patrons**, is kept in the Marienkapelle (Lady Chapel) on the south side of the choir. It was painted around 1442 by Stefan Lochner, the most important artist of the Cologne school of the 15th century, originally for the chapel of the ► city hall. It is a winged altarpiece demonstrating the pride of the citizens, for whom the city patron saints St Gereon and St Ursula, in addition to the Three Magi, intercede directly at the throne of the Virgin, without the intervention of prelates or secular noble rulers. Close to the altarpiece on a pillar by the windows is the greatly revered

*Ludwig I of Bavaria donated these colourful windows in 1848.*

Mailänder Madonna (Madonna of Milan), a graceful, coloured figure with a halo of stars. It was made in Cologne in the late 13th century, probably to replace a Madonna brought from Milan by Rainald von Dassel that was lost through fire.

◀ South transept

A pier close to the crossing bears a 3.7m/12ft-high statue of St Christopher, made around 1470 by Tilman van der Burch. On the east wall is the elaborate **Agilolphus Altar**, carved in Antwerp in 1521.

**South aisle**

On the way back to the west entrance, note the windows of the south aisle, which were donated in 1848 by King Ludwig I of Bavaria and are thus known as the **Bavarian windows**. They depict in glowing colours the origin and spread of the Christian church in the West.

## South Tower

For a wonderful view of the city it is worth climbing the narrow, winding stairs of the south tower – 509 steps from ground level – to the viewing platform at a height of 97m/318ft. Stop on the way to admire the bells, especially the **Petersglocke** of 1923, which at 24 tons is the **largest free-swinging bell in the world**. The seven other bells include the 10.7-ton Pretiosa (1448) and the 5.6-ton Speciosa (1449). Admission to the tower is gained via the new visitor centre, outside the cathedral on its south side.

Opening hours:
Nov–Feb 9am–4pm, March, April, Oct until 5pm, May–Sept until 6pm

## Around the Cathedral

**Cathedral treasury**

The entrance to the cathedral treasury (Domschatzkammer) is on the north side of the choir in modern premises, a windowless brown

Opening hours: Daily 10am–6pm, ours Tue 11am and Thu 3pm

cube clad in bronze panels. On an area of 500 sq m/5500 sq ft some of the most precious items of the cathedral are exhibited: shrines, reliquaries, monstrances, insignia and other liturgical items. The chamber of relics (Heiltumskammer) on the ground floor holds a Baroque shrine with the remains of Archbishop Engelbert, who was murdered in 1225, and relics brought from Rome by Archbishop Bruno in the 10th century: the bishop's crozier of St Peter and links from the chain with which St Peter was imprisoned. The two below-ground floors occupy the cellar of the sacristy, which was built in about 1260.

On the first basement level liturgical items, cups, crosses and monstrances are on display, and a small room contains the original wooden interior of the shrine of the Three Magi. The bottom floor is devoted to an exhibition of richly worked church vestments and mitres, and in a further room sculptures and finds from the 6th-century **Frankish graves** that were discovered in 1959.

**Domplatte**

In the 1970s the steps that led to the cathedral west entrance disappeared under a new raised area of paving known as the Domplatte. To the west of this platform, between the cathedral and the tourist office, is a full-scale copy of the finials from the top of the towers, 9m/30ft high and 4.5m/15ft wide. Close by, and approximately on its original site, is a Roman arch, the side entrance of the 2nd-century **north gate** of the Roman wall.

Parts of the Roman city wall and the foundations of the north gate can be seen in the car park beneath the Domplatte (enter through a metal door next to the U-Bahn steps). The central arch of the gate is now in the ► Römisch-Germanisches Museum. The archaeological discoveries beneath the cathedral, including remains of Roman houses and the 9th-century cathedral, are the subject of an interesting tour (in German: Tue, Thu 4.15pm, Sat 11am; book in advance, tel. 92 58 47 30, or on the day in the Domforum).

*The cathedral is an inspiring backdrop for pavement artists.*

The square on the south side of the cathedral, **Roncalliplatz**, is bounded on the east by the

Römisch-Germanisches Museum, on the west by the Domhotel. The whole area around the cathedral is a stage for street performers of all kinds, pavement artists and skateboarders.

**Cathedral workshops**

The cathedral workshop (Dombauhütte) directly adjoins the south side of the choir. It employs a full-time staff of 90 – stonemasons, roofers, scaffolders, carpenters, painters, electricians, glass restorers and goldsmiths – who preserve and restore the building and its furnishings.

✶ **Heinzelmännchenbrunnen**

Next to Roncalliplatz, on the south side of the Domhotel, water flows in the fountain known as the Heinzelmännchenbrunnen, and Kölsch beer flows in the popular Brauhaus Früh behind it. The fountain was inaugurated in 1899 on the 100th birthday of **August Kopisch**, who wrote a ballad in 1836 on the *Heinzelmännchen of Cologne*, busy elves who came secretly at night to do all the work of the Cologne craftsmen, as depicted by the stone reliefs to the left and right of the fountain basin. The inquisitive wife of the tailor, shown at the centre carrying a lantern, wanted to see who was doing the work and scattered dried peas on the steps of her house. The elves slipped on the peas, fell down the steps and departed in anger, never to return.

# Eigelstein Quarter

F 7

**Location:** Around Eigelstein

**Tram:** 5, 12, 15, 16, 18 (Ebertplatz) or 5, 16, 18 (Breslauer Platz/Hbf)

**The quarter around the street named Eigelstein is a colourful mixture, a traditional Cologne milieu that now gets its character mainly from immigrant groups. The shops and restaurants in the second main street of the quarter, Weidengasse, are mainly Turkish.**

✶ **Eigelsteintorburg**

Eigelstein is the old Roman military road leading north. The name derives from »aquila« (eagle), the banner under which the legions marched. The extension of the city wall in 1106 and the construction of the north gate, Eigelsteintorburg, in the early 13th century as part of a second extension brought the district within the city limits. The massive gate consists of two towers, rounded on the side facing outwards, that flank the central archway. Today they house the Jazzhausschule, providing rehearsal and teaching rooms for musicians. The gate was restored in 1890, and adorned the following year on the side facing the city with the stone figure of the **Kölsche Boor**. This literally means the »Cologne farmer«, but in fact the figure is always represented as a solder and symbolizes the military strength of the city and its loyalty to the German empire. The motto beneath the statue, in local dialect, »Halt fass, do kölscher Boor, bliev beim Reich, et fall sös ov sor!« means »Be steadfast, Kölsche Boor, stand by the empire in good times and bad!«. Today the Bauer is one of the three members of the ruling triumvirate at Carnival time, alongside the prince and the maiden. A large pub furnished in the traditional Brauhaus style close to the gate bears the name Kölsche Boor.

Around Eigelsteintorburg ► Some of the house façades of the streets that radiate from the city gate go back to the expansion of Cologne in the late 19th century, revealing the eclectic mixture of classical and other styles typical of the time. This area did not gain an urban character until after 1860, when industrial growth created pressure to develop the available land.

The cobblestoned alley Stavenhof, a side street of Eigelstein, used to be a red-light district, and the dubious character of the quarter is still maintained by some seedy pubs at the south end of the street, towards the ►main railway station. From the medieval gate walk along Lübecker Strasse to get to the Ring boulevard and on to the ►Mediapark, or continue northwards through the gate to Ebertplatz, from where the large neo-Gothic church of St Agnes is visible straight ahead.

**St Agnes** After the cathedral, St Agnes is the largest church in Cologne. It was built between 1896 and 1902 by Carl Rüdell and Richard Odenthal for the developer **Peter Joseph Roeckerath**, who wished to commemorate his first wife, Agnes. The church with its tall lantern tower is the landmark of the surrounding quarter, known as the Agnesviertel. Some fine house façades in the surrounding residential streets, for example Weissenburgstrasse to the right of the church, illustrate well the architecture typical of the Neustadt, the new residential and commercial quarters that were built in the late 19th and early 20th century when the city finally expanded beyond the medieval wall.

# EL-DE-Haus · NS-Dokumentationszentrum

G 7

**Location:** Appellhofplatz 23 – 25
**Tram:** 3, 4, 5, 16, 18 (Appellhofplatz)
**Internet:** www.museenkoeln.de/ns-dok_neu

**The EL-DE-Haus was used from 1935 until 1945 as the Gestapo headquarters. Since 1981 it has been a place of memorial, also serving as a centre for information on and documentation of the National Socialist (NS) period in Cologne.**

**Memorial site** The Cologne businessman Leopold Dahmen built the house in 1934–35, and it was named EL-DE-Haus after his initials. In 1935 the Gestapo confiscated the building and installed its offices in the upper floors, using the cellars as a prison and place of torture. The ten tiny cells, into which up to 30 persons were crammed at one time, have largely been preserved in their original condition of the years 1944–45. The graffiti on the walls, in a number of languages, tells of the suffering of the prisoners. Many were murdered here, including prisoners of war, forced labourers from eastern Europe and German opponents of the Nazi regime, as well as Jews who were sent to the concentration camps from these cells. Executions were carried out in the back yard.

Opening hours: Tue–Fri 10am–4pm, Sat and Sun from 11am

The EL-DE-Haus is used as a research and education centre on the history of National Socialism in Cologne, and has a permanent exhibition about the Nazi period in the city in addition to special exhibitions about particular aspects of this period.

◄ Documentation centre

# Flora · Botanical Garden

E 8

**Location:** Amsterdamer Strasse
**Bus:** 140 (Zoo/Flora)
**Tram:** 18 (Zoo/Flora)

**This extensive and beautiful park near the zoo has flower beds and ponds, glasshouses and a variety of different gardens with a great range of plant species.**

In 1864 the southern part of the park, known as the Flora, was laid out by the famous garden designer **Peter Joseph Lenné** (1789–1866), as previous botanical gardens had been sacrificed to the expansion of

*An oasis of greenery in the north of Cologne: the Flora*

Opening hours: Daily 8am until dusk; glasshouses: Oct–March daily 10am–4pm, April–Sept until 6pm; free admission

the city. The first botanical garden in Cologne was established around 1250 as a monastery garden by Albertus Magnus (► Famous People), the founder of the science of botany.
From the entrance opposite the zoo in Alter Stammheimer Weg, the Wintergarten catches the eye. It was built as a glass palace in the 19th century, but not restored to its original form after the Second World War, and is now used for events and as a café. In front of it is a parterre garden with flower beds, behind it the Frauen-Rosenhof, an art nouveau building of 1906 that is now used for education in nature and ecology. Beyond this are the large glasshouses with a variety of tropical plants: orchids, cultivated plants such as coffee, tea and cocoa, cactus plants, and many more. The show of camellias early in the year is well worth seeing.
Areas in the style of an English landscape park and an Italian Renaissance garden are close by. The northern end of the park is mainly devoted to a succession of gardens representing different habitats or types of plant, systematically arranged to show selected families of plants, e.g. poisonous and medicinal plants, herbs, plants used by dyers and tanners, and alpine plants.

## ★★ Gross St Martin

G 7

**Location:** Martinspförtchen 8
**Bus:** 132 (Rathaus)
**Tram:** 1, 7, 9 (Heumarkt)

**The massive church tower of Gross St Martin rises majestically from the maze of alleys of the Old Town. Until the 19th century it ranked alongside the unfinished towers of the cathedral as the emblem of the city.**

Opening hours: Tue–Fri 10am–2pm and 3–5pm, Sat 10am–12.30pm and 1.30–5pm, Sun 2–4pm

The church stands on the foundations of a large Roman warehouse, which itself occupied the site of a previous »palaestra«, a Roman sports ground. Excavations under the church uncovered these foundations, part of a 1st-century Roman swimming bath, and remains of the predecessors of the present church. The excavations are open to visitors via steps in the north aisle.
The first records of a church on the site go back to the 10th century, when **Archbishop Bruno** founded a collegiate church for canons, which was converted into a Benedictine monastery a short time later. After a fire devastated this part of the city and destroyed the monastery church, construction of the present building began in 1150. It was consecrated in 1172 and underwent a number of alterations before its completion in about 1250. In the 15th century the Gothic spire of the tower replaced the original Romanesque version; the monastery buildings were demolished after being secularized in 1802.

*The massive church of Gross St Martin towers over the Old Town.*

The main façade, the east front facing the Rhine, is a »trefoil choir« (i.e. its ground plan has the shape of a clover leaf), and is similar to that of ► St Aposteln. The lavish use of decorative elements gives structure to the walls so as to relieve the immense mass of the building. Two arcades run right around the apses. Above them are a dwarf gallery, conical roofs and large triangular gables adorned with fan-shaped blind tracery. At the centre rises the imposing tower, which is also richly adorned with a dwarf gallery and paired lights, and is flanked by four corner turrets. The outer walls of the nave are much plainer.

The lack of decorative **interior furnishing** results from the rebuilding of the church in a simple style after its destruction in the Second World War. Little remains of the medieval wall paintings and furnishings, and the interior conveys only in a much diminished form an impression of the magnificence of a medieval church. Sculptures of the Crucifixion and Deposition by **Tilman van der Burch** (1509) have survived and can be seen behind the font of 1220 in the baptismal chapel in the north aisle.

**Tünnes and Schäl**

In a corner of the courtyard to the west of the church stand two bronze figures, made in 1974 by **Wolfgang Reuter** (► photo p.1). Their names are Tünnes and Schäl (Tony and Squinty), and they represent two different sides of the Cologne character. They are traditional figures in the nearby puppet theatre, Hänneschentheater on Eisenmarkt, and the subjects of countless local jokes and anecdotes. Tünnes is short, plump and has a potato nose. He is good-humoured and harmless, but possesses plenty of native wit. Schäl is tall, thin and cross-eyed. He is cunning, untrustworthy, even malevolent. He likes to play tricks on others and takes nothing seriously. The two complement each other: they seem to be opposites but in fact are conflicting elements of a single mentality.

**Schmitzsäule**

A few yards away a column of masonry, the Schmitzsäule, is an eccentric monument to the foundation of the city. It commemorates the origins of the people of Cologne and the Schmitz family (the most typical Cologne surname) as the issue of Roman legionaries and women from the Ubii tribe who are stated to have met here when the spot was an island in the river. On one side of the column, which is partly built from Roman stonework, an astonishing high-water mark shows the level reached by the worst Rhine flood ever recorded, on 28 February 1784.

# Grüngürtel · Green Belts

E–J 5–8

**Location:** Along Innere Kanalstrasse and Universitätsstrasse; outside Militärringstrasse

**The parks, gardens, lakes and sports facilities of the two green belts that encircle central Cologne are attractive places of recreation and leafy oases close to the bustle of the city.**

**Inner green belt**

The inner and outer green belts were created after the First World War on the site of two rings of fortifications that were then destroyed. The project, planned by mayor **Konrad Adenauer** and city architect **Fritz Schumacher**, originally envisaged a much greater density of buildings on the green belts, but the economic crises of the Weimar Republic prevented the realization of the plans.

The inner green belt (Innerer Grüngürtel) lies within the ring road known as Innere Kanalstrasse/Universitätsstrasse, and extends from Luxemburger Strasse in the south to the railway yards in the north, a length of 4km/2.5mi, with a continuation between Krefelder Strasse and the Rhine. This green belt encloses the area of medieval Cologne and the Neustadt. The **Aachener Weiher** lake, the ► Museum für Ostasiatische Kunst and the university lie within it. Near the Aachener Weiher and further north (across the railway tracks from the Mediapark) are hills consisting of rubble taken from the ruined inner city after the Second World War.

The 243m/797ft-high **Colonius** between Venloer and Subbelrather Strasse is the fifth-tallest telecommunications tower in Germany, built in 1981. The 9m/30ft-high circular platform close to the top contains technical equipment and rooms originally used for a revolving restaurant. The restaurant and viewing platform have unfortunately been closed for many years.

**Outer green belt**

The 12km/8mi-long outer green belt (Äussere Grüngürtel) borders Militärringstrasse and extends from Müngersdorf in the west of the city to Rodenkirchen on the Rhine. It is an ideal area for taking a long walk in grassy and wooded surroundings, for example on the **Decksteiner Weiher** lake in the southwest of Cologne. A tree-lined canal leading out of the city from the Aachener Weiher leads to the Stadtwald park and on to the outer green belt.

# Hauptbahnhof · Main Railway Station

G 7

**Location:** City centre

**Tram:** 5, 16, 18 (Dom/Hbf or Breslauer Platz/Hbf)

**Over 1200 trains arrive at Cologne's main station every day, making it the busiest rail hub in all of continental Europe.**

Cologne's first railway station was built in 1857 on the site of a botanical garden. Of the 19th-century railway buildings, the main hall with platforms (built from 1890 to 1894) remains. With a length of 255m/280yd, a width of 65m/70yd and a height of 24m/80ft it demonstrates the confidence of the period in technical progress. The shape of the steel-frame station roof has similarities with the Gothic architecture of its neighbour, the cathedral. The modern transparent roof of the newer platforms on the north side of the station, with its 46 full cross-vaults and 19 half-vaults of glass and steel, also pays homage to the cathedral. The station concourse of 1957 has a window façade measuring 800 sq m/8500 sq ft, allowing a view of the cathedral. The recent renovation of the station has opened up a large number of passages with shops and places to eat and drink, but for refreshments in elegant surroundings from the grand days of railway travel, the restaurant in the old waiting room (Alter Wartesaal; leave the station and go left) is unsurpassed. The square in front of the station and the steps leading up to the cathedral were remodelled in 2005.

# Hohe Strasse · Schildergasse

G 7

**Location:** City centre

**Tram:** Hohe Strasse: 5, 16, 18 (Dom/Hbf) Schildergasse: 1, 3, 4, 7, 9, 16, 18 (Neumarkt)

**The two long, busy shopping streets in the city centre are closed to traffic. Over 15,000 passers-by per hour make Schildergasse the number one retail location in Germany.**

**Hohe Strasse**

Hohe Strasse (High Street) is reached from the cathedral via Wallrafplatz, site of the headquarters of the broadcaster ►WDR, and from the Heinzelmännchenbrunnen (► Dom) by walking through the Stollwerck-Passage, an arcade with a bronze sculpture of the Greek earth goddess Gaia (1965) by **Gerhard Marcks**. Hohe Strasse was once the finest shopping street in the city, lined with the most expensive stores. The bombing of the Second World War and exorbitant rents changed this, filling the street with the branches of chain stores. Hohe Strasse approximately traces the course of the main north-south Roman road, the cardo maximus, which passed right through the city and continued north to the next military camp, now the town of Neuss, and in the opposite direction to Bonn, the nearest Roman camp to the south.

! *Baedeker* TIP

**Church café**

Café Stanton (a pun on »St Anton«) is the place to take a break from the retail frenzy of Schildergasse. It lies behind the Antoniterkirche (St Anthony's Church; Schildergasse 57, hours: daily 10am–1am, Sat from 9am).

Two historic department stores stand at the junction of Hohe Strasse and the broader **Schildergasse**: the former Palatium, now a fashion store called Hansen, and the old Warenhaus Tietz, now Kaufhof. Both were built between 1912 and 1914 with stone façades in antique style. The Jewish owners of the Tietz department store were dispossessed in 1934 by the National Socialists, who »Aryanized« the company and renamed it Westdeutsche Kaufhaus AG.

In front of Hansen, water flows from the 6m/20ft-high **Bierbrunnen** (beer fountain), which was erected in 1972 to designs by Cologne art students. Beer is said to flow from the fountain once a year, but waiting around for this miraculous event to occur is not recommended. The street is named after the painters (Schilderer) who lived and worked here in the Middle Ages. It, too, follows the course of a major Roman road, the main east-west axis of the city (decumanus maximus); the forum lay at today's intersection of Hohe Strasse and Schildergasse, and modest remains of a semicircular colonnade that bounded the forum can be seen in the Macdonald's hamburger restaurant in the basement of the C & A clothes store.

*The shopping street Schildergasse is a sea of lights at night.*

Halfway down Schildergasse (no. 57) is a small 14th-century basilica, the **Antoniterkirche** (St Anthony's Church). The chapel to the north of the choir commemorates the war dead with a famous work of art, the *Todesengel* (*Angel of Death*) by **Ernst Barlach**. It is a second casting, made in 1942, of a work dating from 1926–27 and bears the facial features of the artist Käthe Kollwitz.

Next to the Antoniterkirche is the Weltstadthaus, a work by the Italian star architect **Renzo Piano**. It was completed in 2005 and houses the Peek & Cloppenburg fashion store. The unusual curved forms of the six-storey building of glass and wood have caused it to be nicknamed »the whale«.

◄ Weltstadtkaufhaus

# ★ Kolumba · Diocesan Museum

G 7

**Location:** Kolumbastr. 4
**Internet:** www.kolumba.de
**Tram:** 5, 16, 18 (Dom/Hbf)

**In 2007 the museum Kolumba, by the Swiss architect Peter Zumthor, opened to critical acclaim. It incorporates a modern chapel built in the ruins of the bombed-out medieval parish church of St Kolumba as well as archaeological finds dating back to the Roman and Frankish periods, and contains a high-quality collection of art on religious themes.**

The museum is devoted to the dialogue between art and religion, with an emphasis on stimulating thought and discussion by presenting modern works on the theme and by juxtaposing old and new. The collection includes early Christian art and painting, sculpture and goldsmith work from the 11th to the 16th century, including such outstanding works as Stefan Lochner's *Madonna mit dem Veilchen* (*Madonna with the Violet*, c. 1440) and the 11th-century Herimannkruzifix, a gilded bronze crucifix with a Roman head of lapis lazuli. The museum also possesses a wide-ranging selection of 20th-century and contemporary work, for example by **Louise Bourgeois**, **Jannis Kounellis**, **Otto Dix**, **Joseph Beuys**, and **Antoni Tàpies**.

Opening hours:
Daily (except Tue)
noon–5pm

**St Kolumba**, the oldest parish church of Cologne, was destroyed by bombing in the Second World War. Excavations on the site uncovered the remains of a Roman house. An apse that was added in the 7th century may mark the first use of the site for Christian worship. The church was altered and expanded in many stages in the following centuries, ending with the conversion of the 12th-century Romanesque basilica to a late Gothic church with galleries and double aisles between 1460 and 1510. After bombing only a pillar bearing a Madonna figure of 1450 remained. In 1950 **Gottfried Böhm** enclosed this within an octagonal, glass-walled chapel that was named **Madonna in den Trümmern**, the »Madonna of the Rubble«. In 1956 the Sakramentskapelle, a chapel with a dark and mystic atmosphere, was added. **Peter Zumthor** has enveloped the whole pre-existing complex in a remarkable new building that combines the post-war chapels, the archaeological site and the museum. The excavations on the ground floor can be viewed from raised walkways, while the sounds of the city filter in through perforated walls of grey brick. The floors

◄ Site, architecture

above combine large and small exhibition spaces in which the works of art have been arranged in a thoughtful manner. Large windows provide magnificent views of the city, and the comfortably furnished reading room is an invitation to linger and study.

**Dischhaus** The shop and office building opposite St Kolumba was built in 1929–30 by **Bruno Paul**. It was one of the most modern works of architecture of inner-city Cologne from the inter-war period. Its striking feature is a rounded façade with horizontal window zones that forms a long curve on the street corner. The Dischhaus was severely damaged in the Second World War and rebuilt to the original plans in the early 1980s.

# Lindenthal

G – H 2 – 4

**Lindenthal, one of the most desirable residential areas of Cologne, was developed to the west of the city centre in the mid-19th century. It is characterized by extensive areas of parkland and attractive avenues.**

**Dürener Strasse** The main shopping street of the district is Dürener Strasse, which is lined by little stores, cafés and restaurants between Universitätsstrasse and Lindenthalgürtel. At the junction of Dürener Strasse and Universitätsstrasse lies the ►Ostasiatisches Museum on the **Aachener Weiher** lake. From here a peaceful, tree-lined path leads about 1.5km/1mi west along a canal to the Stadtwald park.

! *Baedeker* TIP

**For children ...**

... a trip to the Stadtwald animal enclosure is rewarding; the entrance is about halfway along Kitschburger Strasse. Deer, stags, wild boar, goats, peacocks and waterfowl can be seen.

At the end of the first section of the canal, on Bruckner Strasse, stands a church built in 1970 by Gottfried Böhm, **Kirche Christi Auferstehung** (Church of the Resurrection). The façade of concrete and brick is angular, with surfaces protruding or set back, and sections in different materials projecting one into the other. Narrow windows counteract the mass of the structure, and a spiral bell-tower with steps rises to one side.

Inside the church is a place of memorial for the philosopher **Edith Stein**, who was murdered in Auschwitz in 1942 and canonized in 1998.

**Melaten Cemetery** To the north of Aachener Strasse, between Piusstrasse and Melatengürtel, Cologne's **main cemetery**, the 200-year-old Melatenfriedhof, covers an area of almost 40 hectares/100 acres. It is a densely

*For 200 years Cologne's wealthy citizens have been buried at Melaten cemetery.*

planted and shady place with tombs and mausoleums, some of them of considerable artistic merit, along many miles of broad and narrow paths. There are beautiful, touching and curious gravestones from all periods since the foundation of the cemetery in 1810, a measure made necessary by a decree of the Napoleonic government in 1804 to the effect that all burials must take place outside the city walls for reasons of hygiene. On Aachener Strasse within the enclosing wall stands a 15th-century chapel dating from the period (12th–17th centuries) when the site was used as a leper colony. The name of the cemetery, Melaten, probably derives from the sick persons (»Maladen«) who lived here. On specific holy days they were allowed to enter the city, wearing distinctive clothing and carrying rattles to warn of their approach, in order to beg for alms. Until 1801 the site was also used as a place of execution. In addition to many criminals, a number of women accused of witchcraft were burned here at the stake in the early 17th century, as were the two Protestant martyrs of the city, Adolf Clarenbach and Peter von Fliesteden, in 1529.

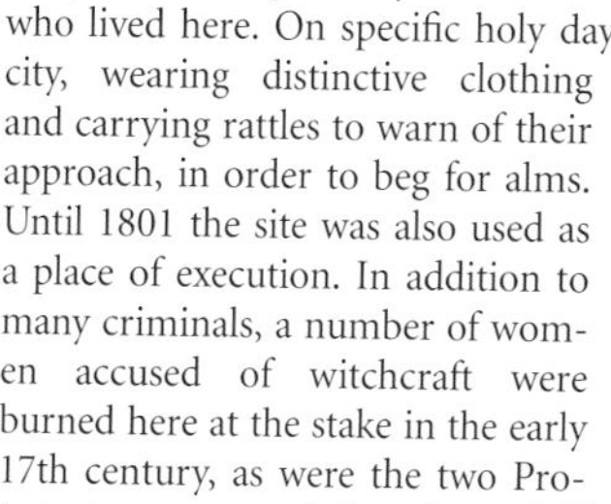

! *Baedeker* TIP

**Flickering candlelight**

If you are in Cologne on 1 November, when Germans tend the graves of deceased relatives and place candles around the headstones, go to Melaten Cemetery at dusk, when thousands of little lanterns create a moving, melancholy atmosphere amidst the autumn foliage.

The pretty little church of **St Stephan** on Suitbert-Heimbach-Platz, close to the junction of Gleueler and Zülpicher Strasse, has its origins in the Carolingian period. The nave was built around 900, the rectangular choir in the late 10th century. In about 1100 the apse and tower were added, in the 13th century the north aisle and on the south side a courtroom that no longer exists. The sacristy dates from the 18th century. St Stephan, also known as the **Krieler Dömchen**, appears in records as a parish church in 1224 and is a popular church for weddings today. The most significant item inside is a 12th-century baptismal font with a horseshoe frieze.

**Stadtwald**

The Stadtwald (»municipal woods«) is a park measuring 2km/1.2mi in length and over 800m/0.5mi in breadth. It lies to the south of Friedrich-Schmidt-Strasse and extends west of Stadtwaldgürtel as far as the outer green belt. It is a fine place for a walk through varied scenery, including wooded areas, open meadows, lakes and a little stream. There is a good view of the park, which is landscaped in the English style, from Hültzplatz at its northeastern corner. The houses of the surrounding streets include large and desirable properties, many dating from the late 19th century.

# Mediapark · Hansaring

F 6/7

**Location:** North of Hansaring, on Erftstrasse and Maybachstrasse

**Tram:** 12, 15 (Hansaring or Christophstr.)
**Internet:** www.mediapark.de

**After a 15-year period of planning and construction in the 1980s and 1990s, the Mediapark district was completed close to the city centre. It has played an important role in Cologne's development as a centre of the media industry.**

**New quarter** The aim behind the creation of the Mediapark was to establish a new residential, leisure and commercial quarter of the city on the site of a former railway goods yard. A number of the buildings have a wedge-shaped ground plan around a semicircular open space next to a lake. About 10 per cent of the workforce in Cologne is employed in media or communications, and almost half of the media companies in North Rhine-Westphalia are based in and around Cologne. Three radio stations have moved into the Mediapark, in addition to the music company EMI Electrola and small music labels. The highly regarded Cologne school of journalism and Bertelsmann Medien AG are also accommodated in the Mediapark.

Cinedom ► The multiplex cinema Cinedom with its 14 screens and seating for 4000 has often hosted film premieres attended by international stars.

Stiftung Kultur ► Tanzarchiv ► The SK Stiftung Kultur, one of Germany's largest cultural foundations, was founded by the local savings bank and is based in the Mediapark, where it runs the Photographische Sammlung, the Deutsches Tanzarchiv Köln and an academy to promote the use of the Cologne dialect.

Photographische Sammlung ► The photographic collection owns the archive of works by the important Cologne photographer August Sander, and also holds high-quality special exhibitions of the works of leading international 20th-century and contemporary photographers. The Museum des Deutschen Tanzarchivs Köln has a permanent exhibition tracing the history of dance (Mediapark 7; hours: daily except Wed 2–7pm; Mon free admission).

KölnTurm ► The most conspicuous building in the Mediapark is the 148m/485ft-high KölnTurm (165.5m/543ft with its antenna). The French architect **Jean Nouvel** was involved in its construction. With its 43 floors the KölnTurm, which opened in 2001, is the tallest office building in Cologne. At the 29th floor the tower is stepped back to

*The KölnTurm is a recent addition to the city skyline – but the architect tactfully kept it lower than the cathedral.*

reduce the floor space, which not only makes the tower more slender, but also creates a terrace on the 30th floor with a wonderful view from the restaurant. At night a changing show of blue-green lights in geometrical patterns makes the KölnTurm prominent on the skyline.

In 2004 construction of the Mediapark concluded with five semicircular buildings on a trapezium-shaped site by the architectural practice of **Herman Hertzberger**. The individual units of the complex face inwards, making it a closed space that also fits in well with the neighbouring buildings.

◄ Filmhaus

Maybachstrasse 111, next to the Mediapark, is the home of the Filmhaus, which screens arthouse movies and organizes film festivals and workshops about the film.

## Hansaring

**Hansa-Hochhaus**

The name of the section of the Ring boulevard between Ebertplatz and Kaiser-Wilhelm-Ring is a reference to the leading position that Cologne held in the organization of merchant cities known as the Hanse. Although much was destroyed during wartime bombing raids and, to an equal extent, by post-war development, a number of fine and well-restored façades of the late 19th century can still be seen on Hansaring and nearby. The 17-storey Hansa-Hochhaus (corner of Ritterstrasse), at 65m/213ft, was Europe's tallest office building at the time of its completion in 1925. The complex is better known now for the media shop Saturn, which stocks an enormous range of CDs and DVDs.

Gereonsmühlenturm ► A short distance from the Hansa-Hochhaus on the opposite side of the ring is Hansaplatz, a small park bounded by a 300m/1000ft-section of the ► medieval city wall. Two of the towers have been preserved; one of them, the Gereonsmühlenturm, was added in the 15th century and served as a windmill.

Memorial ► In front of the wall a bronze memorial by **Mari Andriessen**, *Mother with a Dead Child*, is a reminder of the victims of the Nazi period.

# Medieval City Wall

F – H 6 – 8

**Location:** Individual sections along the Ring boulevard

**In the late 12th and early 13th century the citizens of Cologne built a strong wall that surrounded the city in a semicircle, meeting the Rhine bank in the north and the south. When these fortifications were demolished in the 1880s, the Ring boulevard was built around the medieval city centre, with the Neustadt as a series of new districts outside the Ring. The remaining sections of wall, towers and city gates represent only a small part of the original structure, which was 5.5km/3.5mi long and more extensive than any other in Germany, but they still convey an impression of its size and strength, and make an impressive backdrop to the three squares by the main north, west and south gates.**

**Construction** In 1180 the citizens of Cologne (► plan p.25) pushed through the construction of a new city wall against the will of their ruler, Archbishop **Philipp von Heinsberg**. The growth of trading districts and the existence of monasteries outside the existing wall were the reasons for extending the city boundaries, even though a previous expansion beyond the old ► Roman city wall had been undertaken in 1106, when Emperor **Heinrich IV** granted the right of fortification.

The course of the new wall can be traced in street names such as Severinswall, Kartäuserwall and Pantaleonswall, which run inside and parallel to the Ring. In addition to a number of small entrance ports, there were twelve large gates – the same number as the gates of the heavenly Jerusalem in the Book of Revelations, showing the wish to

! *Baedeker* TIP

**FrauenMediaTurm**

Possession of the 12th-century Bayenturm, once the strongest fortification of medieval Cologne, was regarded as the key to power in the city. Now this tower is firmly under the control of emancipated women. It houses a feminist archive that was founded in 1984 by Alice Schwarzer (►Famous People). Occasional exhibitions are held in the tower, and those who wish to use the library on the top floors should phone in advance (tel. 931 88 10; www.frauenmediaturm.de).

*The 13th-century Eigelstein city gate was the main entrance to Cologne from the north.*

model the holy city of Cologne on the City of God. For much of the period after the building of the wall, which took about 40 years, Cologne was the largest German city by surface area. However, not all of the territory within was built up until the 19th century, and the open land was long used for agriculture. As the population grew rapidly during the period of industrialization (50,000 in 1820, 145,000 in 1880), the wall continued to mark the city boundary and acted as a hindrance to growth. In 1881, after a good deal of lobbying by the city fathers, the Prussian authorities finally gave permission for its demolition.

◄ Remaining sections of wall and gates

The wall on the Rhine front and the wall on the landward side met at the northern end of the fortifications, now the Rhine embankment road Konrad-Adenauer-Ufer. Here the corner of the city was defended by the **Kunibertstorburg**, a stronghold that was supported by two additional towers. One of them, the so-called **Weckschnapp**, survives. The name (»Weck« means a loaf) refers to a story about the cruel use of the tower as a prison whose inmates were starved. A loaf was suspended from the ceiling, but any prisoner who jumped to reach it fell through a trapdoor in the floor and was cut to pieces by sharp blades attached to the sides of the shaft below. The Kunibertstorburg and Weckschnapp were destroyed in flooding in 1784, and the name Weckschnapp was transferred to the only remaining part of the stronghold, a small 15th-century tower that is now part of a residence (Konrad-Adenauer-Ufer 69).

The street Thürmchenswall marks the site of the wall towards the west, and leads to the main northern city gate, the **Eigelsteintorburg** at the edge of the ►Eigelstein quarter. The next surviving part of the medieval wall lies 800m/0.5mi further southwest at Hansaplatz, where a 300m/1000ft section with two towers remains (► Hansaring).

A further 1.5km/1mi along the Ring lies the finest and most important gate of the medieval defences, **Hahnentor** on **Rudolfplatz**. It was the westward city gate, through which German kings entered the city after their coronation in Aachen in order to take up their position as members of the cathedral chapter. The name of the gate derives from the former owner of the surrounding land, Hageno. This was corrupted to Hahnentor (»Cock Gate«). This stronghold dates from 1240. Its west façade, the one presented to approaching royal processions, has two crenellated towers. The entrance arch between them is pointed on the outside and round on the inner side. The arms of the city are attached to the west façade. Note here a memorial plaque to

Hermann Joseph Stübben (1845–1936), the planner of the Neustadt. The three-storey gate was used as a prison, later as an exhibition space, and since 1988 has been the headquarters of the Ehrengarde (»Guard of Honour«), one of the Cologne Carnival societies.

Ulrepforte ► Further south on Sachsenring a further section of wall was saved from demolition for the sake of a monument to a battle of 1268, when forces loyal to the archbishop unsuccessfully attempted to storm the city here. The original monument, considered the oldest secular memorial in Germany and now in the ►Kölnisches Stadtmuseum, has been replaced by a copy. A short distance further south, at the junction with Ulrichgasse, part of a city gate, the Ulrepforte, still stands. It takes its name from the potters (Ulner) who lived here in the Middle Ages, confined to the edge of the city because of the danger of fire from their kilns. Only one of the two original towers remains; in the 15th century it was converted to a windmill, and is now home to a Carnival society, the **Rote Funken**. About 600m/650yd further south, at the end of Severinstrasse, is the south gate of the city, the strong Severinstorburg (►Severinsviertel).

Severinstorburg ►

Bottmühle ► 250m/275yd from here in the direction of the river lies the 17th-century Bottmühle, built on the wall as a windmill and converted into a tower with a medieval appearance in the 19th century.

Bayenturm ► The Bayenturm (►tip p.188) was the southern corner tower on the Rhine. Its outer defences extended into the river. In the 17th and 18th centuries it was a prison, later a museum depot. The upper storeys were destroyed in the Second World War. Since the completion of restoration work in 1994 it has once again had two octagonal upper floors on a square base.

# ★ Museum für Angewandte Kunst · Museum of Applied Art

G 7

**Location:** An der Rechtschule
**Tram:** 5, 16, 18
(Dom/Hbf)

**Internet:** www.museenkoeln.de/museum-fuer-angewandte-kunst

**The Museum of Applied Art exhibits items from all major branches of crafts and design from the Middle Ages to the present, including furniture, fashion, ceramics, glass and jewellery.**

Opening hours:
Tue–Sun
11am–5pm

It was founded in 1888 and since 1989 has occupied the building formerly used by the Wallraf-Richartz-Museum. A statue of the art collector Ferdinand Franz Wallraf (1748–1824) holding an art portfolio stands in front of the museum next to that of the merchant Johann Heinrich Richartz (1795–1861), who donated the original museum building and is shown holding the architect's plans. On the site of

*Design of the early 20th century*

the old museum, which was bombed out, a new building was designed by **Rudolf Schwarz** and completed in 1957. Its lack of adornment pays respect to the simple style of the adjoining Franciscan church and the fact that the museum occupies the site of the former friary. A few remains of the cloister have been integrated into the inner courtyard of the museum.

◄ Collections

The exhibits, which cover 30 different areas of crafts and design, are presented on three floors. The ground floor holds a room for temporary exhibitions and a high-calibre collection on 20th-century interior design.

The first floor is a chronological presentation of **arts and crafts** from the Middle Ages to the present, with an emphasis on furniture since the Gothic period and carpets. Stoneware, porcelain, glass, silver, jewellery and small-scale sculpture are also well represented. The second floor is mainly devoted to the **fashion collection**, which is shown in changing exhibitions.

## Minoritenkirche (Franciscan Church)

**Location:** Minoritenstrasse

**Friary church**

The 13th-century Minoritenkirche, a vaulted basilica that was destroyed in the Second World War and restored in 1958, adjoins the

Museum für Angewandte Kunst to the south. It is the only remaining church of a mendicant order in Cologne. The plain style of the exterior – there is no transept or tower – and interior correspond to the ideals of the Franciscan friars for whom it was built.

Interior ► The winged retable in the choir (1480) originated in Alfeld and was brought to Cologne in the Second World War. The central panel depicts the Virgin as Queen of Heaven. To the south of the choir in the Sakramentskapelle is the tomb of **the blessed Adolph Kolping** (1813–65), who was rector of the church. Note the 14th-century painting of the Crucifixion on the southwestern pillar and, in the north aisle next to the sacristy, the Brauweiler Kreuz, a crucifix that was donated to the monastery in ► Brauweiler in 1024. Only the cross remains from the original donation; the figure of Christ dates from the 14th century. The north aisle also contains the tomb of an important medieval philosopher and theologian, **John Duns Scotus** (1266–1308), who taught at the Franciscan college here in the last year of his life. He is thought to have been born at Duns in the Scottish Borders. He studied and taught at Oxford, Cambridge and the Sorbonne before coming to Cologne.

! *Baedeker* TIP

**Museum café**

The ground-floor café in the Museum für Angewandte Kunst is a pleasant and quiet spot for a break which can be used without paying the museum admission fee. In good weather tables are placed in the courtyard.

Kolping monument ► In front of the church is a statue of Adolph Kolping, »Father of the Journeymen«. In 1849 he founded an influential Catholic social movement, which exists to this day. Its original purpose was to improve the conditions and moral education of journeymen workers.

A heavily weathered fragment of the Roman aqueduct has been placed in the little garden close to the statue.

# ★ Museum für Ostasiatische Kunst · Museum of East Asian Art

G 5/6

**Location:** Universitätsstr. 100
**Internet:** www.museenkoeln.de/museum-fuer-ostasiatische-kunst
**Tram:** 1, 7 (Universitätsstr.)

**Visitors to the oldest European museum dedicated to the art of the Far East not only encounter an excellent collection of Chinese, Korean and Japanese art, but can also enjoy it in fitting surroundings: Japanese architecture that incorporates natural beauty into the building.**

The first museum building was destroyed in the Second World War. Its successor was opened on the Aachener Weiher lake in 1977. The architect **Kunio Maekawa**, a pupil of Le Corbusier, made use of Asian elements in the low, pavilion-like structure, the red-brown ceramic tiles that clad the exterior and the Japanese garden in the inner court.

Opening hours: Tue–Sun 11am–5pm, Thu until 8pm

The expansion of the collection made an extension necessary in 1992. In contrast to the older rooms, which have few or no windows and gain an almost mystical quality through subdued lighting, the new galleries are bright and appear to merge into the garden with their long window fronts.

◄ Tour: old wing

The first exhibition rooms, entered direct from the foyer, are devoted to Chinese sculpture, Buddhist art, Chinese and Japanese painting, and calligraphy. Beyond it are Chinese prints, and a collection of Japanese screens and woodcuts.

◄ New wing

The new wing is an L-shaped gallery around the Japanese garden. The five departments that are housed here attempt to present an all-round view of other cultures by grouping works of art of different types.

The first department is concerned with the **Shang culture** (16th–11th century BC), one of the first civilizations to emerge in China, and combines a unique collection of sacred bronze artefacts with ancient jade items, early ceramics and fragments of bone oracles. The two following sections provide insights into the world of the classic Chinese elite of educated mandarins. Furniture, lacquer work, cloisonné items, jade, porcelain and a mandarin's robe are on view. Next is the **Korean collection** with some valuable celadon porcelain and the Japanese gallery, which contains **arts and crafts of the Edo period** (1603–1868).

**Aachener Weiher**

From the excellent museum café and the outdoor terrace there is a view of the Aachener Weiher, an artificial lake populated by ducks and swans. It is part of the inner ►green belt.

# ★ Museum Ludwig

G 7

**Location:** Bischofsgartenstrasse 1
**Internet:** www.museum-ludwig.de
**Tram:** 5, 16, 18 (Dom/Hbf)

**The Museum Ludwig, at the heart of the city between the cathedral and the Rhine, has a fine collection of 20th and 21st-century art.**

Opening hours: Tue–Sun 10am–6pm, 1st Fri each month until 10pm

Between 1981 and 1986 a large new cultural centre was built to house the Museum Ludwig, Philharmonie and – until 2000 – the Wallraf-Richartz-Museum.

The impulse for this came from the need to accommodate the collection of **Peter and Irene Ludwig**, which included works by Russian avant-garde artists and American Pop Art. This collection was donated to the city on the condition that new premises would be constructed for it.

As the city also wished to have a new concert hall and much-needed space for the art of the Wallraf-Richartz-Museum, a commission was awarded to the architects **Peter Busmann** and **Godfrid Haberer** to combine these functions in a single new complex, to be built on a sensitive site directly east of the cathedral. The silhouette of the museum with its zinc-clad, shed-like roofs forms an interesting contrast to the Gothic cathedral. The construction of the complex created a pedestrian zone that stretches from the Rhine to the cathedral and Hohe Strasse. Below **Heinrich-Böll-Platz**, a square on the north side of the museum designed by the Israeli artist Dani Karavan, is the Philharmonie concert hall. From the square, steps lead down to the river bank.

The museum originally accommodated both the Wallraf-Richartz-Museum and the Museum Ludwig. However, in 1994 Peter and Irene Ludwig offered to donate to the city 90 works by Pablo Picasso and 82 other works of contemporary art, as well as a further 700 as a permanent loan, on the condition that the museum should bear their name alone and be devoted entirely to modern art. The city council accepted this offer, and the ►Wallraf-Richartz-Museum moved into new premises.

**The collection**

The paintings, sculptures, drawings, graphic art and photography in the museum's possession enable it to provide a first-class overview of artistic trends since the early 20th century – from classic modern artists to the contemporary scene. The donation of a further 750 Picassos by Irene Ludwig makes the museum the **world's third-largest Picasso collection** after Barcelona and Paris.

Further strengths of the Museum Ludwig are **German Expressionism**, including works by Nolde, Kokoschka and Beckmann, and **Russian avant-garde** from the period 1906–30, represented by Malevich, Popova, Larionov, Goricharova and Rodchenko. The extensive collection of **American Pop Art** covers the whole spectrum from Johns and Rauschenberg to Warhol, Lichtenstein, Rosenquist, Segal, Kienholz and others. Major **Surrealist** paintings by Ernst, Magritte, De Chirico and Dalí are also on display. **German post-war artists** such as Schultze, Schumacher and Nay are well represented, and trends in German art from the 1960s to the present can be seen in works by Beuys, Klapheck, Graubner, Richter, Kiefer, Baselitz, Penck, Polke and Trockel. The Museum Ludwig attempts to present its art in such a way that recent movements can be seen in relation to the early period of modern art.

Photography, video art ►

The museum also has an extensive and high-quality collection of 20th-century and contemporary photography, as well as video art.

*An eye-catching stairway connects the different levels of the Museum Ludwig.*

**Philharmonie**

The impressive circular concert hall below Heinrich-Böll-Platz has a roof spanning a space of 40m/130ft diameter without central supports. The conductor stands in the middle, with the audience of up to 2000 persons seated around in the manner of an amphitheatre.

# ★ Museum Schnütgen

G 7

**Location:** Cäcilienstr. 29
**Internet:** www.museenkoeln.de/museum-schnuetgen

**Tram:** 1, 3, 4, 7, 9, 16, 18 (Neumarkt)

**The Museum Schnütgen, housed in the church of St Cäcilien and from 2009 also in part of the new Neumarkt cultural centre adjoining the church, is one of the most important collections of medieval art in Germany.**

The basis for the museum were items of religious art, mostly from secularized monasteries and churches, that **Alexander Schnütgen**

Opening hours: Tue–Fri 10am–5pm Sat and Sun 11am–5pm

(1843–1918), a canon of Cologne cathedral, presented to the city in 1906. This core has been extended since then to form an outstanding collection of works in wood, stone, ivory, glass and textiles, as well as goldsmith work, that spans seven centuries of medieval art.

The present church of St Cäcilien is a 12th-century basilica, a collegiate church for a community of canonesses from noble families that was originally founded in 888. Of the 12th-century church, the choir with fragments of friezes and the four eastern bays of the nave remain. In Roman times a large complex of baths occupied the site. With the exception of a single 10th-century arch, the convent buildings have not survived, but the adjacent parish church, St Peter, still stands (►Neumarkt).

**Exhibitions**

A new presentation of the museum treasures was prepared for the opening of the museum extension in 2009. The stated aim is to promote understanding of the medieval way of life and ways of thought, and to present a view of the Middle Ages that is more subtle and diverse than prevailing attitudes to the period. From the entrance in the new museum building, which is shared with the ► Rautenstrauch-Joest-Museum, visitors first enter a room that recreates the atmosphere of a cloister, where some of the finest pieces from the museum's excellent holdings of **stained glass and architectural sculpture** are displayed. These include windows from the abbey at ► Altenberg and carved capitals from the cloister of ►St Gereon (now demolished) and other churches of the region.

Stained glass ►

The large adjacent room is also devoted to stained glass of the 12th to 16th centuries – illuminated by daylight entering through the outer glass walls – and sculpture in stone, including a window from the former chapel of Cologne city hall (►Rathaus) depicting the Three Magi. The sculpture includes Romanesque works such as the tympanum of St Cäcilien and Gothic works, e.g. figures from the high altar of the cathedral.

The exhibition continues in the post-war museum building, taking up the theme of art in the service of liturgy. Illuminated manuscripts, church vestments and items of furniture – pulpits, lecterns, etc – can be seen here, and the museum's **outstanding collection of textiles**, ranging from Coptic and Byzantine to medieval and Baroque items, is presented. The manuscripts also cover a wide spectrum from a late Carolingian gospel to a precious book of hours that was made in Ghent or Bruges around 1500.

The church of St Cäcilien is used to show ivories, goldsmith work, bronzes and sculpture in wood, arranged thematically. The sacristy serves as a church treasury. Here, among ivories from the early Middle Ages to the Baroque period, the **Harrach Diptych** is a highlight. It was made around 800 at the court of Charlemagne, probably as part of the gold cover of a gospel. The crypt, taking »memento mori« as its motto, displays works on the transitory nature of human existence, showing many smaller works that were used for private devo-

Crypt ►

*St Cäcilien church is now a museum for religious art.*

tion. The theme of death, which assumed even greater importance than before after the plague epidemics from 1348 onwards, is illustrated by works portraying the »grim reaper«.

The north aisle is devoted to the childhood of Christ and the Holy Family, with works depicting the Madonna and Child and the Adoration of the Magi, the south aisle to the Passion and Resurrection. On the west gallery an extensive collection of saints' images shows their role as models for humankind; on the galleries at the side reliquaries of gold, crystal and enamel work can be admired. The function of the choir as the most sacred part of the church and stage for liturgy is underlined by choir stalls and works such as the **Altar of St Ursula**, which was made in Cologne around 1170. The original images were lost and replaced in the 15th century by images on a gold background: the Virgin enthroned, surrounded by St Ursula, St Severin and others. ◄ Choir

Among many fine works of sculpture in wood, note a **relief of the Adoration of the Magi**, carved between 1480 and 1485 by Meister Arndt of Kalkar and Zwolle from a single piece of oak. It depicts the Three Magi dramatically in high relief before a landscape and people with their attendants. An outstanding piece of early sculpture from Cologne is the torso of Christ from the **St Georg Crucifix**, made for the church of ► St Georg in about 1067. A cavity in the back of Christ's head was used to store holy relics.

# Neumarkt

G 7

**Location:** City centre **Tram:** 1, 3, 4, 7, 9, 16, 18 (Neumarkt)

**Neumarkt, a long, rectangular square in the heart of the historic city, is a starting point for shopping trips and the venue for a variety of events, such as markets and circuses.**

**Historic market**

Neumarkt (Newmarket) lies on the central east-west axis of the Roman city. The site has not been excavated, but may have been one of the best residential areas of Roman Cologne. It became a marketplace for livestock sales in the 11th century, and was converted to a parade ground in 1815 when the city came under Prussian rule. A few years later the citizens presented their riposte to the military drills of the unpopular Prussian forces by staging the main Carnival parade on the square.

**Neumarkt-Passage**

Käthe-Kollwitz-Museum ►

The Neumarkt-Passage on the north side of the square, near to St Aposteln church, houses cafés, shops and on the top floor the Käthe-Kollwitz-Museum, which is devoted to the work of the artist Käthe Kollwitz (1867–1945). Drawings, printed graphic art and bronze sculptures are on view. Hours: Tue–Fri 10am–6pm, Sat and Sun 11am–6pm

**Olivandenhof**

It is worth making a small detour from the north side of the square along Zeppelinstrasse to the Olivandenhof, where a huge store, Globetrotter, offers sports, camping and outdoor equipment under a glass dome to a backdrop of jungle birdsong. From the open galleries there is a view down to a pool, where customers can try out kayaks and diving kit.

**Neumarkt-Galerie**

Neumarkt-Galerie is a large shopping complex with cafés and bistros between Richmodstrasse and Zeppelinstrasse. It includes the tower of the Richmodishaus, at the top of which two white stone horses' heads can be seen. They are a reminder of the story of **Richmodis von Aducht**, who contracted the plague in 1357 and was quickly buried in the churchyard of St Aposteln after her apparent death. In

*The upturned ice cream on the Neumarkt-Galerie is starting to melt.*

the night grave robbers came to take her rings, but when they raised the coffin lid, she regained consciousness. The robbers fled in terror, and Richmodis was able to walk home and knock at the door. When the news was brought to her grieving husband, he is said to have called »I'd sooner believe that my horses will climb the tower than that my wife could come back from the dead!«. Hardly had he spoken these words than the sound of hoofs was to be heard on the stone steps, and the horses were seen looking out from the top of the tower. In reality the horses are part of the coat of arms of the Hackeney family, who once possessed a fine residence to which the tower belonged. The composer **Max Bruch** was born in the Richmodishaus in 1838.
A large Pop Art sculpture adorns the roof of the Neumarkt-Galerie: an upturned ice-cream cone by the American artist **Claes Oldenburg**.

**Josef-Haubrich-Hof**

The open space at the southeast corner of Neumarkt is named after the art collector Josef Haubrich (1889–1961), who bequeathed to the city many works that are now in the Museum Ludwig. Here a cultural complex is scheduled to open in 2009, including new premises for the ►Rautenstrauch-Joest-Museum and an extension to the ►Museum Schnütgen.

## St Peter

**Location:** Jabachstrasse 1 **Internet:** www.kunst-station.de

Opening hours:
Tue–Sat
11am–5pm,
Sun 1–5pm

St Peter and the neighbouring church St Cäcilien are the only surviving example in Cologne of a collegiate church with its attached par-

ish church. St Peter is known for its exhibitions of contemporary art, which began in 1987 at the instigation of the priest, Friedhelm Mennekes, and have become a Cologne institution.
Of the 12th-century church built on the site of the Roman baths, only the west tower remains. It was incorporated into the present church, a gallery basilica of the early 16th century. The belfry of the tower dates from the 17th century. The greatest treasure inside is an altarpiece of 1638 by **Peter Paul Rubens**. It depicts the *Crucifixion of St Peter*, and was commissioned by the Jabach family, who were wealthy merchants.

# Opera House · Theatre

G 7

**Location:** Offenbachplatz
**Internet:** www.buehnenkoeln.de
**Tram:** 1, 3, 4, 7, 9, 16, 18 (Neumarkt or Appellhofplatz)

**The fine old opera house on Rudolfplatz was damaged in the Second World War. The city authorities decided not to restore it, and commissioned Wilhelm Riphahn and Hans Menne to build a new one between 1954 and 1957 on Offenbachplatz. A few years later the smaller municipal theatre (Schauspielhaus) was built directly to the south of it.**

**Municipal theatre ensemble**

Although the style of the Oper (opera house) is sober, it is designed to impress. The upper tiers of the auditorium project from the wood-panelled walls like drawers, and the generously proportioned foyers are large enough for a small stage with seating to have been inserted for performances of children's opera. Externally, the sloping-sided buildings that flank the stage catch the eye. After over 50 years of use, the opera house was in urgent need of restoration. Demolition was considered, but growing appreciation for the architecture of the 1950s and high regard for the work of Wilhelm Riphahn led to a decision to restore the building. From 2010 to 2013 the opera company will perform at the Palladium in Mülheim on the right bank of the Rhine. The Schauspielhaus is an unassuming building of 1960–62, to the rear of which, in Krebsgasse, there is a small experimental theatre, the **Schlosserei**.

Old synagogue ▸ In Glockengasse on the side of the opera house a memorial plaque recalls the synagogue of 1859, which was devastated in the »Reich pogrom night« of 1938.

Fountain ▸ On Offenbachplatz in front of the opera house, a fountain by **Hansjürgen Grummer** (1966) incorporates mosaic work using material taken from a number of sources, including ruined churches such as the Kaiser-Wilhelm-Gedächtniskirche in Berlin and bathroom tiles from the yacht of Aristotle Onassis.

## 4711-Haus

**Location:** Glockengasse 22 **Internet:** www.4711.com

**Eau de Cologne**

In Glockengasse opposite the opera house stands a decorative neo-Gothic building with a white façade picked out in green and gold, high arcades and little turrets. Every hour between 9am and 9pm a **Glockenspiel** plays, and wooden figures revolve around the clock. The building is a post-war reconstruction of the headquarters of a famous old perfume company that sold eau de Cologne under the brand name »4711«.

◄ Company history

The recipe for 4711 perfume is said to have been given to the founder of the company, Wilhelm Mühlens, in 1792 by a Carthusian monk as a wedding present. In the 19th century, when the company was forced to rename the product for legal reasons, it chose 4711, the number given to the house in 1794, when the French occupying forces numbered all the houses in the city. Inside are sales rooms and a small exhibition about eau de Cologne on a gallery.

# Overstolzenhaus

G 7

**Location:** Rheingasse 8 **Tram:** 1, 7, 9 (Heumarkt)

**The Overstolzenhaus of 1220, now home to a school of media studies (Medienakademie), is the best example in Germany of a Romanesque patrician residence.**

**Romanesque house**

A typical feature of the houses of rich merchants in the Middle Ages was the combination of residential and commercial premises in one building. This is apparent in the imposing gabled façade with fine round-arched windows and the rooms behind it. The ground floor was used as an entrance area with hallways, and the large rooms on the first floor displayed the wealth and status of the Overstolz family. A 13th-century mural depicts a knightly tournament. Above this are four storeys with space to store goods, with an opening at the top for a hoist. The storerooms and the cellars together made up the larger part of the house. Repeated alterations over eight centuries and war damage mean that the interior

*Baedeker* TIP

**Traditional pub**

It is only a few paces from the Overstolzenhaus to the brewery and pub at the corner of Malzbüchel and Paradiesgasse, at the south end of Heumarkt. Named Malzmühle after the malt mill that once stood on this spot, the beer brewed here, Mühlen-Kölsch, is highly prized by locals, and hearty Rhineland meals are served in the wood-panelled rooms. When Bill Clinton came to Cologne in 1999, this pub was chosen to give him a taste of local tradition (hours: Mon–Sat 10am–midnight, Sun 11am–11pm).

has kept little of its original character. It is probable that these were not the rooms in which the family normally ate and slept, but were used for hospitality and ostentation.

### St Trinitatis

**Location:** Filzengraben 6

**First Protestant church in Cologne**

Nearby, on Filzengraben, the Trinitatiskirche was the first church in Cologne to be built for Protestants. Until 1797 only Roman Catholics possessed civil rights in the city. The French occupation changed this, and Protestants were permitted to practise their faith from 1802. In this period the Antoniterkirche on ►Schildergasse was used by the congregation. After 1815 Cologne and the Rhineland were ruled by Protestant Prussian kings and their administrators, but only in 1857–60 were plans for a new church by **Friedrich August Stüler**, a pupil of Schinkel, carried out with the support of the king of Prussia. In order to distinguish the church from the Romanesque places of worship and Gothic cathedral of the Catholic citizens, the style of an early Christian basilica was chosen.

Interior ►

Originally the church interior was brightly coloured, but during restoration after the Second World War a more subdued decorative scheme was preferred.

## ★ Praetorium

G 7

**Location:** Kleine Budengasse
**Tram:** 5, 16, 18 (Dom/Hbf)
**Bus:** 132 (Rathaus)

**Important remains of Roman times lie below the ground close to the city hall: the ruins of the Praetorium, the palace of the governor of the Roman province of Lower Germany.**

Opening hours: Tue–Sun 10am–5pm

During reconstruction of the municipal offices known as the Spanischer Bau (► Rathaus) in 1953, archaeologists uncovered the remains of the Praetorium, the **centre of military and civil government** for Lower Germany, the region west of the Rhine from Remagen (south of Bonn) to the North Sea. Four phases of construction from the early 1st to the mid-4th century AD have been identified. An area measuring 180 × 180m (200 × 200yd) was investigated, and in 2007 renewed excavations in the area began in preparation for an archaeological zone which may open in 2011. At present a small part of the site is accessible to visitors beneath the Spanischer Bau.
An exhibition space next to the excavations is devoted to displays on Roman building, including a dedicatory inscription on the occasion

of the restoration of the Praetorium in AD 184–185. There are also changing exhibitions on themes such as Roman glass and tableware, charts showing the history of the province and a model of the Praetorium building.

*The centre of power in Roman Cologne, now open for visitors beneath the city hall square*

A tour of the excavations reveals the foundations and some small parts of the above-ground walls of the palace, which had a 90m/100yd-long Rhine façade and an octagonal hall at the centre. A large crack in the foundations is thought to be the result of an earthquake around the year 800. The remains of stone wells can be seen amidst the Roman masonry: after the disintegration of Roman power, the building was probably occupied by Merovingian kings until the 7th century, and from the 9th to the 14th century this was the densely populated Jewish quarter (► Rathaus).

**Roman sewer**

From the exhibition room steps and a low concrete tunnel lead to a Roman sewer, largely intact despite alterations and its use as a cellar in later centuries. It consists of large blocks of tufa stone, and is between 2m/6ft 6in and 2.5m/8ft high inside, which makes it possible to walk a length of over 100m/100yd. The sewer drained waste water from the streets above and effluent from Roman homes into the harbour. A section of the sewer has been placed above ground at the corner of Budengasse and Unter Goldschmied.

## Roman Aqueduct

On the wall next to the steps that lead to the sewer is a slice from the aqueduct of Roman Cologne. In the 1st century a short aqueduct channelled into the city the water of streams that flowed 10km/6mi to the west. In the 2nd century it was replaced by a major work of engineering, over 95km/60mi long, beginning at springs in the Eifel region at an altitude of 420m/1400ft and crossing hilly landscape and the watershed between the rivers Maas and Rhine by means of bridges and tunnels. It carried almost 20 million litres (over 5 million US gallons) of water each day.

The cross-section of tunnel in the Praetorium is well enough preserved to show the structure of the aqueduct: a U-shaped concrete channel covered by a concrete tunnel vault, with a red waterproofed layer at the bottom and a layer of brown lime deposit that indicates the water level.

After Roman times the aqueduct decayed, and pieces of the lime deposit were removed, polished, and used as a substitute for marble to decorate churches throughout the region. Its remains were regarded in the Middle Ages as the work of the devil. Names along its course such as Teufelsrinne (Devil's Channel) or Teufelsgraben (Devil's Ditch) testify to this, as does a popular legend about the first cathedral architect, Meister Gerhard. He is said to have wagered with the devil that the cathedral would be finished before the aqueduct. He lost the bet, and plunged to his death from the scaffolding on the cathedral choir.

# ★ Rathaus · City Hall

G 7

**Location:** Rathausplatz
**Bus:** 132
**Tram:** 5, 16, 18 (Dom/Hbf) or 1, 7, 9 (Heumarkt)

**Cologne's city hall occupies approximately the site that was used in Roman times as the centre of administration. In its present form it originated between the 14th and 16th centuries, and was rebuilt, partly in modern style, after severe damage in WW II.**

**Germany's oldest city hall**

A »house of the citizens in the Jewish quarter« mentioned in a document of 1135 makes the Rathaus of Cologne (»Rat« means »council«) the oldest city hall in Germany. The rich merchant families (patricians) gained far-reaching political independence from the rule of the archbishops in the late 13th century, and the old city hall was succeeded by a more imposing building around 1350. In 1396 the craft guilds took power and, to mark their victory over the patrician families, built the tower between 1407 and 1414. In 1540 the Löwenhof (Lion Court) was added, and from 1569 to 1573 the Rathauslaube (loggia), which is regarded as **the most beautiful example of Renaissance architecture in the Rhineland**.

◄ Tour

A guided tour of all historic parts of the city hall can be organized through KölnTourismus (► Practicalities, Information). Visitors are permitted to enter the lobby and gallery of the Lion Court without a guide: Mon, Wed and Thu 8am–4pm, Tue 8am–6pm, Fri 8am–noon.

◄ Renaissance loggia

The upper storey of the richly adorned Renaissance loggia on the west of the city hall was used to proclaim the decisions taken by the council. Behind it steps lead to the Hansasaal. All three sides of the two-storey loggia have round arches with columns, and are decorated by friezes. At the front a relief depicts the legend of **Mayor Gryn** fighting a lion, an allegory of the struggle of the citizens for freedom from clerical rule. The story relates that Gryn was tricked by two priests into entering an inner court in which a hungry lion was kept.

← *The Renaissance loggia and 15th-century tower of the city hall*

# CARNIVAL TIME

**Carnival is the »fifth season of the year« for the people of Cologne, an occasion for uninhibited celebrations that show their love of a party and their passionate attachment to their home town. For visitors the days before Ash Wednesday, when the Carnival celebrations spill out onto the streets, seem like an eruption of madness in every corner of the city.**

At Carnival time the whole of Cologne is a scene of costumed revelry, the city centre is closed for parades, and unsuspecting strangers who enter a pub can hardly believe their eyes. The origins of the event lie far back in the mists of time.

The ancient Romans held boisterous celebrations named **Bacchanals** or **Saturnalia**, at which the established social order was up-ended for a limited time. Bacchus was the god of wine and ecstasy, Saturn the god of agriculture and fertility. A second influence on Carnival – which today takes place between the end of January and early March, depending on the date of Easter – is the driving out of the spirits of winter and the ushering in of spring.

Carnival also seems to have served as a valve, a social mechanism for relieving tensions. The name of the festival shows that it was adapted to

the purposes of Christianity: Carnival is derived from »carne vale«, meaning »farewell to meat«. The name is known from the 12th century to describe the period of unrestrained carousing before the beginning of Lent, the 40-day period of fasting that preceded Easter.

## Prince, Maiden, Farmer

Carnival in its present, institutionalized form dates back to the early 19th century, when the first big parades were organized. The precursors of these processions in the Middle Ages were the activities of guilds, families and neighbourhoods, whose members donned masks and paraded through the streets making music. The biggest parade of modern Carnival, on the Monday before Ash Wednesday (Rosenmontag), was held for the first time in 1823, also the year when the ruling triumvirate of the Carnival season – prince, maiden and farmer – first appeared. The three figures, known collectively as the Dreigestirn, have medieval-style costumes. The prince wears a doublet and hose, and sports a fine cap adorned with long peacock feathers. The maiden (Jungfrau), who is always a man wearing a blonde wig with pigtails, represents Colonia, the city of Cologne. The farmer (Bauer) is a sturdy figure who traditionally symbolizes both the ability of the city to defend itself stout-heartedly, and also the coarser side of Carnival. The uncontrolled drinking of earlier times was channelled into entertainments (Sitzungen) for respectable middle-class citizens in the 19th century. The participants, usually costumed, sit at long tables under the presidency of a Committee of Eleven and are treated to dancing, singing, humorous declamations and comedy acts.

Many citizens are members of Carnival associations such as the **Rote Funken** (literally »Red Sparks«). They originated as a parody of the soldiers who defended the city walls, and to this day parade in fine red-coated uniforms with braiding and medals. The **Blaue Funken** started out as an ironic comment on the unpopular Prussian forces, mocking a regiment of dragoons in their blue coats. Many other associations, each with its own

uniform and traditions, have sprung up since the 19th century. The practice of throwing sweets and flowers into the mass of spectators at parades also derives from a love of mocking established institutions: in earlier centuries, nobles would throw money and food into the crowds.

Alongside the official Carnival the old, carefree revelry goes on in the pubs and on the streets of all the quarters of the city. This spontaneous singing and dancing, and the costumed groups who march around banging drums and making music, reflect the origins of the festival more accurately than the big parades and the organized entertainments.

## Eleven: the Crazy Number

In the Rhineland, the number eleven is regarded as the crazy number. The Carnival season starts long before the outdoor celebrations in February, with an official opening on 11 November at 11.11am. From January entertainments begin behind closed doors, and everything culminates in the **days of street festivities** all over the city before Lent begins. This begins on the Thursday, called Weiberfastnacht, the day when women rule the city. Long before the official start – again at 11.11am – crowds of costumed women gather on Alter Markt, linking arms to sway to the music and sing. There is a large number of Carnival hits, usually sung in the Kölsch dialect. New songs appear every year, but the old favourites keep their popularity, and many fans of Carnival know all the words, or at least the chorus, by heart. On Weiberfastnacht it is not advisable for men to wear a tie, as the women carry scissors to cut them off.

In the afternoon at 3pm the story of Jan and Griet that is depicted on the

*Carnival festivities in the Gürzenich hall*

monument at Alter Markt is played out in the south of the city at the medieval gate, Severinstorburg. Shops and most offices close at midday, and in the evening a round of masked balls and entertainments gets under way. Pubs are packed to the doors, even though many of them remove all their tables and chairs as a precaution.

On the Saturday the Carnival associations set up tents on Neumarkt, and in the evening the Geisterzug, the »parade of ghosts«, sets off through the streets to provide a flesh-creeping spectacle. This parade is an anarchic rebellion against the official Carnival of the establishment. It is staged under a political motto, and is often accompanied by demonstrations.

On Sunday an attractive parade known in dialect as the »Schull- und Veedelszöch« (**parade of the schools and city quarters**) takes place. It is a colourful sight, with many decorated floats on a particular theme chosen for that year, as the schools and other groups go to great lengths to make interesting costumes and banners.

The highlight of the »fifth season« is **Rosenmontag, the day of the biggest parade**. It lasts for several hours and draws hundreds of thousands of spectators, who take pre-booked seats in the stands or simply line the roadside. Those who still have the energy sing and dance in the pubs until the early hours, or don their best costume for a ball.

## Ash Wednesday

A true Carnivalist needs stamina. On Shrove Tuesday more parades are held, this time not in the centre but in other neighbourhoods, and the days of madness end at midnight, when a straw effigy named Nubbel is burned following a mock funeral procession. Nubbel is the scapegoat for the sins committed in the previous days. On Ash Wednesday the celebrations are over and, officially, the period of fasting begins. The people of Cologne like to mark this occasion by going out with friends for a hearty meal of fish and exchanging tales of how they spent this year's Carnival.

For those who aren't able to see it all live, the excellent Karnevalsmuseum (►p.113) will give more information.

He slew the lion, and the priests were hanged from the city gate. Medallions of Roman emperors above the columns are a reference to the Roman origins of the city.

The central arch of the loggia leads to the modern lobby, where a copy of the *Altar of the City Patrons* by Stefan Lochner has been placed. The original is in the ► Dom. Beyond is the **Piazzetta**, a large covered space built after most of the city hall was destroyed by bombs. Here the walls are decorated with portraits of mayors, and the original figure of the Kölscher Boor (► Eigelstein Quarter) can be seen. To the north is the gallery of the **Löwenhof**, where the **Petrusbrunnen** (St Peter's Fountain), the remains of an alabaster altar to the Virgin of 1662 from the cathedral, has been placed.

! *Baedeker* TIP

### Flowers and confetti

In Germany all marriages must be sealed in a civil ceremony. The most popular registry office in Cologne is the Rentkammer in the tower of the city hall. On Fridays and Saturdays, especially in May and June, the little square outside the city hall is the scene of colourful celebrations, as bridal couples are greeted by their friends with confetti, flowers, champagne and music.

The hall above the foyer was named **Hansasaal** in the 19th century as a reminder of the Hanseatic League, which met there to decide on a war against Denmark in 1367. The restored north wall is adorned with a rosette of Gothic tracery and wooden figures of the Eight Prophets (1410), which once stood in the Prophetenkammer. On the south wall are the 14th-century statues of the **Nine Heroes**, three each from ancient heathen times (Alexander the Great, Hector, Julius Caesar), the period of the Old Testament (Judas Maccabeus, David, Joshua) and Christian times (Gottfried of Bouillon, King Arthur, Charlemagne). Above are Emperor Ludwig the Bavarian and two personifications of the rights granted to the city by Ludwig (the Right of Staple is a figure with a river, the right of fortification has a tower).

Prophetenkammer ► To the north the Prophetenkammer connects the Hansasaal to the Senatssaal in the tower.

Muschelsaal, Weisser Saal ► The modern wing of the city hall, giving onto Alter Markt, houses offices. The Muschelsaal (Shell Room) and Weisser Saal (White Room) were rebuilt with alterations after the war, and are decorated with plasterwork and tapestries.

✶ **Tower**

The 61m/200ft-high tower was the tallest building in the city when it was completed in the early 15th century, as it originally surpassed both the tower of Gross St Martin and the unfinished cathedral.

Tower statues ► The tower was reduced to rubble in the Second World War and rebuilt between 1950 and 1975. The statues were added in 1995, but had to be remade in 2008 due to the poor quality of the stone and mistakes in treating it. They represent 124 persons who were influential in the 2000-year history of the city. Christ, surrounded by apostles and saints, looks down from the top storey. Beneath him are ar-

## *Rathaus* Plan

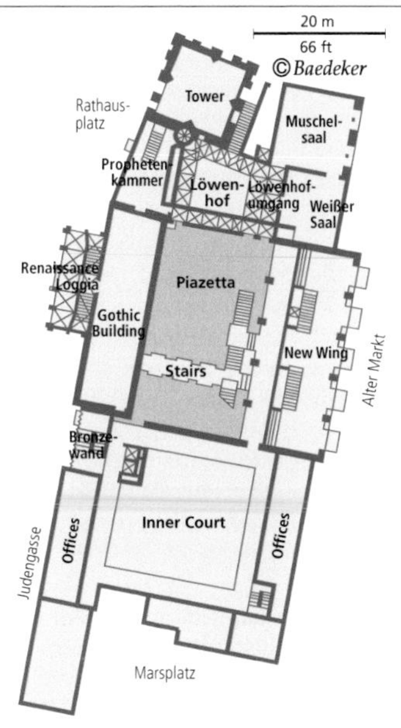


**Gothic Wing**
Ground floor: vestibule
Ist floor: Hansasaal

**Tower:**
Basement: Turmkeller
Ground floor: Rentkammer
1st floor: Senatssaal

tists, politicians, industrialists, priests and others, including **Heinrich Böll** and **Irmgard Keun** as the most recent personalities, **Karl Marx** and **Konrad Adenauer**, **Stefan Lochner**, **Sulpiz Boisserée** and **Jacques Offenbach**. The ground floor is devoted to emperors and kings, among them Emperor **Augustus**, **Charlemagne** and **Henry II of England**, the first English king to confer trading privileges in his kingdom on the merchants of Cologne.

The rooms of the tower, from which a Glockenspiel plays each day at 9am, noon, 3pm and 6pm, are the Senatssaal, an archive and arsenal, and the city wine cellar. The Rentkammer on the ground floor (so called because the municipal finances were once administered from there) is now a registry office.

**Spanischer Bau**

In the early 17th century a building was constructed opposite the city hall. It became known as the Spanischer Bau, because in 1623 an alliance of Catholic states, the Spanish League, convened here. It served various functions as well as being the seat of the city council. In the Second World War it was destroyed. The rebuilt Spanischer Bau of 1953 houses the council chamber and municipal offices. With its restrained brick exterior and carefully designed interior spaces, it is regarded as a highlight of 1950s architecture in the city. Below it lie the remains of the Roman ►Praetorium.

## Mikwe

**Location:** Rathausplatz

Opening hours: Fri 11.30am–4pm, Sat and Sun 10am–4pm (key available in the Praetorium)

The main surviving structure of the medieval Jewish quarter, which occupied the site of the Spanischer Bau and the square in front of the city hall, is the Mikwe (mikva), a **bath for ritual ablutions**. It was discovered during excavations of the 1950s, which dated the bath and the adjacent synagogue to the 9th century. In its present form the mikva dates from around 1170. Believers who had touched a corpse or offended against dietary regulations, and women after their period or the birth of a child, were considered unclean. Cleansing took place through immersion in »living water«, i.e. water that had collected naturally; the Hebrew word »mikva« means »a collection of water«. To gather natural ground water, a 16m/52ft-deep shaft was dug. Stone steps lead down around the walls of the shaft to the basin, which can be full of water or almost empty depending on the level of ground water and the river Rhine. Originally there was probably a tower above the shaft.

**Synagogue**

The synagogue next to the mikva was re-excavated in 2007–08 to prepare an archaeological zone that will combine the Roman structures beneath the city hall and Spanischer Bau with remains of the medieval Jewish quarter; it is scheduled to be completed in 2011. A planned new Jewish Museum may be incorporated in the complex. It is known that there was a Jewish community in Roman Cologne. It was first documented in AD 321 and the city's Jewish quarter is considered to be the oldest north of the Alps.

## Museum of Eau de Cologne

**Location:** Obermarspforten (Farina-Haus) **Internet:** www.farina1709.com

**An Farina**

Opening hours: Mon–Sat 11am–6pm

Opposite the city hall stands a 1980s development named An Farina. It accommodates offices, shops and flats. In the inner court the **Frauenbrunnen** (Women's Fountain) portrays Cologne women from Roman times to the present. An Farina takes its name from the adjoining building at the corner of Unter Goldschmied and Obenmarspforten. A previous house on this site was used for the production and sale of the first Cologne perfume, which was invented in 1709 by an Italian immigrant, **Giovanni Maria Farina** (1685–1766). The premises are still in the possession of his descendants, who sell perfume made to the original recipe in the **world's oldest perfume factory**.

Production no longer takes place here, but an interesting exhibition displays pictures, documents showing that the Farinas supplied the royal courts of Europe, and historic perfume bottles (guided tours on request).

# Rautenstrauch-Joest-Museum

G 7

**Location:** Cäcilienstr.
**Internet:** www.museenkoeln.de/rautenstrauch-joest-museum
**Tram:** 1, 3, 4, 7, 9, 16, 18 (Neumarkt)

**From summer 2009 Cologne's ethnological museum displays its huge collection on themes from a wide range of non-European cultures in new premises.**

The museum opened in 1906 with a collection largely donated by the scientist and traveller **Wilhelm Joest** and his brother-in-law **Eugen Rautenstrauch**. The museum holdings encompass 65,000 objects, about 100,000 historic photographs and an extensive library, including an excellent **Oceania department** with 20,000 items from Australia, Melanesia, Micronesia and Polynesia. Africa, the Near East and pre-Columbian civilizations of South and Central America are also well represented. The aim of the museum, one of the leading institutions of its kind in Germany, is not only to engage in research,

Opening hours:
Tue–Fri 10am–4pm,
Sat 11am–4pm,
Sun 11am–6pm

*Stored in the Rautenstrauch-Joest-Museum*

but to promote understanding of and respect for other peoples by presenting their culture. In the new premises areas on the upper floors will be organized thematically, permitting a comparison of the attitudes in different cultures to such issues as social identity, death and religion.

# Rhine Promenade

F–J 8

**Location:** between Zoobrücke and Severinsbrücke

**At weekends and on holidays the people of Cologne love to walk and cycle along the tree-lined promenades on both sides of the Rhine.**

**Left bank** For visitors the most attractive part of the left bank lies between the Zoobrücke in the north and the Severinsbrücke, although it is possible to continue much further in both directions. Here strollers have a good view of the river shipping and the opposite bank, and many opportunities to take refreshments in the cafés and traditional pubs of the Old Town.

Konrad-Adenauer-Ufer ► At the Zoobrücke, close to the ►Flora and ►Zoo, the embankment road called Konrad-Adenauer-Ufer leads south to the Hohenzollernbrücke by the cathedral. Walking south, note the **Bastei** (Konrad-Adenauer-Ufer 80), an Expressionist-style circular building of 1924 by the Cologne architect **Wilhelm Riphahn** with a star-shaped platform that projects over the promenade. It was once a gourmet restaurant, and is now used for conferences and other events. A little further on are the twin towers of ►St Kunibert. On the opposite side of the Rhine there is a good view of the Tanzbrunnen in the Rheinpark and the old trade fair buildings (►Deutz). The imposing stone building further along at Konrad-Adenauer-Ufer 3 was the seat of the royal Prussian railway company from 1913. South of the Hohenzollernbrücke the Rhine promenade is called **Frankenwerft** (►Altstadt · Old Town). Just beyond the bridge, steps lead up to the ►Museum Ludwig, and the following section of the Rhine promenade as far as the Deutzer Brücke has as its backdrop the little gabled houses of the Old Town in the shadow of the tower of ►Gross St Martin and a row of garden cafés and restaurants.

Between the Deutzer Brücke and the Severinsbrücke lie the ►Schokoladenmuseum, on the left across the old harbour swing-bridge, and the little pink-coloured church ►St Maria Lyskirchen on the right across the embankment road. To see the part of the city that is developing most dynamically, with an interesting mix of old and new architecture and good river views, it is well worth extending the walk southwards through the harbour area (►Schokoladenmuseum · Rheinauhafen).

# ★ Römische Grabkammer · Roman Burial Chamber

Excursion

**Location:** Aachener Str. 1328, Köln-Weiden

**Bus:** 141, 963 from Weiden-Zentrum to Frechener Weg: tram 1 to Weiden

**The burial chamber of a Roman land-owning family with its original artefacts, which dates from the 2nd century AD and is in an excellent state of preservation, is one of the most remarkable Roman tombs outside Italy.**

The burial chamber was discovered in 1843, but the Roman villa rustica to which it belonged has not so far been identified. Steep, dark steps lead down to a chamber about 12 sq m/130 sq ft in size and 6m/20ft below the ground. Its arrangement as a Roman dining room expresses the hope of enjoying a pleasant afterlife: three couches, on which diners lay, have been cut into the wall and clad with marble. In the corners of the room are two basket chairs carved from limestone. Portrait busts of a couple and a young woman are placed on the couches. The 29 small niches in the walls held urns with the ashes of the deceased. The **marble sarcophagus** dates from the 3rd century and originally stood in a small funerary temple above the chamber. It has depictions of the deceased couple and the seasons of the year. When the grave site decayed and the roof collapsed, the sarcophagus fell into the chamber below. The sarcophagus and the lower chamber represent two different traditions of burial: from the 2nd century the dead were no longer buried but cremated. The niches for urns thus belong to the more recent, the sarcophagus to the older practice.

In the room above the chamber, grave goods are on display, and photographs and charts explain the origin and meaning of the tomb.

Opening hours:
Tue–Thu 10am–1,
Fri 10am–5pm,
Sat and Sun 1–5pm

# Römische Stadtmauer · Roman City Wall

F – H 6 – 8

**Location:** see plan p.27

**The Roman city wall was probably built soon after AD 50, when the »oppidum ubiorum« was elevated to the status of a Roman colonia with municipal rights at the wish of Agrippina, the wife of Emperor Claudius. It was almost 4km/2.5mi long, and had 9 gates and 19 defensive towers. Remains of the wall can be seen in many places in the city.**

**Method of construction** The wall consisted of an inner and an outer shell of regularly shaped greywacke stones, and an inner core of cement mixed with rubble. It was 2.4m/8ft thick, about 7.8m/26ft high, and protected the city until the building of the ►Medieval City Wall in 1180. The most important remains of the wall are described below.

North gate ► The north gate was close to the cathedral, roughly opposite the entrance to the tourist office. It had three entrances: two side entrances about 2m/6ft 6in wide, and a central opening 5.60m/18ft wide and 8.60m/28ft high, the arch of which is today in the ►Römisch-Germanisches Museum. In the 12th century the gate was converted into a house for the cathedral dean and retained this function until 1826, when the middle arch was demolished. In the 1970s one of the two side entrances was erected close to its original position opposite the north tower of the cathedral.

Underground car park ► Some foundations of the north gate and a section of wall can be inspected in the car park that lies below the cathedral square. This is the best place to see how the wall was built. Here a shaft-like structure can be seen that was clearly built onto the wall at a later date, leading beneath its foundation. This is believed to have been the route by which **Archbishop Anno**, threatened by angry citizens, escaped from the cathedral precinct during a revolt in 1074. The circular stone shaft visible close by in the car park belongs to a well that stood in the atrium on the west side of the 9th-century cathedral. A fragment of the wall further to the east can be seen inside the cathedral cellars, now the treasury (Domschatzkammer).

Lysolphturm ► From the north gate walk west along Komödienstrasse. At the junction with the busy north-south traffic artery (Nord-Süd-Fahrt) are parts of a tower, named **Lysolphturm** after a family that lived in it in the Middle Ages. The sections of wall immediately adjacent on both sides were demolished in the 1960s to make way for the Nord-Süd-Fahrt and U-Bahn.

Wall of Zeughaus ► The south wall of the ►Zeughaus facing the street An der Burgmauer has a Roman core, which is not visible. The fountain to the east of the Zeughaus, the Römerbrunnen, was created in 1915 with the ground plan of a Roman tower, and restored in 1955 after severe damage in the Second World War. On its walls are portraits of Roman emperors and an inscription from the *Annals* of **Tacitus** relating to Cologne. The wall to the west of the Zeughaus is Roman.

Helenenturm ► At the Römerturm (►Zeughaus), which marks the north-west corner of the Roman city wall, turn left into St.-Apern-Str. It is only a few paces to the Helenenturm at the corner of St.-Apern-Str. and Helenenstr., which was probably the only semicircular tower of the Roman wall and was open on the city side. Follow St.-Apern-Str. and Apostelnstr. to the east end of the church St Aposteln, where a walled-up doorway about 2.35m/8ft above street level has a curious origin. The last above-ground remains of the Roman wall were not demolished here until 1835. The walled-up opening in the east apse of the church is believed to have been used by the canons of St Apos-

*The Römerturm, the tower at the northwestern corner of Roman Cologne, is the best-preserved part of the Roman city wall.*

teln as a convenient entrance, and its position is a clue to the height of the wall over which they passed: 7.8m/26ft.

◀ Mauritiussteinweg

Continue south into Mauritiussteinweg, where a 140m/460ft-long section of wall has been preserved between no.18 and no. 52 – to the east, behind the houses.

◀ Duffesbach

The busy road at the end of Mauritiussteinweg is called, from west to east, **Rothgerberbach (red tanners' stream)**, **Blaubach (blue stream)** and **Mühlenbach (millstream)** after the trades of leather-tanning, dyeing and milling for which the now subterranean Duffesbach stream was once used. The elevated north bank of this stream was the site of the southern section of the Roman wall. This is evident when walking from Mauritiussteinweg towards the Rhine, as fragments of walls and towers, and the height difference in the terrain, are clearly visible.

◀ Ubiermonument

Beneath the house An der Malzmühle 1 at the corner of Mühlenbach are remains of a square tower that has been dated with some certainty to AD 5, i.e. to the beginnings of the »oppidum ubiorum«. It may have been built to guard the entrance to the Roman harbour, but was partially destroyed and the ground here raised by in-filling when the wall was built later in the 1st century. It is considered to be the first defensive tower in Germany, indeed perhaps the country's earliest Roman stone building. The high quality of the masonry is a clear indication that it was the work of Roman military architects. It stands on a concrete platform measuring 10.90 × 10.60m (35 × 36ft) and is now 6.5m/21ft high, but was originally certainly much taller. There is a small exhibition room with architectural fragments from nearby Roman buildings. The key can be obtained from the Praetorium.

# ★★ Römisch-Germanisches Museum

G 7

**Location:** Roncalliplatz 4
**Tram:** 5, 16, 18 (Dom/Hbf)
**Bus:** 132
**Internet:** www.museenkoeln.de/roemisch-germanisches-museum

**Cologne's museum devoted to the Roman and early Germanic period stands next to the cathedral on the site of a 3rd-century villa. In addition to Roman and Merovingian finds, including outstanding ancient glass and jewellery, it has an extensive prehistoric collection.**

Opening hours: Tue–Sun 10am–5pm

The large windows on Roncalliplatz allow visitors to see the two largest exhibits, the Dionysos Mosaic and the Poblicius Monument, from outside.

## Museum Tour

**Dionysos Mosaic**

The exhibits are thematically grouped to provide information on such subjects as art, commerce, travel, war and religion in Roman times.

From different levels of the staircase there is a view of the Dionysos Mosaic, which was uncovered in its present location in 1941 when an air-raid shelter was built. The 10.5 × 7m/34 × 23ft mosaic consists of about 1.5 million stone, glass and ceramic pieces. It was the floor of one room of a peristyle house (i.e. with an arcaded inner courtyard) of the 1st to 3rd centuries, which measured 40 × 65m/130 × 215ft, and thus had approximately the dimensions of the present museum. The excellent state of preservation of the mosaic is probably due to the fact that it was buried when the house collapsed as the Franks overran the city in 355. The scenes on the mosaic, which was clearly executed by highly accomplished artists, depict dancing satyrs and maenads, fruit and animals, all of which were associated with the cult of the wine and fertility god Dionysos. The god himself is shown in the middle, drunk and leaning on a satyr for support. It is not known whether the room was simply an impressive dining room for celebrations and banquets, with the mosaic as an invitation to enjoy life's pleasures, or was primarily used for rites of the Dionysian cult. One one recent occasion it has been used as a dining room: when the G8 summit was held in Cologne in 1999, a glass table was placed over the mosaic so that the world leaders could lunch there in style.

**Poblicius Monument**

Next to the Dionysos Mosaic a huge funeral monument rises to the roof of the museum. Part of it was found in 1884, the rest between 1964 and 1967 on Chlodwigplatz, close to the main Roman road leading south. Although many stones are missing, the 14.6m/48ft-high monument and its inscription have been reconstructed. It was erected, probably around AD 40, by **Lucius Poblicius**, who had served in the 5th Legion and must have had considerable wealth. The figure of Poblicius stands on the upper storey between Corinthian columns, clad in a toga and holding a scroll. Reliefs with scenes and figures from the cult of Dionysos on the sides of the monument stand for the hope that the deceased would have eternal life and happiness.

The ceramic items, furniture, toys and kitchen utensils exhibited on the **lower floor** illustrate different aspects of everyday life in Roman times. The numerous stelae and grave goods throw light on the Roman funeral cult.

On the **upper floor** different groups of exhibits are devoted to particular themes: religion, streets and town planning, architecture, crafts and trade, travel, etc.

*The highlights of the Römisch-Germanisches Museum: the funeral monument of Poblicius and the Dionysos mosaic*

The **collection of Roman glass**, the largest of its kind in Europe, is a highlight of the museum. Note in particular the unique **cage glass** (Diatretglas), which was probably made about AD 340. The clear inner body of the glass is covered with a fine outer network of green glass, created with almost incredible skill and patience by first covering the inner layer with the green glass, then grinding away the green outer layer until it remained only as a delicate cage or net, attached to the body of clear glass within by means of thin ties. The cage glass in the museum bears the Greek inscription »Drink, and you will always live well«. It is likely that Cologne was the sole place of production for such glasses. A further speciality of the Cologne area in Roman times was the manufacture of **snake-thread glasses,**, cups and bottles that were decorated by adding coloured threads of glass to the surface.

◄ Philosophers' Mosaic

The Philosophers' Mosaic opposite the glass collection dates from the 3rd century and was found in the city centre in 1844. It measures 7 × 6.8m/23 × 22ft. Its almost 2 million pieces form a complex geometrical pattern portraying the Greek philosophers and poets Diogenes, Cleobulos, Socrates, Cheilon, Sophocles, Plato and Aristotle; the last two portraits were added in the 19th century to fill gaps.

One of the themed blocks provides information on the ruling imperial house, including busts of **Augustus** and his empress **Livia**, who were in power when Cologne was founded, and one of Emperor **Claudius**, who granted Roman municipal rights to the settlement. The reconstruction of a covered Roman carriage is also a remarkable exhibit.

North gate ► The central arch of the north gate of the Roman city (►Roman City Wall) has been erected behind the imperial busts. It bears the letters CCAA, the abbreviation of the name of Roman Cologne and at the same time the story of its foundation: C(olonia) = city with Roman municipal rights; C(laudia) = founded in the reign of Emperor Claudius; A(ra) = with an altar for the imperial cult; A(grippinensium) = at the behest of Agrippina (who was born in Cologne, married Claudius and initiated the granting of colonia status). Behind the arch, the reconstruction of a tower from the city wall is used a space for temporary exhibitions. On this floor **Roman and Germanic jewellery** are on display.

Museum branches ► The outside branches of the Römisch-Germanisches Museum shed further light on the Roman period. They include the ►Praetorium, the Ubiermonument (►Roman City Wall), the Roman and Frankish cemetery below ► St Severin church and the ►Römische Grabkammer in Köln-Weiden.

Directly to the south of the museum, part of a Roman road that led down to the harbour has been relaid close to its original position – unfortunately with less skill than that of Roman engineers, as the poor state of the road shows. Next to it is part of a sewer that lay beneath the road.

! *Baedeker* TIP

**Culinaria Romana**

Whether a luxurious dinner or solid home cooking, after learning about the culinary culture of Caesar's time visitors to the Römisch-Germanisches Museum can cook their own authentic Roman meal (infos at tel. 22123468 and www.museenkoeln.de/museumsdienst).

# ★★ Schloss Augustusburg

Excursion

**Location:** Brühl, 13km/8mi southwest of Cologne
**Train:** Brühl Bf. (the palace is opposite the station)
**Tram:** 18 (to Brühl Mitte)
**By car:** via autobahn A 553 to exit Brühl-Ost
**Internet:** www.schlossbruehl.de

**The palaces of Augustusburg and Falkenlust, in the small town of Brühl halfway between Cologne and Bonn, are jewels of Rococo architecture and interior decoration, which served as models for many German princely courts of the 18th century.**

*Schloss Augustusburg was a model that 18th-century princes were keen to emulate.*

In 1984 the two palaces and their gardens were recognized as UNESCO World Heritage monuments. A moated castle built on the site in 1284 was one of the residences of the archbishops of Cologne after they lost control of the city in 1288; in 1689 this castle was destroyed by French troops. Prince Elector **Clemens August**, Archbishop of Cologne (1700–61), a member of the Wittelsbach family, laid the foundation stone for today's palace in 1725. He was a lover of the arts and of hunting with falcons, but in political matters he was not a skilful ruler. The original design of the palace by the Westphalian Baroque architect **Johann Conrad Schlaun** was considerably altered by **François de Cuvilliés**, who took charge of the work in 1728. Prominent artists were employed to decorate the palace: **Balthasar Neumann**, for example, for the staircase and the Lombard painter **Carlo Carlone** for some of the ceilings. Construction was completed in 1768.

Tours: Tue–Fri 9am–noon, 1.30–4pm, Sat and Sun

From the avenue leading to the palace Schlaun's U-shaped plan is apparent. A north and a south wing flank the court of honour. Schlaun's Baroque design for the east façades of both wings survives. Under Cuvilliés the south side became the main façade, but because his work consisted of alterations to the existing fabric of the palace, this façade remained asymmetrical.

◀ Interior

The entrance is in the north wing. Balthasar Neumann's magnificent staircase is the most notable feature of the building. It celebrates the splendour of a ruler in the age of Absolutism with a display of mar-

**! Baedeker TIP**

**Concerts in the palace**

From May to September concerts are regularly performed in Schloss Augustusburg. Baroque music often features on the programme. For information: tel. 022 32 / 94 18 84 or www.schlosskonzerte.de).

ble, plasterwork and caryatids, and Carlo Carlone's ceiling fresco of the *Magnanimity of Clemens August*. On the upper floor there is a succession of lavishly decorated and beautifully restored rooms in the west and south wings. This part of the palace was often used to entertain state visitors when nearby Bonn was the capital of the Federal Republic of Germany. The lower floor, which opens onto the gardens, was used as the summer quarters of the prince bishop. Here the use of blue and white tiles on the walls gives the apartments a cool atmosphere.

**Park**
Opening hours: Daily 7am–6pm, in summer until 9pm

The palace gardens typify the style of a **French Baroque garden**. In its arrangement around a central axis, with swirling symmetrical patterns of low box-tree hedges in the style of a broderie parterre (i.e. designed to imitate embroidery) and mirror ponds with fountains, the gardens embody the spirit of the 18th century, which aimed both to subdue nature and to rule the state with absolute power. The garden designer was **Dominique Girard**, a pupil of André Le Nôtre, who worked on the gardens at Versailles and elsewhere. In 1842 the palace grounds were remodelled, and beyond the Baroque parterre gardens **Peter Joseph Lenné** created a landscape park in the English style with woods, clearings and avenues.

**Falkenlust hunting lodge**
Opening hours: As Schloss Augustusburg

Only 1.5km/1mi to the southeast of Schloss Augustusburg stands the hunting lodge built by Clemens August in 1729. He had a passion for falconry, which he saw as symbolic of the perspicacity and discipline needed to rule a state. He used Falkenlust not only for hunting, but as a discreet place for conducting secret negotiations and amorous adventures. It was built in Rococo style by **François de Cuvilliés** and **Michel Leveilly**. The most noteworthy features of the interior are the lacquer cabinet, the tiled staircase and the cabinet of mirrors.

## Max Ernst Museum

**Location:** Comesstrasse 42 **Internet:** www.maxernstmuseum.lvr.de

**Artist from Brühl**

A museum to honour Brühl's most famous son, the artist Max Ernst, opened in 2005 in a 19th-century building next to Schloss Augustusburg. The Dadaist and Surrealist Ernst (1891–1976) had little sympathy with the place of his birth, moving to Cologne after the First World War and spending most of his life in France and the USA. Nevertheless, his home town has assembled a collection of paintings, collages and sculptures dating from seven decades, as well as graphic works and photographs on the life of the artist.

# ★ Schokoladenmuseum · Rheinauhafen

H 8

**Location:** Rheinauhafen 1a
**Tram:** 1, 7, 9 (Heumarkt) or 15, 16 (Ubierring)

**Internet:** www.schokoladenmuseum.de

**The extremely popular »museum of chocolate past and present« established by Hans Imhoff, owner of Cologne's Stollwerck chocolate factory, is a treat for all fans of chocolate. It occupies one end of the Rheinauhafen, an extensive harbour where a new residential, leisure and commercial district has arisen in recent years through the conversion of old warehouses and construction of some interesting new buildings.**

Opening hours:
Tue–Fri
10am–6pm,
Sat and Sun
11am–7pm

The museum opened in 1993 at the harbour just south of the city centre. With its porthole windows and slanting glass sides that taper like the bows of a ship at the end of the quay, it makes a nautical impression. When approaching across the swing bridge that spans the harbour entrance it becomes apparent that the architect, **Fritz Eller**, cleverly combined modern architecture with the old buildings that were once used by the customs office.

*Visitors to the Schokoladenmuseum queue at the chocolate fountain.*

The **world's first chocolate museum** uses photographs, displays and exhibits, but above all production machinery, to initiate its visitors into the world of the cocoa bean and its products. The exhibition begins with the cultivation of cocoa beans in the hot, humid equatorial regions, and explains how they are made into cocoa mass and cocoa butter. Cocoa trees and other exotic plants grow in a small tropical hothouse. An extensive machine park then shows how cocoa is rolled, refined and aerated, then processed into chocolate bars and truffles or formed as Father Christmas figures and Easter eggs. There is an array of mould-filling and packaging machines, where school groups and adults alike watch fascinated as the chocolate moves on turntables and along conveyors. For generations the Stollwerck company was a major employer in Cologne (►Severinsviertel), but the museum is now the only remaining site in the city where chocolate is manufactured.

Having learned about the production from start to finish, visitors proceed to the gilded **chocolate fountain** containing 200kg/450lb of warm molten chocolate, and are given a wafer that is dipped into the flowing mass. The rooms of the upper floor revert to an educational mission: artefacts from pre-Columbian civilizations are the starting point for a tour through the cultural history of chocolate, which includes fine porcelain used in previous centuries for the luxurious pursuit of drinking chocolate, historic advertising posters, chocolate vending machines, and a fully furnished old-world chocolate shop. Private tours in English can be arranged: tel. 93 18 880.

The inevitable conclusion to a visit is the well-stocked **museum shop**, where the museum sponsor Lindt presents a huge range of products. The café, which is open to all without paying museum admission and from which there is a wonderful view of the Rhine, serves meals, snacks and creative variations on hot and cold chocolate drinks.

## ✶ Deutsches Sport & Olympia Museum

**Location:** Rheinauhafen 1
**Tram:** 1, 7, 8, 9 (Heumarkt)
**Internet:** www.sportmuseum.info
**Tours:** tel. 336 09 59

Opening hours: Tue–Fri 10am–6pm, Sat and Sun 11am–7pm

To counteract the massive calorie intake that a visit to the Schokoladenmuseum may have caused, look no further than the neighbouring building, a harbour warehouse that has been converted to a museum of sport. Over 3000 exhibits, as well as models, films and displays, trace the history of sport from ancient Greece to the present day. An English betting shop has been reconstructed, highlights of the history of German, international and Olympic sports are presented, and visitors have an opportunity to try out a range of sports for themselves.

## ✶ Rheinauhafen

The harbour was constructed from 1892 to 1898, taking its name from a small island known as the Rheinau. At the north end of the harbour a swing bridge leads to the Schokoladenmuseum. The machinery to move the bridge is in the brick tower known as the **Malakoffturm**, which was built in 1855 as part of the Rhine fortifications. At the approach to the bridge is a sculpture of 1908 by **Nikolaus Friedrich**, *Der Tauzieher* (*The Rope-Puller*).

On the 2km/1.25mi-long area to the south of the two museums, large-scale building activity that began in 2002 has turned a derelict harbour into a top-class residential area, with offices, shops, galleries and restaurants. The renovation of old warehouses and harbour installations and the construction of new buildings have made the Rheinauhafen a rewarding place for a long stroll with a view of the river and a good deal of historical and architectural interest. The whole project is scheduled for completion in 2010.

*Baedeker* TIP

**Outdoor cinema**

On evenings in August the Schokoladenmuseum hosts open-air cinema. The beer garden opens at 7pm, and films are screened when it gets dark.

Beyond the Sport & Olympia Museum a 19th-century warehouse in the shadow of the Severinsbrücke is destined for conversion to a ground-floor store and first-floor flats. Further along lies the most spectacular modern development, the three 58m/190ft-high **»crane buildings«** (Kranhäuser), which project daringly over the quayside on a single slender support in a form reminiscent of historic harbour cranes. They were designed by the Hamburg firm Bothe, Richter and Teherani, and have made an instant and unmistakable contribution to the Rhine panorama of Cologne.

At the south end of the harbour basin the **Hafenamt** of 1898, the old harbour office, is resplendent following the restoration of its neo-Romanesque façade of red brick and stone. The adjoining buildings, closer to the Rhine, are the Krafthaus, the power station that once provided energy for 24 hydraulic cranes, and the locomotive shed.

◄ Info-Pavillon

Next to the Hafenamt a container-like pavilion (Wed–Fri 10am–6pm, Sat, Sun noon–6pm) serves as an information centre on the development of the Rheinauhafen; there is a good view from its 10m/33ft-high platform, which is open round the clock.

**Luxury waterfront accommodation**

The long, six-storey block on the Rhine front called Wohnwerft (»residential wharf«) set the tone for the modern architecture of the harbour, which with the exception of the conspicuous »crane buildings« is intended to remain discreet, in order not to steal the limelight from the historic buildings. The apartments in Wohnwerft all extend through the building from front to back, so that everyone has a river view. To the south is the Bayenturm (►Medieval City Wall), followed by two further new blocks with luxury flats and an open square named Elisabeth-Treskow-Platz after a notable 20th-century goldsmith; the building with rounded corners and outside steps here, the **Bastion**, was built in 1891 with thick concrete walls to house artillery, and is now a goldsmith's workshop. The red-painted building with a little tower and gables is the Rheinkontor of 1909. It now houses a Greek restaurant, Limani, offices and five large, luxurious penthouses.

**Siebengebirge warehouse**

A row of tall, steeply-pitched gables and round towers with conical roofs characterize the building that extends south from the Rhein-

kontor. The eye-catching roofscape has given it the name Siebengebirge (»seven hills«, the name of an area on the right bank of the Rhine to the south of Bonn). This enormous and impressive warehouse of 1909, the first steel-framed concrete building in Cologne, has been converted for residential use and offices, a task that required some skill, as the depth of the building (22m/72ft from the Rhine façade to the west façade) made lighting difficult and required the insertion and enlargement of windows and addition of balconies, while preserving the historic character of this listed monument.
Continue south past Silo 23, once a grain store, and the modern ECR (Event Center Rheinauhafen, used for exhibitions and events) to the southern end of the complex, **KAP am Südkai**, a 130m/425ft-long modern building with a glass façade. The showrooms on the ground floor are intended to present the latest developments of companies in the field of architecture, design and technology. Those who have come this far will be ready for a rest in the café with a great view of the river. Nearby stands **Herkules**, one of three harbour cranes that have been left on this part of the quay. Herkules was the strongest of them all, able to raise a load of 30 tons. The most famous item that it lifted ashore was »Dicker Pitter«, the cathedral's largest bell (►Dom), in 1924. Herkules was in service from the early 20th century until the 1980s.

# Severinsviertel · Severin Quarter

H/J 7/8

**Location:** Around Severinstrasse
**Bus:** 132, 133 (Severinskirche, Rosenstrasse, Severinstrasse)
**Tram:** 15, 16 (Chlodwigplatz)

**Many inhabitants of Cologne identify strongly with their own quarter (Viertel) of the city. The Severinsviertel, known as »Vringsveedel« in the local dialect, is one of the liveliest and has preserved a traditional atmosphere with many pubs, cafés and small shops and a well-balanced mixture of native Kölner and newcomers.**

**Roman origins**

In the 10th century the district now known as Severinsviertel corresponded to the land owned by the church of **St Severin**, below which the remains of a 4th-century church have been excavated. The discovery in the 1960s of the Poblicius Monument (►Römisch-Germanisches Museum) at Chlodwigplatz also drew attention to the long history of the quarter: in Roman times the dead were buried outside the city in cemeteries along Severinstrasse, the main route leading south parallel to the Rhine.

**✶ Severinstorburg**

Taking Chlodwigplatz as a starting point for a tour, enter Severinstrasse with its shops and cafés through the impressive medieval city

gate. The polygonal tower above the arch was built in the late 12th century, a few decades after the lower storeys. By the 15th century the age of gunpowder had arrived, and chambers for cannon were added. Excavations since 2004 have uncovered evidence of the Roman road, a Roman cemetery, and fortifications of the late medieval period below and around Chlodwigplatz.
Like the Hahnentorburg (►Medieval City Wall), the central opening of the gate has a pointed arch on the outside and a round arch on the inner façade. Inside the gate turn right into Severinswall to see the **Bottmühle**, one of the four windmills constructed on the city walls in the 17th century. At Severinstor, on the Thursday before Ash Wednesday at 3pm, the first parade of the Carnival period begins. It goes along Severinstrasse to Alter Markt.

**Haus Balchem**

Severinstrasse no. 15 is the broad, white-painted Haus Balchem. It is considered the **finest remaining Baroque house in Cologne** and was built, as the date on the gable testifies, in 1676 by the brewer H. Deutz; the name of the house derives from the Balchem family, who once ran an inn on the site. Although the façade has a Baroque design, the arrangement of the storeys is that of a medieval Cologne dwelling: above the ground floor is a mezzanine floor, to which the richly decorated bay window belongs, and the main living accommodation was situated on the next floor above. The upper storeys served as storage space. Today the building accommodates a branch of the municipal library.

**Chocolate girl and Stollwerck factory**

A little way along Severinstrasse lies Severinskirchplatz. Here, on the open space in front of the church, stands a fountain with the figure of the Schokoladenmädchen (chocolate girl), a reminder of the existence of the old **Stollwerck chocolate factory**, which employed many women from this area from the mid-19th century and was the most important company in this part of the city until it closed in the 1970s. The huge works site, to the east around Dreikönigenstrasse, is now largely a residential development.

## St Severin

**Location:** Severinstr./Im Ferkulum 29
**Bus:** 132, 133 (Severinskirche)
**Tram:** 6, 15, 16, 17 (Chlodwigplatz)

Opening hours:
Mon–Sat 9am–6pm,
Sun 9am–noon, 3–5.30 pm

By the end of the 4th century there was a small church on the Roman cemetery that stretched along the road to the military camp at Bonn, now Severinstrasse. In the following centuries aisles and a narthex were added. This first place of worship made way in the 9th century for a large basilica, which was oriented to the east and was dedicated by **Archbishop Bruno** in 948. In the 11th century further additions were made, by lengthening the choir and constructing a large hall crypt. More major alterations followed in the 13th century:

the choir was given vaulting, an apse flanked by two towers was added, and the nave was restored. The structuring of the apse of the choir in two storeys corresponds to the usual practice in Cologne churches in this period. The late Gothic modernization of the nave with a net vault and tracery windows dates from the 15th and early 16th century. The west tower was completed in 1526.

## DID YOU KNOW ...?

- ... that St Severin was bishop of Cologne in the late 4th century? When the saint's wooden shrine was opened in 1999, precious Byzantine textiles were found, and an examination of the human remains confirmed that the person who has been revered in the church since the early Middle Ages died around the year 400 at the age of about 55, supporting the tradition and legends about Severin.

The only surviving medieval stained-glass window (1508) is at the western end of the south aisle. It is probably a work of the **Master of the Legend of St Severin** and depicts the Crucifixion. The name given to the artist derives from 20 panels dating from about 1500 that show scenes from the saint's life; they can be seen in the first bay of the choir. St Severin was a collegiate church; some fine funeral monuments for the canons are in the church aisles. There is a graceful late 13th-century Madonna statue in front of the northwest pier of the crossing. The floor of the west bay of the choir, which is decorated with geometric patterns in black and yellow marble, was laid in the 12th century. The 13th-century choir stalls, with 62 seats and beautiful carvings, are the oldest in Cologne. The **shrine of St Severin** stands behind the high altar, elevated on four small columns. It was made in 1819 to replace the precious 11th-century shrine that was broken up and melted down in 1795. Of the medieval shrine there remains only a round enamel depicting St Severin, which is kept in the choir.

Crypt ►

Tours: Information from Domforum and www.romanische-kirchen-koeln.de

The crypt and the excavations, which can be viewed only as part of a guided tour, are accessed from the north aisle. The main crypt below the choir has remains of **13th-century murals**. The impressive excavations make it clear that the number of burials along the old Roman road was large. The most interesting grave goods found here are on display in the ► Römisch-Germanisches Museum. The foundations of the previous churches are recognizable among the confused pile of sarcophaguses.

**University buildings**

The area immediately to the south of Severinsviertel, beyond the medieval city gate, is a fashionable residential quarter known as the Südstadt. In Claudiusstrasse close to the Rhine a college of higher education occupies the Alte Universität, dating from 1905–07. The buildings originally housed a school of commerce. In 1919 the newly refounded university moved in, but due to lack of space transferred to its new site in Lindenthal (► University) in 1935. During the »Third Reich« the gauleiter of the Köln-Aachen Gau used it as his headquarters.

The neo-Baroque old university buildings open onto the Römerpark, which was laid out in 1895–98 to compensate for the loss of green space when the harbour was built on the Rheinau island. ◄ Römerpark

To the south of the Römerpark is the larger Friedenspark (Peace Park). It surrounds a Prussian fort of 1825 that was converted into a place of memorial for fallen soldiers in 1926. Although the park was fitted into the existing plan of walls and ditches of the fort, its design followed the geometrical principles of art nouveau. ◄ Friedenspark

## Stadtgarten · Neu St Alban

G 6

**Location:** Venloer Strasse/Spichern-Strasse

**Tram:** 3, 4, 5 (Hans-Böckler-Platz)

**The Stadtgarten is not just a lovely park, but is also much visited for its beer garden and the Kölner Jazzhaus, which runs a highly regarded programme of concerts.**

**Oldest park in Cologne**

The Stadtgarten was founded in 1827–29, which makes it the oldest park in the city. It was not created to satisfy the pride of a prince, but by the citizens of Cologne themselves. It is a leafy area with the character of an English landscape garden. At the northwest corner lies a much-admired modern church, Neu St Alban.

**Neu St Alban**

The remarkable architecture of Neu St Alban is the work of **Hans Schilling**, who built it in the years 1957–59 to replace Alt St Alban (► Wallraf-Richartz-Museum), which was destroyed by bombs.

*Shady trees, cooling beer: the Stadtgarten in summer*

Bricks from the old opera house were used. The ground plan takes the parabolic form that had been usual since the 1920s.
The interior was designed in accordance with liturgical practices that were then new in the Catholic church: the altar is positioned so that Mass can be celebrated towards the congregation, which was not officially the case until the Second Vatican Council of 1962–65. A sacrament chapel was added to the north. Some items of furnishing from the old church, Alt St Alban, came into the new church: a 16th-century Crucifixion scene, figures of the apostles on the organ loft, a 15th-century Pietà below it, and the Baroque pulpit.

## ★ St Andreas

G 7

**Location:** Andreaskloster (near cathedral)
**Bus:** 132
**Tram:** 5, 16, 18 (Dom/Hbf)

**St Andreas, a Dominican church, attractively contrasts Rhenish late Romanesque with French Gothic style. Its octagonal Romanesque central tower is the most conspicuous feature of the area around the cathedral. The best view of the church is from the north side of the cathedral square on Komödienstrasse.**

Opening hours: Mon–Fri 7am–7pm Sat and Sun from 8am

The church was built from 1200 on the site of a 10th-century monastery church and underwent many changes up to the mid-17th century. In 1414 the Romanesque choir was replaced in the Gothic style and the crypt was filled in; this crypt, which probably dates from the 11th century, was not rediscovered until 1953. From the 14th to the 16th century, chapels were added to the aisles. Although St Andreas suffered considerable damage from bombing, in the post-war years it was used at times as a substitute for the cathedral, where services could not be held until 1948.
The narthex in the west is a **superb example of Rhenish late Romanesque architecture**. The massively built nave has a Romanesque elevation that emphasizes the horizontal lines and fine ornamentation of the capitals. The crossing is domed, and lower than the nave – probably following the height of the 10th-century choir. The elevated choir with richly ornamented consoles, on the model of the Sainte-Chapelle in Paris, gives maximum space to the windows.

Furnishings ►

According to legend, the blood of St Ursula and her martyred companions is said to have been shed over the so-called **blood basin of St Ursula** in the narthex. In fact it is a 15th-century reliquary. The altarpiece of the Brotherhood of the Rosary in the first chapel on the right in the south aisle of the nave was painted by the Master of St Severin around 1500 to give thanks for victory over Charles the Bold of Burgundy. It celebrates the foundation of the brotherhood by **Jakob Sprenger**. Sprenger was a Dominican whose name appeared as

*The restorers chose a tasteful colour scheme for the pillars and shafts of St Andreas church.*

co-author of the notorious *Hexenhammer* (*Hammer of the Witches*) of 1487, a manual for the fight against witchcraft. Pope Sixtus IV and Emperor Friedrich III are kneeling at the feet of the Virgin; Jakob Sprenger is depicted at the bottom left wearing a black cap. On the opposite wall is a 16th-century winged altar painting of the crucifixions of Christ and St Andrew by **Barthel Bruyn the Elder**.

In the chapel to the right before the transept 14th-century murals have survived: a fresco behind the altar on the east wall portrays *Christ as Judge of the World*. The fine choir stalls of 1420 have carved figures of saints (the apostles and patron saints of Cologne churches). In the north transept note the *Pietà* of about 1380, the *Crucifixion of St Andrew* (1658) and a 16th-century altarpiece of the *Resurrection of Christ*. The 15th-century figure of St Michael on the northwest pier of the crossing and the over-life-size St Christopher (*c*1490) are probably the work of the Cologne sculptor Tilman van der Burch. The 14th-century scenes from the life of the Virgin in the Marienkapelle (Lady Chapel) on the north side of the church are important and beautiful examples of Gothic painting.

In the south transept, which is known as the **Choir of the Maccabees**, stained-glass windows by Markus Lüpertz (2005–08) are devoted to the theme of redemption. The depictions include the story of the seven Jewish Maccabee brothers and their mother, who are considered as proto-Christian martyrs. According to tradition the golden shrine in this transept contains their relics; it was completed in 1527 and depicts scenes of their martyrdom in parallel with scenes of Christ's Passion. Further windows by Lüpertz on the theme of creation are planned for the north transept.Karl Band provided the crypt with a new concrete vault, one of the more interesting pieces of 1950s reconstruction. Under the older vault of the crypt a Roman sarcophagus contains the remains of the great scholar and philosopher **Albertus Magnus** (►Famous People).

Crypt ►

## St Mariä Himmelfahrt

**Location:** Marzellenstrasse 32

**Former Jesuit church**

Two minutes' walk from St Andreas, the former Jesuit church of St Mariä Himmelfahrt (Assumption of the Virgin) reflects the spirit of the Counter-Reformation. The lavishly decorated interior is regarded as an important example of Jesuit early Baroque. Construction began in 1618 and was completed in 1678, but the presence of the Jesuit order in Cologne is documented as early as 1544. The church was designed by **Christoph Wamser** and financed by generous donations from the house of Wittelsbach, from whose ranks the prince archbishops of Cologne came in the 17th century.

The architecture illustrates how the Jesuits saw their mission: as the vanguard of the movement to revive the old and »true« faith, i.e. that of the Roman Catholic Church, they had recourse to styles of the pre-Reformation period, especially Gothic, but combined it with elements of the contemporary Baroque style.

Interior ►

The furnishings, done in a unified style by **Jeremias Geisselbrunn** and **Valentin Boltz**, are entirely devoted to the veneration of the Virgin Mary. A Madonna in Glory crowns the high altar of 1628, and the altar painting of 1643, which was made for St Aposteln church by **Johann Hulsmann**, depicts the Assumption of the Virgin. The statues on the piers of the nave (the twelve apostles, and Christ as Redeemer and the Virgin as the Queen of Heaven on the piers of the crossing), are a conscious reference to Cologne Cathedral and the Catholic architectural tradition in the city.

# ★★ St Aposteln

G 7

**Location:** Apostelkloster 10 (on Neumarkt)

**Tram:** 1, 3, 4, 7, 9, 16, 18 (Neumarkt)
**Bus:** 136, 146

**The Church of the Apostles, a masterpiece of Romanesque architecture, is famous for its trefoil choir – its east section with a cloverleaf ground plan, probably the most harmonious and beautiful example of such a design.**

*Octagons: the tower above the crossing of St Aposteln and one of the two turrets that flank it*

The first church on the site was built in the 10th century. In the 11th century **Archbishop Pilgrim** built a basilica here just outside the Roman wall, which remained in place as the boundary of the monastery precinct until 1802. Pilgrim's church had both an east and a west choir, and the archbishop chose the west transept as the site for his grave. The west tower was built in the 12th century. From 1192 the **trefoil choir** at the east end was added. Like that of ►Gross St Martin it took the church of ►St Maria im Kapitol as its model. In the early 13th century the church was given a stone vault.

**Famous trefoil choir**

Opening hours: Wed–Mon 10am–noon, 3–5pm

The main façade of St Aposteln faces east, towards ►Neumarkt. The three rounded apses – at the east, as at the north and south end of the transept – form the trefoil shape. The octagonal crossing tower between them is crowned by a lantern. At the corners where the apses meet, two octagonal flanking towers with steeply pointed roofs reinforce the effect of the central tower. The façade is structured horizontally by division into two storeys, above which a dwarf gallery runs around all three apses. When the church is viewed from Neumarkt, the west tower in the background adds its weight to that of the east end; from the other direction, the fortress-like appearance of the western ensemble makes a strongly contrasting impression. The lozenge-shaped roof of the west tower is considered the original model for all subsequent towers of this kind.

◄ East façade

Although they belong to different phases of construction, the enormous rectangular space of the west end and the trefoil choir in the east form a harmonious whole. Below the organ is the 11th and 12th-century crypt, which was revealed during restoration in 1955. The sandstone pillars in the arcade of the nave date from the 11th

◄ Interior

century; the friezes and cornices of trachyte stone were added in the 13th century when the vault was built. The step-by-step construction of the vaulting helped to achieve the skilful integration of different spaces into a whole. The horizontal structure of the church exterior in two storeys is reflected inside, especially in the trefoil choir, where the lower level is given depth by niches, the upper level by a gallery.

Furnishing ► In comparison to the appearance of the church before the Second World War, the furnishings and decoration are sparse today. On the south side of the west transept statues of the fourteen auxiliary saints (16th–18th century) can be seen.

As the 19th-century mosaics that covered the vaults were destroyed in the bombing, **Hermann Gottfried** was commissioned to paint the ceilings of the trefoil choir and crossing, and carried out the work, with the exception of the underside of the octagonal dome, between 1988 and 1994. A painting in the south aisle and a surviving mosaic in a tympanum at the north end of the west transept give an idea of the pre-war interior. In the eastern apse a modern retable holds 14th-century oak figures of the apostles. On the piers of the crossing are statues of St Paul and the Virgin, the two principal patrons of the church (*c*1480), and a 15th-century figure of St George.

**Statue of Adenauer**

At the corner of Apostelnstrasse a statue of Konrad Adenauer, the former mayor of Cologne and first chancellor of the Federal Republic, was unveiled in 1995 (► Famous People). Apostelnstrasse and the nearby Mittelstrasse are among the most attractive shopping streets of the city.

# St Engelbert

E 8

**Location:** Riehler Gürtel 12 **Tram:** 13, 16 (Amsterdamer Str./Gürtel)

**When it was completed in 1931, St Engelbert made its mark as the first example of modern church architecture in Cologne. On New Year's Eve 1946 it was the site of a famous sermon preached by Cardinal Frings (► Famous People), which was taken to mean that theft as a means of survival, henceforth known locally as »fringsing«, was condoned by the church.**

**»Lemon squeezer«**

The architect, **Dominikus Böhm**, designed the church on a central plan consisting of eight parabolic walls above a circle and covered by a lead roof that continues the parabolas. Its appearance quickly earned it the name »lemon squeezer«. The tall, angular, free-standing tower, which like the main building is clad in brick, forms a contrast to the rounded forms of the church itself. The interior gains its atmosphere from the dim light entering through small windows and the dramatic illumination of the choir.

# ★ St Georg

H 7

**Location:** Waidmarkt

**Tram:** 3, 4 (Severinstr.) or 3, 4, 16, 18 (Poststr.)

**Behind military-looking outer walls an 11th-century basilica with a beautiful addition of 1180, the west choir, awaits discovery. The church also possesses two fine medieval crucifixes and interesting pre-war stained glass.**

Opening hours: Daily 8am–6pm

The site of the church of St Georg lay just outside the south gate of the Roman city on the road to Bonn. Excavations uncovered remains thought to derive from a Roman police station that was built here to secure the route and the settlement outside the city wall. In Merovingian times a chapel dedicated to St Caesarius was built over the Roman structure. In 1059 Archbishop Anno founded a collegiate church that was consecrated eight years later and, apart from the west choir, has largely been preserved. Roman columns were reused to support the arcades of the nave, which makes St Georg the only Romanesque church in Cologne or the Rhineland designed as a basilica with columns instead of piers. Beneath the raised choir is a five-aisled crypt. In the mid-12th century cross-vaulting was added to the nave, which entailed placing rectangular piers between the columns of the arcade. Between 1180 and 1188 the old western choir was replaced by the present one, which externally has the appearance of a fortress, probably because a strong base was required for a tower that was never completed. The walls are almost 4m/13ft thick. The domed interior, however, is a **harmoniously proportioned space** of two storeys: at the lower level a larger central niche is framed by two smaller ones on each of the three walls, while a gallery above gives depth and windows placed between double-arched openings provide light.

◄ Furnishings

When the church was restored in the late 1920s, new windows were designed by Jan Thorn-Prikker. The church was severely damaged in the Second World War, but stained-glass windows depicting St Anno, St George and St James were remade on the basis of the original cartoons for the west choir. The mosaic of the Virgin Mary in the south aisle (1913) is also the work of Thorn-Prikker. An expressive medieval work has been placed at the centre of the west wall: a **»plague cross«** of around 1380, a harrowing depiction of the crucified Christ that reflected the sufferings of the population in a time of pestilence. The crucifix in the eastern choir was probably made in the late 11th century; the original is in the ►Museum Schnütgen.

The 14-storey building opposite St Georg was constructed in the 1950s as the police headquarters – shortly before discovering that the Roman remains below the church may have been a police station. The fountain on Waidmarkt is the **Hermann-Joseph-Brunnen** of 1894. It represents the legend of the young saint who brought an apple to the statue of the Virgin and Child in ►St Maria im Kapitol.

# ★★ St Gereon

G 7

**Location:** Gereonshof 4 **Tram:** 12, 15, (Christophstr.)

**Late Roman times and the Middle Ages come together in this unusual church, which is named after the martyr Gereon, later a patron saint of the city. The heart of the building, a late Roman oval, was integrated in the early 13th century into a tall ten-sided space with a dome, the largest such structure to be attempted between the building of Hagia Sophia and the dome of Florence cathedral.**

Opening hours: Mon– Sat 10am–6pm, Sun 12.30–6pm

The original building was constructed on a Roman cemetery outside the city walls, probably in the second half of the 4th century. It had an oval ground plan with a large niche in the east and eight smaller ones, four each to the north and south. To the west was an atrium. It is not known who built this unusually shaped structure and for what purpose. It is thought to have served as a mausoleum or place of memorial, and its magnificence – golden mosaics adorned the vault, and coloured marble the walls – indicates that a high-ranking person, perhaps close to the imperial family, commissioned it. According to a medieval legend **St Helena**, the mother of Emperor Constantine, built the oval on the site where Gereon and other soldiers of a Roman legion were martyred and thrown into a well. However, a coin minted in AD 345 or later was discovered in the foundations, dating the building after St Helena's time. Excavations found no trace of a well, but the Roman masonry can clearly be seen inside the niches. In following centuries the building, known as »the golden saints«, was used by Frankish kings, possibly for coronations, and was the burial place of Hildebold, the first archbishop of Cologne. From the 9th century a college of canons was attached to the church. In the 11th century **Archbishop Anno II** added a crypt and a choir for the canons in the east. Archbishop **Arnold von Wied** extended the choir and built the fine east façade in the 12th century. The most significant architectural alternations, the conversion of the Roman oval space to a decagon and the construction of the great dome above it, were undertaken in the early 13th century. A few years after the completion of the dome in 1227, the baptistery was added to the south. The 14th-century sacristy has fine Gothic tracery.

**Façade**

The main façade of the church, in the axis of an ancient processional way leading from the cathedral, is a four-storey apse flanked by two towers. The 48m/158ft-high decagon, which has small flying buttresses between the late Roman niches and pointed lancet windows crowned by trefoils, is an impressive example of the transition from Romanesque to early Gothic style.

← *The core of St Gereon is a 4th-century Roman building.*

## St. Gereon *Phases of Construction*

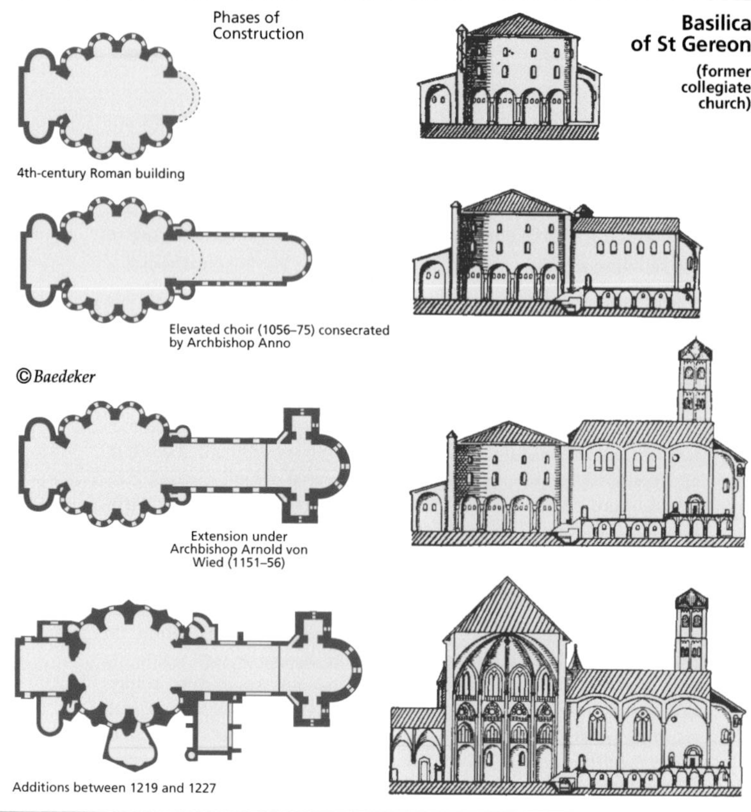


Interior ► The vault of the dome has a span of 21m/69ft and a height of 34m/113ft. It was painted glowing red with golden drops in 1979 to represent martyrdom and the Pentecost. Between the piers, whose shafts rise to form the ribs of the vault, the wall has a four-part elevation: the Roman niches, a gallery, fan-shaped windows and clerestory windows. The beheading of St Gereon is depicted at the centre of the modern floor. The windows of the decagon and the apse of the choir were installed in the 1980s; the designs are by **Georg Meistermann** and **Wilhelm Buschulte**. Steps lead up to the long choir, which is elevated as the crypt lies beneath. The Romanesque murals of the apse have partly survived. On the south side a painting from the St Sebastian altar (1635) has an interesting bird's-eye view of Cologne, above which Archbishop Anno, accompanied by St Sebastian and St Gereon, shows St Helena his additions to the church. The beautiful

*The ribs of the red-painted dome of St Gereon meet 35m/115ft above the floor of the ten-sided space.*

Gothic sacristy may well have been built by craftsmen from the cathedral workshop; its finely carved doors date from the early 16th century.

◀ Crypt

In the crypt large sections of the 11th-century **floor mosaics** survive. They were originally made for the choir, and depict scenes from the lives of Samson and David. The west end of the crypt opens onto the confessio, where the bones of supposed Roman martyrs lie in stone sarcophaguses. It is also worth taking a look at the Romanesque baptismal chapel (1230–40) to the south of the decagon.

## ★ St Kunibert

F 8

**Location:** Kunibertskloster 2 **Tram:** 5, 16, 18 (Breslauer Platz)

**St Kunibert is the last and stylistically purest of Cologne's Romanesque churches.**

Opening hours:
Mon–Sat
10am–1pm,
3–6pm,
Sun 3–6pm

From about 1215 the present church, a vaulted basilica with east and west transepts, was constructed over a previous building that **Bishop Kunibert** chose as the site of his grave in 663. It was consecrated in 1247, though not yet complete. For centuries the three towers of St Kunibert have been the dominant feature of the Rhine panorama to the north of the cathedral. The reconstruction of the west tower, not finished until 1993, restored the original appearance of the church and brought to an end the programme of post-war rebuilding of Cologne's Romanesque churches.

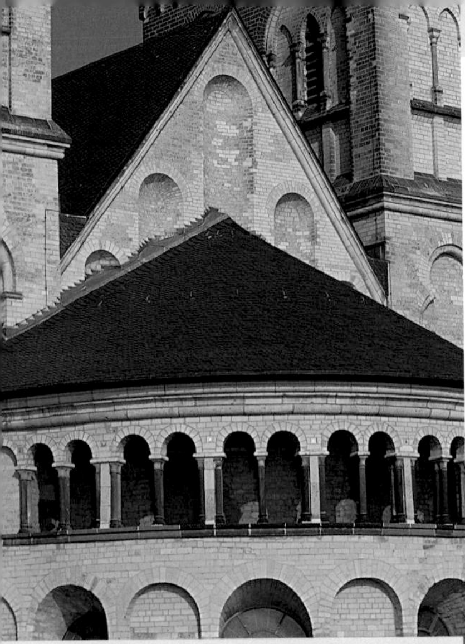

*The well-proportioned east façade of St Kunibert*

The most impressive view of St Kunibert is from the Rhine bank. The **richly decorated façade** is typical for the Romanesque church choirs of Cologne: a choir apse flanked by two towers, with two storeys pierced by windows and surmounted by a dwarf gallery. Galleries between the inner and outer walls give depth to the apse on both the upper and lower storeys. The choir windows of about 1230 are the most important part of the medieval furnishings, as they contain the **oldest surviving stained glass in Cologne**. The upper window at the centre depicts the Tree of Jesse, i.e. the family tree of Christ, with scenes from the Old and New Testaments; to the left and right the legends of the two patron saints of the church, Clemens and Kunibert, can be seen; in the lower row of windows are St Cordula (left) and St Ursula (right). Note also the remains of medieval stained glass in the southern east transept (*c*1260) and in the northern choir niche (*c*1250). The 19th-century reliquary shrines in the choir hold the bones of St Kunibert and two Anglo-Saxon missionaries, both named Ewald, who were killed while preaching to the heathen Saxons. An Annunciation scene of 1439 encompasses the crossing: the figure of the Virgin is on the southwest pier, that of the angel on the northwest pier. Both are thought to be the work of cathedral architect **Konrad Kuyn**. The donor, **Hermanus de Arcka**, is shown as a small figure at the feet of the Virgin.

Kunibert's well ►

A lattice-like slab of slate in the choir covers the shaft of a well known locally as Kunibertspütz. It is 17m/56ft deep and pre-dates the Christian period. It is associated with fertility rites; according to an ancient popular belief, babies in Cologne are not brought by a stork, but come from this well.

## Ursuline Church St Corpus Christi

**Location:** Machabäerstr. 75

Nearby in Machabäerstrasse stands the Baroque Ursulinenkirche (1709–12). In 1639 the Ursuline Sisters from Liège took refuge from the Thirty Years' War in neutral Cologne, where they founded the first secondary school for girls in Germany. Elector Johann Wilhelm sponsored the construction of the church, which was designed by his

Venetian court architect **Matteo Alberti**. The two towers of the façade are reminiscent of north Italian hall churches of the period after Palladio; the interior and colouring of the façade are modern.

# ** St Maria im Kapitol

H 7

**Location:** Kasinostr. 6
**Tram:** 1, 7, 9 (Heumarkt)
**Bus:** 132, 133, 250, 260, 978

**St Maria im Kapitol was built above a Roman temple dedicated to the Capitoline gods Jupiter, Juno and Minerva. The 11th-century church with its trefoil choir, a space of great beauty, was a pioneering work of Rhenish Romanesque architecture and served as a model for other churches in Cologne.**

Opening hours:
Daily 9am–6pm

The 1st-century Roman temple lay in the southeastern corner of the city. The temple had imposing dimensions: a building measuring 33 × 30m (36 × 32yd) in a 97 × 69m (106 × 76yd) precinct. In the 7th century the Merovingian mayors of the palace took possession of the temple precinct. **Plektrudis**, wife of palace mayor Pepin of Herstal, lived here in exile and was buried in a small church on the site. In the mid-10th century Archbishop Bruno provided funds for a new church, of which few remains have been found, and established a Benedictine nunnery. The impetus for construction of the present church came in the 11th century from **Abbess Ida**, a granddaughter of Emperor **Otto II** and his wife **Theophanu**. The consecration of the altar in the nave in 1049 by **Pope Leo IX** in the presence of Emperor **Heinrich III** testifies to the importance of the church, which was completed and received its final consecration in 1065 from **Archbishop Anno II**. In the 12th and 13th centuries the crossing and later the nave were provided with vaulting. The west tower collapsed in 1637 and was not rebuilt.

◄ Trefoil choir

The nave, which gained a wooden roof in place of the earlier vault during post-war restoration, is divided from the east end by the fine Renaissance screen, but the continuation of the aisles of the nave as an ambulatory around the three apses of the choir binds the two spaces together. The ground plan of the choir of St Maria im Kapitol (known as a trefoil choir on account of its clover-leaf shape) was an architectural innovation in its time. In shape and dimensions it is closely similar to the choir of the Church of the Nativity in Bethlehem, which is considered to have

! *Baedeker* TIP

**Romanesque night**

Once a year, music lovers can enjoy concerts of ancient and modern church music in St Maria im Kapitol until 2am. For a break between the musical offerings, beer is served in the cloister (further information: www.romanischer-sommer.de).

# ST MARIA IM KAPITOL

★★ **The church takes its name from the Roman temple over which it was built. The temple was dedicated to Jupiter, Juno and Minerva, who were known as the Capitoline deities.**

Hours:
daily 9am–6pm

① **Wooden doors**
The two doors dating from about 1060 are carved with scenes from the life of Christ. They were once the north entrance.

② **Tombstone of Plektrudis (*c*1160)**
This slab honours the founder of the church, described here as a saint and queen, and is inscribed with a verse from Psalm 26: »Domine dilexi decorem domus tue« (»Lord, I have loved the habitation of thy house«).

③ **Tombstone of Plektrudis (*c*1280)**
The second tombstone portrays Plektrudis holding a model of the church that she founded.

④ **Limburger Madonna**
This wooden sculpture of the late 13th century comes from the monastery of Limburg.

⑤ **Screen, crypt**
The screen separates the altar from the nave. It was made in present-day Belgium in 1523, but not erected in the church until 1525. The materials are limestone and sandstone, which were intended to imitate marble and alabaster. The crypt is the second-largest in Germany after that in Speyer.

⑥ **Plague cross**
This crucifix of 1304 is held to work miracles.

⑦ **Madonna (*c*1180)**
St Hermann Joseph is said to have laid an apple at the feet of the Virgin in thanks for hearing his prayer. There are almost always apples here.

*The statue of »The Mourner« at the northeast side of the church was made in 1949 by Gerhard Marcks. It commemorates those who died in the Second World War.*

*he donors of the screen were the ackeney, Salm, von Straelen and on Berchem families. Above it is the organ.*

*The musical highlight of the year in the basilica is the annual Romanesque Night.*

*Because the church is built on a slope, the crypt is illuminated by windows. Here, too, services are regularly held.*

*The doors are almost 5
16ft high and once stood
the entrance in the north
apse. The carved panels
of walnut wo*

been the inspiration for it; alternatively, the trefoil plan may possibly have been invented here independently. The harmony of the interior is enhanced by the fact that the choir is not elevated, but has the same floor level as the nave. This was possible because the ground slopes away to the eastand the **crypt** thus lies lower. It is an impressive aisled crypt with cross vaults that are supported on massive columns and cushion capitals. The crypt of Speyer Cathedral was the model.

The gallery for the canonesses at the west end of the nave is a conscious quotation of the octagon of Charlemagne's palace chapel in Aachen and thus emphasizes the imperial descent of Abbess Ida.

Furnishings ► The most remarkable items inside the church are **wooden doors dating from about 1060**, which once formed the entrance to the north apse and have now been placed at the west end of the south aisle. They are almost 5m/16ft high and are decorated with 26 scenes from the life of Christ, carved in walnut wood with some traces of the original colours. Two **slabs for the tomb of the supposed church founder Plektrudis** can also be seen: the older one of about 1160 is in the north aisle, while the other, which dates to about 1280 and depicts Plektrudis with a model of the church, is in the south aisle.

Three Madonna statues are on view in the course of a tour of the church: a Virgin with glass eyes (1150/1160) on the west wall of the north aisle that reveals Byzantine influence was originally placed on the eastern gable outside the church; a coloured, late 13th-century figure, which came from a monastery in Limburg, close to the Renaissance screen; and a standing figure of the Virgin with Child at the entrance to the eastern apse on the north side. It dates from 1180 or 1190 and is associated with a popular pious legend, according to which St Hermann Josef, a 12th-century Premonstratentian monk and mystic, once offered the Virgin an apple on his way to school; she reached over and took it from him. To this day apples are placed on the plinth of the statue, and the name Hermann Josef is common among Catholic families in Cologne.

Renaissance screen ► The Renaissance screen was made in 1517 in Mechelen (in Belgium) using black and white limestone and sandstone to imitate marble and alabaster, and was brought to the church in 1525. It is one of the few surviving architectural works of the Renaissance in Cologne. 22 figures of prophets and saints alternate with scenes from the New and Old Testament. The arms of the Hackeney and Hardenrath families refer to the donors. In the chapel between the north and east apses is a highly expressive **forked crucifix** of 1304.

»Mourner« ► Outside the church to the east on the court named Lichhof is **Gerhard Marcks'** *Mourner*, an Expressionist sculpture made in 1949 as a memorial to the horrors of war. The southern entrance to Lichhof is the Dreikönigenpförtchen (Gate of the Three Magi). It was built in 1330 to mark the place at which the relics of the Three Magi were believed to have entered the city in 1164.

*The paintings on the vault of St Maria Lyskirchen, which date from the 13th century, were not rediscovered until 1880.*

# St Maria Lyskirchen

H 7

**Location:** An Lyskirchen 12
**Bus:** 132, 133, 250, 260, 978
**Tram:** 1, 7, 9 (Heumarkt)

**This church near the harbour is modest in size, but its well-preserved late Romanesque painted ceiling, the only one remaining in the city, gives it a unique position among the churches of Cologne.**

Opening hours:
Daily 10am–6pm

Recent excavations have shown that the site of the church was not in the bed of the Rhine in Roman times, as was previously believed, but at the southern tip of an island in the river. This gives some support to the legend that the first bishop of Cologne, **Maternus**, who lived in the early 4th century, founded the church. Little has been discovered, however, about previous buildings on the site, and St Maria Lyskirchen is first documented in 948 as a church outside the city wall, in the suburb of Noithusen. It is thought to have been the chapel of a wealthy merchant called Lysolfus; the name Lyskirchen that derives from this does not appear until the 11th century. The present church was built between 1210 and 1220, with additions including the apse in the 17th century. St Maria Lyskirchen sustained little damage in the Second World War. The original plans, as for St Kunibert, foresaw a Rhine façade with two towers, but the south tower was not completed. The church has the form of a basilica with galleries. The lower floors of the towers open onto the choir as chapels.

◀ Interior

The **colourful 13th-century paintings on the walls and vault** were rediscovered in 1880. The earliest is probably the *Adoration of the Magi* of about 1220–30 on the west wall of the nave. The vault of the

nave was painted around 1250 with corresponding scenes of the Old Testament on the north side and the New Testament on the south side – for example, in the third bay the promise to Isaac is paired with the Annunciation to the Virgin Mary. The paintings thus represent a theological programme based on the belief that the New Testament was the fulfilment of signs present in the Old Testament. The vaults of the tower chapels, too, are decorated with cycles of paintings: those in the north relate the legend of St Catherine of Alexandria, those in the south tower the story of St Nicholas.
Note also the 13th-century baptismal font, the graceful Madonna (2nd half of the 13th century) above the high altar and a further sculpture of the Virgin that dates from about 1420. It is known as the Schiffer-Madonna (boatmen's Madonna), a reminder that Noithusen was once a settlement of fishermen and Rhine boatmen.

## ★★ St Pantaleon

H 7

**Location:** Am Pantaleonsberg 6

**Tram:** 12, 15, 16, 18 (Barbarossaplatz) or 3, 4, 16, 18 (Poststr.)

**This former Benedictine church ranks high among the historic sights of the city, as one of the oldest churches of Cologne and at the same time an outstanding work of 10th-century architecture.**

Opening hours: Mon–Fri 9am–6pm, Sat 9am–4pm, Sun noon–6pm

Soon after 955 **Archbishop Bruno** founded a Benedictine monastery on the site of a Roman villa suburbana and a small church dedicated to the Greek martyr **Pantaleon** that is first mentioned in records in 866. The new church was consecrated in 980. Empress **Theophanu**, a Byzantine princess who was the wife of Emperor Otto II, was responsible for the enlargement of the nave and the construction of the westwork, which was completed in 996. To this day St Pantaleon lies somewhat sheltered from the bustle of the city inside the walled precinct of the former monastery. The complex of buildings, now used as a home for senior citizens, is the only place in Cologne where the original character of a monastery founded outside the gates of the Roman city can still be appreciated.

Architecture ►

The impressive bulk of the **westwork** is reminiscent of a fortress, but to medieval eyes was an image on earth of the »heavenly Jerusalem«. It is flanked by two towers for stairs, polygonal at the bottom and circular at the top. The westwork was originally much taller than the rest of the building, a hall church; alterations in the 12th century changed this situation. The gabled narthex and the two lower storeys of the towers are adorned with friezes of rounded arches that incorporate Roman tiles.

Interior ►

The two-storey interior of the westwork corresponds to its monumental exterior. The upper storey is open to the nave in the form of galleries, whose pillars and round arches have the alternating red and white colours that characterize the façade. The magnificence of this part of the church suggests that the gallery was intended to accommodate members of the emperor's family at services. The imperial manner is also evident in the nave, where the wall structure refers to the architecture of Roman palaces. The nave was vaulted in the 17th century, but in reconstruction after the Second World War the vault was replaced by a flat ceiling.

◄ Furnishings

Various eras from the Middle Ages to recent times have left their mark in St Pantaleon. The modern post-war work includes the **painted ceiling of the westwork** (*Heavenly Jerusalem*) and painted coffered ceiling (1992–93) of the nave. In the choir the late Gothic and Baroque styles are dominant: the screen of 1503 with its delicate open-work tracery and the Baroque organ case of 1652 combine harmoniously. The shrines of Maurinus (1170), a 9th-century abbot, and Albinus (1886) have been placed in front of the screen. The saint known here as Albinus is St Alban, the 3rd-century British martyr; Theophanu brought his remains from Rome, and in 2002 a shoulder blade was removed from the shrine and donated to St Albans Cathedral in England. The choir stalls date from the 14th century, the high altar from 1747. In the south transept note the modern sarcophagus (1965) of **Theophanu** and murals of the 12th and 13th century that have been taken from the crypt.

◄ Treasury, crypt

The north transept gives access to the treasury, formerly the chapterhouse, which can be viewed only as part of a guided tour. Some remains of the Romanesque sculptural decoration are on display in the lapidarium in the westwork. The crypt, which can also be entered only during guided tours, has remains of the Roman villa and the Roman sarcophagus that contains the bones of **Archbishop Bruno**.

*The late Gothic rood screen of St Pantaleon with its elaborate tracery dates from the early 16th century.*

# ★ St Ursula

F 8

**Location:** Ursulaplatz 24

**Tram:** 5, 16, 18 (Breslauer Platz)

**The church of St Ursula, which in its present form dates from the 12th to 17th centuries, is a remarkable testimony to the importance of the cult of holy relics in the Middle Ages and early modern times.**

Opening hours: Mon–Sat 10am–noon, 3–5pm, Sun 3–5pm

The first church was built here in the 4th century to honour the memory of late Roman female martyrs, as a Roman inscription walled into the south side of the choir states and archaeological excavations have confirmed. However, the earliest records of a cult of the martyred virgins date from the 9th century; the well-known **legend of St Ursula** (► Baedeker Special p.250) originated in the 10th century. In 1106, when the city limits were being extended and a new defensive wall built, the discovery of many graves from a Roman cemetery bordering the main route north gave a decisive impulse to the cult of the relics and resulted in a brisk trade in holy bones that reached as far as Finland, Portugal and Venice. The Roman skeletons were interpreted as the bones of 11,000 virgins who accompanied Ursula on her pilgrimage to Rome. The building of the present basilica in the early 12th century testifies to the importance of this cult. The altar was consecrated in 1135, the west tower constructed in the early 13th century, the Gothic choir and Marienkapelle (Lady Chapel) to the south in the late 13th century. Further extensions on the south side of the church in the 15th century gave the Lady Chapel the appearance of a second south aisle. In the 17th century the famous **Goldene Kammer** (Golden Chamber) was built, and a Baroque crown added to the tower. The unimpressive appearance of the west façade is due to the fact that the nunnery cloister stood here and was demolished following the secularization of the religious houses of the city in 1802.

After heavy damage in the Second World War, reconstruction work aimed to restore the Romanesque appearance of the nave as a basilica with galleries. Instead of replacing the Gothic vaulting, of which the small consoles are still visible, a modern wooden ceiling was installed that reveals the wall elevation of the basilica. Beyond the transept the choir in High Gothic style adjoins the Romanesque nave. The stained glass of the eleven choir windows – the number is a reference to the 11,000 virgins of the legend – date from the 19th and 20th centuries.

Furnishings ►

The rich furnishings and fittings of the church are – it almost goes without saying – largely related to St Ursula. Five medallions on the west door (1959–60) depict scenes from the saint's legend. A 15th-century Pietà adorns the southern central pillar of the narthex. On the balustrades of the nuns' galleries in the nave are late Gothic reliquary busts of the holy virgins that have faces both at the front and back of the heads. Next to the first northern pier of the nave, little columns bear the sarcophagus of Viventia (*c*1100); above it is a 16th-century relief of Carrying the Cross. A 17th-century tomb of St Ursula is in the north transept (the sarcophagus dates from the 15th century). On the walls of the choir hang 19 panels that represent the most complete depiction of the legend of St Ursula. They were painted in 1456 by an unknown artist working in the tradition of Stefan Lochner. The figure of St Ursula extending her cloak for protection, also in the north transept, is probably the work of the Cologne sculptor **Tilman van der Burch**, carried out around 1460. In the apse to the south of the choir a fine scene of the Crucifixion has been created by adding figures of St John and the Virgin that date from around 1500 to a 14th-century plague cross. Here, note a 17th-century alabaster relief (*Outpouring of the Holy Spirit*) and ten slate slabs painted with figures of the apostles (13th century). The shrine of St Ursula in the choir was made between 1887 and 1893, incorporating some medieval parts. The figures in the niches of the altar retable also date from the late 19th century. Next to it is the **shrine of Aetherius** (*c*1170), who in the legend was betrothed to St Ursula.

*Decorative patterns made from human bones cover the walls of the »Golden Chamber« of St Ursula.*

✶ ◄ Goldene Kammer

A heavy iron door in the south wall of the narthex leads into the Goldene Kammer. Today this room seems morbid and extremely strange, but in the Baroque period it was simply a product of the veneration of relics. In order to house the numerous relics associated with the cult of St Ursula and the 11,000 virgins, the imperial counsellor **Johann von Crane** and his wife Verena donated the chamber in 1643. The lower part of the walls is covered with a total of 122 reliquary busts of various dates in small niches surrounded by gilded Baroque floral scrollwork. Above this a huge number of bones – arm, leg and hip bones, and smaller items – have been arranged in patterns and mottoes to form a bizarre ornamentation. The altar on the east wall dedicated to St Ursula contains some of her relics.

The **Abbesses' Room** on the gallery contains further treasures, including textiles and goldsmith work. It was reopened in 2005 after restoration work that lasted seven years. The former treasury has been converted to a sacristy.

# THE PRINCESS AND HER PILGRIMAGE

**In 12th-century Cologne there was a flourishing trade in holy relics, supposedly the bones of 11,000 virgins who died for their faith with St Ursula. Strictly speaking this trade was not permitted, but when the bones were placed in reliquaries – wooden busts that depicted the holy virgins, with an opening at the front through which the relics could be seen – the church authorities gave their approval.**

When the city was extended in the early 12th century and a new wall built near the church of St Ursula, the bones that were taken to be those of Christian martyrs were found on the site of a Roman cemetery. The cult reached unprecedented dimensions: by the late 14th century 12,000 relics of St Ursula and her companions had reached all parts of Europe, and were later taken to India, China and South America. Although the sale of these bones spread the cult of St Ursula and increased the fame of Cologne in all parts of the known world, the citizens came to fear that they would soon have no holy relics left for themselves, and in 1393 asked the pope to ban further exports.

## Chamber of Bones

A visit to the **Goldene Kammer**, the Golden Chamber of the church of St Ursula, suffices to show that enough relics remained in the city. The walls of this remarkable room are decorated to the ceiling with thousands of human bones. On the lower walls reliquary busts are arranged in niches, and above them a mosaic of bones has

*St Ursula and her followers as depicted on the »Altar of the City Patron Saints« by Stefan Lochner*

been made in spiral and criss-cross patterns, or forming Christian mottoes and symbols. It is the only room of its kind in Europe outside the Mediterranean region.

## The Legend of St Ursula

Ursula was a British princess who vowed to devote her life to Christ. When the neighbouring heathen king threatened Ursula's parents with war unless she married his son, the princess agreed on the condition that she should be allowed to undertake a pilgrimage first and that the groom, Aetherius, should be baptized.

With ten companions she set out for Rome, and each of the pious girls was joined by a further 1000 companions, making a total of 11,000 virgins. On the way to Rome they sailed across the sea and up the Rhine, and stopped in Cologne. Here an angel visited Ursula in a dream and told her that she would return to the city and die a martyr's death. Two pagan Roman commanders, who feared that this host of pilgrims would ensure the spread of Christianity, sent a message to the Huns who were besieging Cologne. On their way back from Rome Ursula and her companions disembarked outside the city and were slaughtered by the Huns. Ursula herself was spared, as Attila, the king of the Huns, wished her to be his wife. She refused and was killed by an arrow.

A host of angels appeared from heaven and drove the besiegers from the city. In gratitude for their deliverance, the people of Cologne built a church in honour of Ursula and made her their patron saint. And the ancient cemetery beneath the church ensured a steady supply of holy relics.

# Synagogue

H 6

**Location:** Roonstrasse 50
**Bus:** 136, 146 (Roonstrasse)
**Tram:** 1, 7, 12, 15 (Rudolfplatz)

**The synagogue in Roonstrasse, built in 1895–99 by Emil Schreiterer and Bernhard Below, is the only synagogue in Cologne to have been reconstructed after destruction in the Reich pogrom night of 1938 and the Second World War bombing.**

**Rebuilt synagogue**

During reconstruction in 1958 the original appearance of the exterior was retained, but a number of alterations had to be made inside in order to accommodate rooms for the congregation and a small **museum** on the history of Jews in Cologne; the museum is open only as part of a group guided tour (tel. 921 56 00). The high interior was divided to create an additional floor, and the elaborate murals were not restored.

The synagogue was built in neo-Romanesque style on the plan of a Greek cross. The complex has a central dome (not visible from out-

*The façade of the synagogue has a large rose window.*

side) and the north and south wings, originally containing the galleries with seating for women, illuminate the interior with their large rose windows.

**Rathenauplatz**

Rathenauplatz was laid out in 1881. It was then called Königsplatz and was intended as the place of assembly for Carnival parades. A number of fine late 19th-century façades surround the square. In the little park at the centre of Rathenauplatz there is a shady beer garden, and around the square are good bars and cafés, in addition to the synagogue restaurant, which serves kosher food (reservations necessary; tel. 240 44 40).

# University

H 5 / 6

**Location:** Köln-Lindenthal, main building on Albertus-Magnus-Platz

**Tram:** 9 (Universität)
**Bus:** 130

**With about 48,000 students, Cologne University is the largest in Germany. The largest faculty, with 20,000 students, is the Humanities Faculty.**

**First municipal university**

Corresponding to its size, the buildings of the university and the attached university clinic occupy a large area, extending east-west from the inner green belt to Lindenthalgürtel, and north-south from Gyrhofstrasse and Gleueler Strasse to Kerpener Strasse. The Faculties of Natural Science occupy an adjacent site between Zülpicher and Luxemburger Strasse.

The university was founded in 1388 as the first-ever municipal university. It was the fourth-largest in Germany and was renowned far and wide, especially in the late Middle Ages. The university was closed down in 1798 by the French occupying authorities and did not reopen until 1919, at the site now known as the Alte Universität (►Severinsviertel).

The main building of 1929 with its large portal lies parallel to Universitätsstrasse, which here runs through a tunnel in order to keep Albertus-Magnus-Platz as an open square. Six lateral wings attached to the main building extend into the park of the green belt.

On Albertus-Magnus-Platz stands a bronze statue of the medieval philosopher of the same name (►Famous People), made in 1956 by **Gerhard Marcks**. He looks across to a building constructed in 1964–67 to house lecture theatres, opposite which is the Philosophikum (1971–74).

Further south lies the university library. The brick-clad nine-storey building to the north of the main building houses the Faculty of Economics and Social Sciences.

# Volksgarten

J 6 / 7

**Location:** Volksgartenstrasse

**Tram:** 12 (Eifelplatz)

**The Volksgarten is an oasis of green for the residents of the Südstadt quarter. Boats can be hired for paddling on the lake, and the beer garden and restaurant that overlook the lake are popular on summer evenings.**

History

The land for the park was donated to the city by a private benefactor, and it was laid out in 1887–89 as part of the Neustadt development. It extends between Volksgartenstrasse, where a number of imposing villas of the late 19th-century have been preserved, Vorgebirgsstrasse, Vorgebirgswall and Rolandstrasse. Pleasant paths meander between trees, lake and meadows, and past a fort, part of the Prussian defences that has now been converted to artists' studios. In the fort there is also a pretty rose garden; the Volksgartenrestaurant and beer garden provide seats and refreshments.

# ★★ Wallraf-Richartz-Museum · Fondation Corboud

G 7

**Location:** Martinstr. 39
**Bus:** 132, 133

**Tram:** 1, 7, 9 (Heumarkt)
**Internet:** www.museenkoeln.de/wallraf-richartz-museum

**The Wallraf-Richartz-Museum, which for many years shared premises with the Museum Ludwig next to the cathedral, moved to its own new building close to the city hall in 2001, fittingly occupying a site where goldsmiths and painters worked in the Middle Ages.**

Opening hours: Tue, Wed, Fri 10am–6pm, Thu 10am–8pm, Sat and Sun 11am–6pm

All the municipal museums of Cologne once originated in the various departments of the Wallraf-Richartz-Museum; today, however, it is devoted only to painting and drawing from the Middle Ages to the 19th century. A particular strength is medieval painting of the Cologne school, a field in which the collection is the largest in the world.

Art collected by **Ferdinand Franz Wallraf** (1748–1824), rector of the university, formed the basis of the museum. His work in saving items from secularized monasteries and churches during the French occupation between 1794 and 1814 was of great importance. The merchant **Johann Heinrich Richartz** (1795–1861) donated a large sum in 1851 for the construction of a purpose-built museum on the site of today's ►Museum für Angewandte Kunst. After occupying this

*Oswald Mathias Ungers designed the clear lines of the Wallraf-Richartz-Museum, where treasures of medieval art are displayed.*

19th-century building and its post-war successor, the Wallraf-Richartz-Museum moved into the new premises with the ►Museum Ludwig in the 1980s. The expansion of the Museum Ludwig finally made it necessary to construct a new home for the Wallraf-Richartz-Museum.

◄ New architecture

**Oswald Mathias Ungers** (1926-2007) designed a cuboid structure with clear lines and few windows, clad in basalt lava and tuff stone from the Eifel region. It was opened in 2001. The 3300 sq m/36,000 sq ft of exhibition space occupy three floors.

Inside the museum, too, Ungers paid homage to the square and the rectangle, as the ground plan, ceiling heights and ceiling lighting show. The floors are devoted to periods from the Middle Ages to the 19th century in chronologically ascending order. The rooms have individual ground plans but are all grouped around a central space. The second floor, where medieval art is displayed, has a cross-shaped central room in reference to the altars that are exhibited there. The walls were painted using the traditional fresco technique by an Italian family business, with a different colour for each floor: a light terracotta red for the Middle Ages, »Veronese green« for the Baroque period and marble grey for the 18th and 19th centuries. The staircase approximately occupies the site of an ancient lane called In der Höhle, in the 15th century the address of the most famous Cologne painter, **Stefan Lochner**.

◄ Fondation Corboud

In 2001, 170 Impressionist and post-Impressionist paintings were donated to the museum by the Swiss collector **Gérard Corboud**. This new department has many works by Gustave Caillebotte, but **Paul Signac**, **Paul Gauguin** and **Emile Bernard** are also well represented.

*The medieval section of the museum has an unrivalled collection of works by masters of the Cologne school.*

## Tour

**Medieval art** 950 sq m/10,000 sq ft of space on the first floor present medieval art. The room at the centre contains large-format altarpieces from the 14th to the 16th century; note the monumental **Altar of St Sebastian** at one end. A tour of the room reveals the development of altar paintings in Cologne. The twelve smaller rooms display individual works from 13th-century Italian painting to the Renaissance in Cologne. Stefan Lochner's *Madonna of the Rose Bower* (*c*1450) is a highlight. Note too the outstanding works by anonymous painters known as the Master of St Veronica, the Master of the Small Passion and the Master of the Legend of St Ursula. The transitional period to Renaissance art is superbly represented, for example by **Albrecht Dürer's** *Piper and Drummer* and by such artists as Lucas Cranach the Elder, Joos van Cleves and Barthel Bruyn.

**Baroque art** The third floor, arranged chronologically and thematically, is dedicated to the Baroque period and holds works by great masters of the period 1550–1750. The central room presents large-format painting with historical and mythological subjects, starting with **Peter Paul Rubens'** ***Juno and Argus*** (*c*1610). There are also fine works by van Dyck, Jordaens and Heemskerck.

Italian art is represented by works of Titian, Tintoretto, Strozzi, Piazzetta and Paris Bordone, Spanish art by major works of Ribera, Mu-

rillo, Collantes and Meléndez. The room at the northwest corner shows developments in French painting of the 17th and 18th centuries, with works by Rigaud, Le Nain, Boucher, Claude Lorrain and Lancret.
The fourth corner room is devoted to works of Flemish and Dutch artists, including van Dyck, Jordaens, Rubens (*Self-Portrait with Friends from Mantua*, 1602) and Rembrandt (*Self-Portrait as Zeuxis*, 1663).

**18th and 19th centuries**

A wealth of outstanding art is to be found on the third floor, where painting and sculpture of the 18th and 19th centuries is displayed. Important works of Symbolism by Munch, Ensor, Gauguin and Redon hang in the small entrance room. The central space is used to exhibit French Impressionist and post-Impressionist works, e.g. by Monet (*Water Lilies*), Manet, Cézanne, Sisley, Renoir (*The Sisleys*) and Degas. There are also wonderful post-Impressionist paintings by Seurat, Signac, Luce, Rysselberghe and Cross.
In the corner room to the left works by Hackert, Caspar David Friedrich and Menzel trace the development of landscape art up to the mid-19th century. Biedermeier interiors are presented in a separate room: Fries, Spitzweg, Begas and others. The following corner room is devoted to large-format pictures of the first half of the 19th century by Ramboux, Bendemann, Steinle, Simon Meister and Schick. A further room exhibits the work of the great German Realist **Wilhelm Leibl**, who was born in Cologne; paintings by Gustave Courbet can also be seen here. The third corner room presents the Barbizon artists Daubigny, Corot and Troyon, as well as German painters who were active in Rome: Feuerbach, Marées and Böcklin. The third floor also shows work by German Symbolists such as Max Klinger and Franz von Stuck, and the last corner room is an opportunity to admire the art of Liebermann, Slevogt, Baum and Lovis Corinth.

## ✶ Gürzenich

**Location:** Martinstr. 29

**Celebrations and congresses**

The Gürzenich is the most significant secular historic building of Cologne after the city hall. It lies to the south and east of the Wallraf-Richartz-Museum, and is known all over Germany as the venue for Carnival celebrations that are broadcast on television. It was constructed between 1441 and 1447 on land originally owned by the patrician Gürzenich family as a public multi-purpose building for the city of Cologne. The ground floor was used as a warehouse and sales space, the upper floor for a great banqueting hall measuring 23 × 53m (75 × 175ft) that was open to the roof. Several emperors were welcomed here: Friedrich III in 1474, Maximilian I in 1486 and in 1505 for a Reichstag, Charles V in 1520. Later the Gürzenich was

*The Gürzenich was built in the mid-15th century for banquets and celebrations.*

used for storing and selling goods, until it was restored to its original function as a venue for festivities in the 19th century. Following modernization in 1996–98 it now serves as a congress centre (e.g. for the G8 summit in 1999), and for events such as Carnival celebrations and concerts.

The Gothic architecture mixes secular and religious elements: crenellations, corner turrets and decorative motifs. The main façade is on the eastern side. Statues above the entrances depict Marcus Vipsanius Agrippa, who was traditionally regarded as the founder of the city, and Marsilius, hero of a legend much propagated in medieval and early modern Cologne that asserted the free status of the city in the Roman period. After the Second World War the lobby areas and the bombed-out 19th-century wing were reconstructed – work now recognized as excellent 1950s architecture. More recent renovations have added a glass lift suitable for transporting large items on the south façade.

**Alt St Alban** The Gürzenich backs onto the ruined church Alt St Alban; the two buildings share a wall, the upper part of which is visible in the staircase of the Gürzenich. From here and from the street Quatermarkt it is possible to glimpse the devastated interior of the church, which was restored as a **place of memorial** for the dead of the two world wars. It is open to the sky. The sculpture *Grieving Parents* is a copy in stone of a work of 1931 by **Käthe Kollwitz**.

# ★ Zeughaus · Kölnisches Stadtmuseum

G 7

**Location:** Zeughausstr. 1 – 3
**Tram:** 3, 4, 5, 16, 18 (Appellhofplatz)

**Internet:** www.museenkoeln.de/koelnisches-stadtmuseum

**The Zeughaus (arsenal) of the city has been converted into a museum that illuminates the political, economic and social history of Cologne from the Middle Ages to the present day.**

**Former arsenal**

The Zeughaus was built between 1594 and 1606 to store the weapons of the Free Imperial City of Cologne. It is a plain, early Baroque brick structure. The beautiful Renaissance-style entrance is crowned by the heraldic arms of the city, adorned with a helm and surrounded by allegorical symbols. A staircase lies within a tower at the west wall. The window shutters in the city colours, red and white, were added in the restoration of 1980–84. The side facing the street An der Burgmauer rests on the foundations of the ►Roman city wall. Since 1991 an unexpected object has perched on the tower of the Zeughaus: a gilded and winged Ford Fiesta car, the work of the Cologne artist **HA Schult**. This ***Goldener Vogel*** (*Golden Bird*) with a wingspan of 10m/33ft is one of ten sculptures from a series of 1989 entitled *Fetisch Auto*, and caused years of controversy in the city after it was placed on the tower.

*HA Schult's winged and gilded car is parked on the tower of the Zeughaus.*

*The Zeughaus, the old city arsenal, still houses a collection of arms and armour.*

The **Römerbrunnen** (Roman Fountain) of 1915 to the east of the Zeughaus was made by Franz Brantzky using remains from the Roman city wall. A double column bears the Capitoline wolf, and twelve reliefs show the heads of Roman emperors from Augustus to Theodosius. The text above the reliefs is a passage from the *Annals* of Tacitus relating to Cologne. The Prussian **Alte Wache** (guard house) of 1840–41 to the west of the Zeughaus is used for temporary exhibitions.

## Kölnisches Stadtmuseum

Opening hours: Tue 10am–8pm, Wed–Sun 10am–5pm

The Stadtmuseum surveys the eventful history of Cologne from the Middle Ages to the present, with an emphasis on everyday life in past centuries in addition to politics and economics. Only a fraction of the museum holdings, which comprise about 200,000 items, can be shown on the two floors of the Zeughaus, which have an exhibition area of 2000 sq m/20,000 sq ft. Exhibits from Roman and post-Roman Cologne are held in the ►Römisch-Germanisches Museum.

On the ground floor a good deal of space is devoted to the political history of Cologne, but the exhibition begins with items which are **typical of Cologne**: the hand-carved puppets of the Hänneschen-

Theater, eau de Cologne, Carnival requisites, Kölsch beer and a car made by the biggest local employer, the Ford factory. Paintings, photographs and documents outline the history of the city from the First World War and Weimar Republic to the »Third Reich« and post-war period.

There is a large and detailed **model of Cologne in 1571**, prepared on the basis of Arnold Mercator's bird's-eye view of the city. The original of a monument from the medieval city wall commemorates the battle at Ulrepforte in 1268, an important step on the road to independence from the rule of the archbishops. A fine variety of exhibits – tools, banners, weapons and armour, seals and documents – presents the period from the 13th century to the era of French and Prussian rule and the age of imperial Germany in the late 19th century. Two important items are the Gothic **city seal of 1268** and the **Verbundbrief**, the constitution that came into force when the guilds took power in the city in 1396.

The upper floor is dedicated to the cultural, economic and social history of Cologne. There is an excellent collection of historic scientific instruments and globes, furniture, household items and models of ships to illustrate such themes as »Religion, Superstition and Science«, »Cologne in 1900« and »Trade and Transport«. The religious customs of Cologne's Jewish community, the importance of shipping on the Rhine, childhood and the world of labour in the early 20th century, and the completion of the cathedral are also explained.

✶ **Römerturm Roman Tower**

The Roman tower (Römerturm, ► photo p.217) to the west of the Zeughaus on the corner of Zeughausstrasse and St.-Apern-Strasse was once the northwest corner of the ► Roman city wall. It is well preserved and decorated with circular and diamond patterns formed from stones of different colours. A stylized temple can be made out on the upper row. In the Middle Ages the tower, whose walls are 2.5m/8ft thick, was used as a latrine by the Franciscan nunnery of St Clare. This saved it from demolition. It was converted to a house in 1833 and passed into municipal ownership in 1873. The band of ashlar stone at the top and the crenellations above it were added around 1900. The adjoining neo-Gothic house was built in 1896 for the cathedral architect. Today the tower is a gallery showroom.

## St Maria in der Kupfergasse

**Location:** Neven-DuMont-Strasse 7

**Former Carmelite church**

A short walk south from the Zeughaus leads to a church that formerly belonged to a Carmelite convent. The order of Discalced Carmelite Sisters, which was established in Cologne in 1637, initially built the **Loreto Chapel** in 1673–75. It was based on the Casa Santa of Loreto, an Italian place of pilgrimage, to house a votive image known as the **Black Madonna**. In 1705–11 the chapel was incorporated into a new church. Architecturally it is in the Dutch Baroque style, a tradition that the Carmelite sisters brought from their original home in s' Hertogenbosch.

The 17th-century statue of the Black Madonna (Schwarze Muttergottes), which is carved from lime wood, was presumably brought to Cologne by Carmelite sisters who were forced to flee from the Netherlands. As it is believed to work miracles, it has long been a destination for pilgrims, and now stands in the old chapel at the entrance to the church. It has a prominent role in local popular piety, and is said to have turned black when it was carried through the streets of Cologne in order to protect the city from an outbreak of plague.

# ★ Zons

Excursion

**Location:** 25km/15mi north of Cologne **By car:** B 9 to Dormagen-Zons

**The little town of Zons, which has been incorporated into the district of Dormagen, is known for the best-preserved medieval fortifications of the Rhineland, the picturesque appearance of the town centre and performances on its open-air stage.**

History

Zons was originally a **manor of the archbishops of Cologne** and is first mentioned in records in the 11th century. In 1372 the customs post for Rhine traffic was moved from the town of Neuss to the north to Zons, which then lay directly on the river. The settlement received a municipal charter and was fortified. A castle, Burg Friedestrom, was also built to protect it. All goods transported on the Rhine were subject to customs duty amounting to 2–10% of their value, and more than half of the archbishops' income derived from customs.

From 1463 the chapter of Cologne Cathedral owned the town. A dispute over the rights to Zons between Archbishop **Ruprecht von der Pfalz** and the cathedral chapter escalated to a full-scale war when Charles the Bold of Burgundy joined the conflict on Ruprecht's side and Emperor Friedrich III supported the cathedral chapter. The war ended in 1475 with the defeat of Charles the Bold, and Zons remained in the possession of Cologne. However, the economy of the little town suffered from devastating fires in the 15th and 16th centuries, from outbreaks of plague in the 17th century and sieges during the Thirty Years' War. The customs post was abandoned in 1796 at the time of French occupation.

»Rothenburg on the Rhine«

The impressive medieval wall, which is over 1km/1100yd in length, with its towers, gates and ditches, as well as the narrow streets of the town and the lovingly restored timber-framed houses have given Zons the nickname »Rothenburg on the Rhine«. The south tower

*This tower, once part of the fortifications, was converted to serve a peaceful purpose.*

was converted to a windmill in the 15th century. The neo-Gothic church of 1875 to the north of Schlossstrasse, which leads to the Rhine, occupies the site of its 14th-century predecessor. Just to the south of Schlossstrasse a 14th-century tower with a Baroque roof named Juddeturm has survived. It was a corner tower of the old barbican. The marketplace was at the junction of Schlossstrasse with Rheingasse and the Rhine wall. The town hall that once stood on the north side has not been preserved.

◀ Rhein-Kreis-Museum

A 17th-century manor house in Schlossstrasse is now the Rhein-Kreis-Museum. It is worth entering to see the largest collection of art nouveau pewter in Germany and documents on the history of the town (hours: Tue–Fri 2–6pm, Sat and Sun 11am–5pm).

Of the main castle, which lay further south, some parts remain: the south gate, which led to the barbican; the gate tower, which was the principal entrance; and the Schlossturm, the tower at the southeast corner of the town wall.

◀ Rheingasse

Pretty old houses and the former Rhine wall give Rheingasse a pleasant atmosphere. Beyond the wall, where the Rhine once flowed, cows graze today. The square, six-storey tower at the north end of Rheingasse, known as the Rheinturm or St.-Peters-Turm, housed the customs post. On the inside of the Rhine gate next to it is a relief of Archbishop **Friedrich von Saarwerden**, who gave the town its charter in 1373, above an inscription dated 1388.

The former castle bailey outside the wall is the site of a popular **open-air theatre** (Freilichtbühne Zons). There are parking spaces close by to the west and next to the Rhine dike. Ensembles from neighbouring cities perform here in summer.
Along the top of the **Rhine dike** between the town and the river runs a path and bicycle track with a good view of Zons and the gently sloping river meadows.

# ★ Zoo · Aquarium

E 8

**Location:** Riehler Str. 173
**Bus:** 140
**Tram:** 18 (Zoo, Flora)
**Internet:** www.zoo-koeln.de

**Cologne Zoo is one of the largest and most attractive in Germany. It has over 500 species of animals from all parts of the world. The large new elephant park, the modern primate house and the rain-forest zone are among the highlights.**

Opening hours: Daily; summer 9am–6pm, winter until 5pm
Aquarium: daily 9am–6pm

Cologne Zoo was one of the first in Europe when it opened in 1860. Since then it has seen many changes, not only in its size and the species represented, but also in the aims of the zoo: in addition to showing a broad cross-section of the animal world, the protection of nature and preservation of species has become a priority. In Cologne European buffalo, lion tamarins, Bali starlings and Przewalski horses are bred in order to save the species and reintroduce them to nature. More than 30 outdoor compounds are designed to meet as far as possible the conditions that the animals need. The architecturally impressive buildings from the early period of the zoo convey an idea of changing attitudes to the purpose of a zoo. The oldest, a protected monument of 1863, was the giraffe and later elephant house, built in the style of an Indian temple. In the light of modern zoological knowledge it was considered unsuitable for the elephants, which can now roam over an area of about 2 hectares/5 acres in a modern **elephant park**. The former bird house of 1898–99, which resembles a Russian church and is now used as a monkey house, reflects the 19th-century idea that a variety of architectural styles should correspond to a wide range of animal species. A further survival from the founding years is the neo-classical director's residence. The **sea-lion rock** of 1882 and the **monkey rock (Affenfelsen)** of

## i Feeding times

- 10.30am: birds in rainforest
- 10.45am: penguins
- 11.30am: sea lions
- Noon: common otters
- 2pm: crocodiles (Monday only)
- 3pm: baboons, small clawed otters and (Monday only) piranhas
- 4pm: sea lions
- 4.30pm: penguins, common otters

*The sea lions in Cologne zoo draw the crowds with their circus tricks and earn an extra helping of fish.*

1914 are worlds apart: the sterile, stony terrain of the former was primarily intended for the amusement of spectators, who had an excellent view, while the latter lives up to the philosophy of Hagenbeck's zoo in Hamburg: »animals in the landscape«. The baboons and lemurs can retreat into the hollow rock, which contains cages that are not visible from outside. Here the spotlight is on observation of animal life, and the monkey rock, along with the **primeval forest house (Urwaldhaus)** for primates is one of the zoo's main attractions.

About one third of all the mammal species of Cologne zoo are apes and monkeys. The Urwaldhaus of 1985 is home to gorillas, orangutans and rare bonobos. To the left of the main entrance is the **house for lemurs** from Madagascar.

**Other compounds**

To the right of the main entrance pass the camels, pandas and cockatoos on the way to the **South American house**, where primates from the New World live. Big cats, too, are well represented: in addition to lions and tigers, there are cheetahs in an area that is based on African savannah. At the north end of the zoo, two compounds for big cats were built in the 1990s so that leopards and snow leopards can live in highly authentic habitats (high altitude and forest landscapes respectively).

There is also a **children's area (Kinderzoo)**, where petting and feeding the animals is allowed, and a **zoo school** for visiting classes.

**Aquarium, terrarium, insectarium**

Opposite the main entrance is the aquarium, which includes an insectarium and terrarium. The aquarium is a dimly lit room with several tanks on the side walls, home to colourful tropical fish and turtles. Crocodiles, snakes and lizards can also be seen here. The upper floor is the realm of insects, millipedes and spiders. Preying mantis, locusts, large cockroaches, dragonflies, beetles, mosquitoes and bugs of all kinds crawl and fly in their glass cases. Visitors can look inside a bee hive and enter a room in which butterflies flutter about.

**! *Baedeker* TIP**

**Reduced admission fee**

On Mondays and from Tuesday to Friday after 4pm the entrance tickets are cheaper than at other times.

# Zülpicher Strasse · Latin Quarter

K / L 6 / 7

**Location:** Neustadt-Süd

**Tram:** 9, 12, 15 (Zülpicher Platz)

**Zülpicher Strasse on the southwest edge of the inner city is the main street of a district of pubs and restaurants that goes locally under the name »Latin Quarter« (»Kwartier Lateng« in dialect).**

*Students' haunt: the »Latin Quarter« is just a stone's throw from the university.*

**Student quarter**

The proximity of the area to the university prompted comparison with the students' Quartier Latin in Paris, and this is one of Cologne's liveliest districts at night. There are bars, pubs and restaurants along Zülpicher Strasse and in side streets such as Dasselstrasse, Kyffhäuserstrasse and Hochstadenstrasse. A few high-quality restaurants are to be found around the nearby Rathenauplatz (► Synagogue).

◄ Herz-Jesu-Kirche

The Herz-Jesu-Kirche (Church of the Sacred Heart) of 1893–1900 on Zülpicher Platz is one of Cologne's most significant neo-Gothic buildings. Its architecture was clearly influenced by that of the cathedral, which was finished in 1880. The nave is largely a post-war structure, but the tower gives an impression of the style of the original church.

# INDEX

# LIST OF MAPS AND ILLUSTRATIONS



# PHOTO CREDITS

AKG p.29, 63, 251
Barisch p.58
Barten p.69, 206
Barten / Stadt Köln p.191
Branscheid p.1, 7, 156, 231, 252
Buness p.14 (center), 43, 98, 100, 119, 177, 187, 199, 245, 255, 266
Damm p.64
Dieterich p.49
dpa / Litzmann p.30
F1 online / Büth p.236
Freyer p.97, 174, 242, 243 (below), 260
Gerling / Steffen Hauser p.51
Hackenberg p.92, 152, 161, 239, 240
HB Verlag / Fischer p.3, 13 (above and center), 16, 20, 34, 124, 134/135, 140, 167, 221, 229, 259, inside front cover
HB Verlag / Penzl p.208
Horrocks / Stadt Köln p.88
Koelnmesse p.6 (right above), 9, 55, 258
laif / Gaasterland p.70, 185
laif / Gollhard & Wieland p.14 (above), 74, 122, 142, 145
laif / Huber p.37, 103
laif / Linke p.2 (right above), 5 (left above), 8, 10/11, 12, 39, 56, 57, 71, 114, 146/147, 179, 213, 243 (right below), 256
laif / Ogando p. 46, 68/69, inside back cover
laif / Specht p.22, 40, 171 (left above and right below), 166
laif / Tueremis p.14 (below)
laif / Zanettini p.15
picture-alliance p.91
picture-alliance / akg-images p.6 (left below), 26, 62, 159
picture-alliance / akg-images / Werner Forman p.11
picture-alliance / akg-images / Erich Lessing p.44
picture-alliance / dpa p.13 (below), 60, 171 (left below), 182
picture-alliance / dpa / dpaweb p.65, 197
picture-alliance / KNA-Bild p.149
Sackermann p.2 (left below), 5 (right below), 32, 50, 52, 76, 82, 86, 135, 136, 147, 155, 171 (right above) 173, 189, 195, 204, 217, 223, 233, 243 (left above and right above), 244, 247, 249, 265
Schiestel / Stadt Köln p.219
Ventur / Stadt Köln p.4, 87
Zegers p.165, 263

Cover photo: mauritius-images / age

# PUBLISHER'S INFORMATION

**Illustrations etc:** 135 illustrations, 15 maps and diagrams, one large city plan
**Text:** Achim Bourmer, Ursula Branscheid, Wilhelm Branscheid, Jutta Buness, Thomas Corzelius, Andrea Hollmann, Dieter Luippold, John Sykes, Andrea Wurth
**Editing:** Baedeker editorial team (John Sykes)
**Translation**: John Sykes
**Cartography:** Christoph Gallus, Hohberg; Franz Huber, Munich; MAIRDUMONT/Falk Verlag, Ostfildern (city plan)
**3D illustrations:** jangled nerves, Stuttgart
**Design:** independent Medien-Design, Munich; Kathrin Schemel

**Editor-in-chief:** Rainer Eisenschmid, Baedeker Ostfildern

1st edition 2009

Based on Baedeker Allianz Reiseführer »Köln«, 10. Auflage 2007



Printed in China

# BAEDEKER GUIDE BOOKS AT A GLANCE

## Guiding the World since 1827

- Andalusia
- Austria
- Bali
- Barcelona
- Berlin
- Brazil
- Budapest
- Cologne
- Dresden
- Dubai
- Egypt
- Florence
- Florida
- France
- Greece
- Iceland
- Ireland
- Italy
- Japan
- London
- Mexico
- New York
- Norway
- Paris
- Portugal
- Prague
- Rome
- South Africa
- Spain
- Thailand
- Tuscany
- Venice
- Vienna

# DEAR READER,

**We would like to thank you for choosing this Baedeker travel guide. It will be a reliable companion on your travels and will not disappoint you.**
**This book describes the major sights, of course, but it also recommends interesting events, as well as hotels in the luxury and budget categories, and includes tips about where to eat or go shopping and much more, helping to make your trip an enjoyable experience. Our authors Dieter Luippold and John Sykes ensure the quality of this information by making regular journeys to Cologne and putting all their know-how into this book.**

Nevertheless, experience shows us that it is impossible to rule out errors and changes made after the book goes to press, for which Baedeker accepts no liability. Please send us your criticisms, corrections and suggestions for improvement: we appreciate your contribution. Contact us by post or e-mail, or phone us:

▶ **Verlag Karl Baedeker GmbH**
Editorial department
Postfach 3162
73751 Ostfildern
Germany
Tel. 49-711-4502-262, fax -343
www.baedeker.com
www.baedeker.co.uk
E-Mail: baedeker@mairdumont.com